Everyday Literacies

COUNTERPOINTS

Studies in the
Postmodern Theory of Education

Joe L. Kincheloe and Shirley R. Steinberg
General Editors

Vol. 80

PETER LANG
New York • Washington, D.C./Baltimore • Boston
Bern • Frankfurt am Main • Berlin • Vienna • Paris

Michele Knobel

Everyday Literacies

Students, Discourse, and Social Practice

PETER LANG
New York • Washington, D.C./Baltimore • Boston
Bern • Frankfurt am Main • Berlin • Vienna • Paris

Library of Congress Cataloging-in-Publication Data

Knobel, Michele.
Everyday literacies: students, discourse, and social practice / Michele Knobel.
p. cm. — (Counterpoints; vol. 80)
Includes bibliographical references (p.   ) and index.
1. Sociolinguistics—Australia—Case studies. 2. Students—Australia—Language—Case studies. 3. Language and education—Australia—Case studies. I. Title.
II. Series: Counterpoints (New York, N.Y.); vol. 80.
P40.45.A87K58   306.44'0994—dc21   97-44506
ISBN 0-8204-3970-3
ISSN 1058-1634

Die Deutsche Bibliothek-CIP-Einheitsaufnahme

Knobel, Michele:
Everyday literacies: students, discourse, and social practice / Michele Knobel.
–New York; Washington, D.C./Baltimore; Boston; Bern;
Frankfurt am Main; Berlin; Vienna; Paris: Lang.
(Counterpoints; Vol. 80)
ISBN 0-8204-3970-3

Cover design by Andy Ruggirello.

The paper in this book meets the guidelines for permanence and durability
of the Committee on Production Guidelines for Book Longevity
of the Council of Library Resources.

∞

© 1999 Peter Lang Publishing, Inc., New York

All rights reserved.
Reprint or reproduction, even partially, in all forms such as microfilm,
xerography, microfiche, microcard, and offset strictly prohibited.

Printed in the United States of America.

To Heidi, Jean-Paul, Lorna, and Nathanael

and

Betty and John Knobel
who encouraged me to Discourse surf from a very young age

Contents

Acknowledgments ix

1. Language education in new times 1
2. Researching D/discourses 21
3. Nicholas 71
4. Jacques 101
5. Layla 125
6. Hannah 157
7. Doing school 187
8. D/discourse research and education 207

Reference list 241

Index 269

Acknowledgments

To Colin Lankshear, whose life and work inspire everyone who knows him or who reads his writings. His ideas and keen understandings of the world sustain and enrich my own endeavors.

To Nicholas, Layla, Jacques, and Hannah, their families, and their teachers. I am deeply grateful for their generous commitment to this project—it could not have done without them.

This book also owes much to the research and scholarship of James Paul Gee and Judith Green. The conceptual and theoretical ground that each has laid continues to be of enormous value to language and literacy researchers and educators throughout the world. I acknowledge without reservation my debt to them and my ongoing appreciation of their work.

Writing, like life, never occurs in a vacuum and there are many other people who have contributed directly to writing this book. In particular, I am especially grateful to: Patricia Irvine, Marcia Moraes, Margaret LeCompte, Kris Gutierrez, Cathie Wallace, Sarah Michaels, Edgar González Gaudiano, Alicia de Alba, Chris Searle, Donaldo Macedo, Michael Peters, David Bloome, Nick Burbules, Peter McLaren, Glynda Hull, Ludmila Doneman, Michael Doneman, Neil Anderson, Lean Putney, Bob Bleicher, and the Santa Barbara Classroom Discourse Group. Grateful thanks are due to Sharan Merriam for her generous collegiality in making available her most recent work as pre-publication proofs, thereby accommodating my own deadline. In addition, of course, there are many others too many to mention here whose work has created a fine tradition to follow and learn from. These people include: Ludwig Wittgenstein, Shirley Brice Heath, Dell Hymes, Courtney Cazden, Kevin Harris, Henry Giroux, Linda Brodkey, Conchita Delgado-Gaitan, Luis Moll, Barbara Rogoff, Angela McRobbie, Norman Fairclough, and Gunther Kress.

To Joe Kincheloe and Shirley Steinberg for the opportunity to put this book in place. Their commitment to an ongoing critical dialogue between theory, education, and everyday life provides support and encouragement for educators everywhere. Thanks are also due to Chris Myers, Seth Ditchik, Jacqueline Pavlovic, Karla Austin, and others at Peter Lang Publishing for their tireless help and work in seeing this book through to completion.

Many thanks are due to Shirley Keun and Ruth Haycock, for so cheerfully and professionally formatting my text, and to Eileen Honan for bringing her valuable and expert knowledge of teaching and literacy to her reading and re-reading of my manuscript. To the School of Language and Literacy Education, Queensland University of Technology, my thanks for your support in the form of a grant to complete this project. I also acknowledge the goodwill of the following journals for granting permission to publish excerpts from their pages: *Linguistics and Education* (for table 2.1 on page 54), and *The Australian Journal of Language and Literacy* (for table 2.2 on page 56).

CHAPTER ONE

Language education in new times
The larger context

We are living in times of great, often radical change. The globalization of marketplaces means that nations are controlled no longer by their governments alone, but increasingly by multinational corporations. At the same time, economic production in the "developed" world is shifting from high-volume to high-value outputs, and workers are expected to be multiskilled and trainable. However, much of this high-value production is occurring in countries where labor is cheap, and performed by people who have little hope of purchasing or enjoying the kinds of goods they are producing. At the same time, changes in global demographics have generated a greater need for understanding and negotiating different languages, along with diverse cultural and social meanings and practices, in everyday interactions. Indeed, singular and stable identities are no longer the assumed norm in social research, but are conceptualized increasingly as multiple and shifting in physical and virtual contexts.

At present, this complexity comes hand-in-hand—somewhat paradoxically—with global shrinkage. Computer-mediated networks and other technological media are bringing the world into the living room, workplace, classroom, and home office in a seemingly anarchic explosion of services and information. Previously, much of this information might have taken weeks or even longer to travel from one country to another, or certain services were simply not available. Now, for many people in postindustrial countries, information about all manner of things is readily and easily accessed almost as it happens, and access to services around the world is only a key press away.[1] In keeping with this context, there is general agreement that the nature of knowledge and expertise is rapidly changing. Louis Perelman claims, for example, that knowledge is increasing at such a rate that expertise "now has a shelf life measured in days" (1992, 22). This has profound implications for education.

The New London Group (1996, 60), among others, declares that the fundamental purpose of current education should be to "ensure that all students benefit from learning in ways that allow them to participate fully in public, community, and economic life." If this is the case, and I believe it is, then schools have a significant role to play in embracing and critiquing "new times" (Hall 1991; Lankshear and Knobel 1998), rather than trying to enclose them or keep them at bay. What students now need to learn is—and should be—vastly different from what was required in the not-so-distant past for maximizing quality of life chances (however these are measured).[2]

Language education is a case in point.[3] Traditionally, language teaching in schools aimed at standardizing the national language, and promoting homogenized and monocultural perspectives on events and acceptable social practices[4] by means of this standardized language. Currently, language and literacy standards are writ large in education policy agendas, but now with an emphasis on achievement and excellence rather than on literacy "basics" (Lankshear 1997c). For example, the new national literacy goal for Australian education claims "every child leaving primary school should be numerate, and able to read, write and spell at an appropriate level" (Curriculum Corporation 1997a, n.p.).[5] Appropriate levels will be based on the forthcoming results of the National School English Literacy Survey, which was conducted in 1996 and surveyed a representative sample of at least 4,500 year 5 students (i.e., 9–11 years old). Findings from this survey will present estimates of national literacy achievements for these students. Indeed, the current Australian government has anticipated survey outcomes and has already drafted sets of literacy standards or benchmarks for literacy achievement for students in years 3 and 5 (and later, years 7 and 9). These benchmarks are aimed at improving "student learning in literacy and numeracy, and school performance" and will be used to inform "Australian governments and the community about student achievement in literacy and numeracy" (Curriculum Corporation 1997b, 2). Examples of draft benchmark standards set for writing in year 3 are presented in Table 1.1 below.

Table 1.1   **Sample of Draft Benchmark Standards for Year 3 Text Writing**

Benchmark standard	Proficient	Exceptional
Composes simple texts that convey meaning to others, incorporating a few related ideas in logical order. For example, reports, narratives, instructions, recounts, explanations, poems, and/or descriptions.	Composes texts that convey a view to others, incorporating several related and developed ideas. For example, reports, narratives, instructions, recounts, explanations, poems, descriptions, and/or arguments.	Composes texts which convey a view to others and which have clear and developed main ideas and relevant supporting details. For example, reports, narratives, instructions, recounts, explanations, poems, descriptions, and/or arguments.

Standards setting brings into play certain sets of values and assumptions, and warning bells clang when the genealogy of the National Literacy Survey is traced back to the national English curriculum statement and profiles (Curriculum Corporation 1994).[6] These documents are grounded in sets of somewhat idealized literacy competencies that identify what students "should" be able to demonstrate. Progenitors of the literacy survey can also be located in government policies that construct explicit and causal relationships between literacy, employment, and the health of the national economy (cf. Birch and Smart 1990; Ozolins 1993). Looking forward, Colin Lankshear (1997c, 7) views competency standards as a key move in the current and profound commodifications of literacy that are beginning to proliferate in the form of "evaluation packages, validation packages, remedial teaching packages, packaged standards, profiles, and curriculum guidelines, textbook packages, and teacher professional development packages promising recipes and resources for securing the required performance outcomes."

Strikingly similar turns to education standards and benchmarks for literacy (and numeracy) performance are evinced in the United States of

America. President Clinton, for example, used his annual State of the Union address (1997) to launch a "national crusade for education standards." "Inaction" has become the national enemy, and Clinton vowed that the launch of the America Reads campaign will mobilize a "citizen army of one million volunteer tutors to make sure every child can read independently by the end of the third grade." He exhorted states and schools to (re)shape their curricula to "reflect" these national standards which represent "what all our students must know to succeed in the knowledge economy of the 21st century." To "help" schools meet these standards and to ascertain and evaluate student performance, national tests in reading will be set for all fourth grade students and in mathematics for all eighth grade students. Clinton also explicitly links standards with curriculum and school reform: "Raising standards will not be easy and some of our children will not be able to meet them at first. The point is not to put our children down, but to lift them up. Good tests will show us who needs help, what changes in teaching to make, and which schools need to reform."

Academic debates over standards and standardized curricula rage more publicly in the U.S. than in Australia at present, although much of the U.S. debate appears to focus on national test scores within an international arena more so than on how these standards are selected and what may be their potential long-term effects in education, employment, and civic sectors (cf. Stedman 1997a, 1997b; Baker 1997; Bracey 1997; and criticisms in Larson and Peckham 1997). Indeed, directing public attention to standards and test outcomes often deflects much needed attention from more pressing issues and problems, particularly when standards and benchmarks embody a government's economic rationalist goals for the nation. This is not a startling, new claim. Thomas Popkewitz, in his prescient critique of education reform initiatives, reminds us that "the social and epistemological assumptions circulating as current reform standards mystify the problems of schooling and decontextualize the profound and complex issues of curriculum" (1991, 211). Clinton's State of the Union speech, as one example among many,[7] was grounded in calls to action to "keep our economy and our democracy strong" and his reference to the "knowledge economy" stands as a trope for policy trends worldwide that bank on posited causal connections between education and a prosperous national economy (cf. Ozolins 1993).

This brings us to the heart of the matter. Few could argue against "lifting our children up"; however, setting standards and benchmarks always brings into question what it is that students should know and are able to do, to what ends, and how these things are measured most effectively (cf. Shepard and Bliem 1995, 25). To this I add questions about what it is that students *already* know and do, and what value—if any—this is accorded in schools and education policies. Again, Popkewitz's voice rings loud and true when he asserts that "the selection and organization of school knowledge contains dispositions and values that handicap certain groups while they benefit others" (1991, 151). For example, recent, well-publicized attempts at defining a discrete body of knowledge for North American students (e.g., E.D. Hirsch's *Cultural Literacy* of 1987) or establishing templates for ascertaining and validating students' academic performance and streaming (e.g., Herrnstein and Murray's *The Bell Curve* of 1994) are chilling reminders of what school knowledge and performance standards look like in the hands of ultraconservatives intent on reinvoking a misremembered nostalgia for White America past, or who are revamping scurrilous White supremacist theories in order to further disadvantage already marginalized groups.[8]

However, and starkly juxtaposed with the rush to set across-the-board literacy standards and benchmarks in many countries, theories and conceptions of "language and literacy" and "being literate" have changed dramatically in the past two decades. Likewise, language and literacy practices have altered in myriad ways. These changes have brought with them a flurry of new ways of thinking about and conceptualizing language. This is demonstrated in particular by new and emerging concepts and categories for talking about literacy in schools and elsewhere (e.g., multiliteracies, intercultural literacies, technological literacies, to name only a few). In addition to more complex ways of perceiving language practices, being able to merely encode and decode texts is no longer regarded as a sufficient education goal by most educators and education commentators (cf. Freebody 1993; Lankshear 1997a, 1997b). Educators and theorists interested in literacy as a complex phenomenon claim that students now need to learn more than ever before ways of thinking analytically and critically about relationships among discourses, information, social practices, and meaning-making as part of accessing worthwhile employment opportunities and becoming effective citizens,[9] while at the same time maximizing opportunities for becoming full participants in a wealth of cultural and social activities.[10] Yet despite a raft of theoretically-grounded innovations directed at improving language education in the past thirty years, and the latest round of literacy standards, it seems that very little has actually changed in most classrooms (cf. Cook-Gumperz 1993; Cook-Gumperz and Gumperz 1992; Cummins and Sayers 1995).

For example, language education in Australian primary schools has engaged variously with: whole language approaches, process writing, literature-based learning, learning-to-learn-through-reading, genre theory, critical literacy, and a profusion of other approaches. None of these appears to have "worked." In response, the New London Group calls for a shift in focus from debates over the form and content of language and literacy education—the kind of knowledge brokering that is rapidly superseded—to the *social outcomes* of language and literacy learning. This outcomes-based perspective focuses on the kinds of citizens and workers that are produced by schools. In terms of research, this necessarily brings into play analyses of relationships among school experiences and everyday life experiences in any consideration of what counts as an effective language and literacy education for young people.

Accordingly, this book is—in part—an introduction to research procedures that enable researchers and educators to identify and examine sets of language and social practices enacted in young people's everyday lives, and in the process, narrates actual lived experiences of four young adolescents in their final year of primary school. These experiences generate substantive content that speaks directly to the issues that lie behind this book; namely, what *is* the relationship between school learning and students' everyday lives, and what might an effective relationship between them be.

FRAMING THE STUDY

D/discourses and Event Mapping

The investigations in this book are framed by James Paul Gee's theory of D/discourses[11] and by social constructionist approaches to ethnographic and sociolinguistic data analysis developed by Judith Green and her colleagues. Employing both approaches enables close examination of social and language practices on a moment-to-moment basis, set within larger contexts of sociohistorical institutions, conventions, and meanings.

In brief for now, **D**iscourses (with an upper case *D*) are "inhabited" and "operated" by socioculturally defined groups of people. These people act as—and are accepted as—members of the Discourse, and each Discourse is constituted by particular "ways of talking, acting, valuing, and believing, as well as the spaces and material 'props' the group uses to carry out its social practices. Discourses integrate words, acts, values, beliefs, attitudes, social identities, as well as gestures, glances, body positions, and clothes" (Gee 1992b, 107; also 1996a, 122–148). **d**iscourses (with a lower case *d*) are the "language bits" of **D**iscourses (Gee 1991a, 1992/3). Gee's theory is explored in more detail in the following chapter.

Judith Green and the Santa Barbara Classroom Discourse Group's conception of event mapping provides a fruitful method for examining young people's language and social practices in everyday contexts.[12] "Contexts," from this perspective, are conceptualized as more than the physical sites of events (Green 1990, 105); they are spaces of negotiation, interaction, and "inter(con)textuality" (Floriani 1993, 271). An "event" is defined, for now, as a "bounded activity around a particular topic on a given [school] day" (Santa Barbara Classroom Discourse Group 1995, n.p.), and an event may bear more than one meaning or interpretation. Event mapping and discourse analysis procedures, I argue, can be used to identify and scrutinize patterns of events across times and places, tensions and contradictions between events, unique or startling events, and displays of Discourse membership constituting students' everyday lives in school and out of school. This approach to D/discourse research is addressed in more detail in the following chapter.

An Ethnographic Multiple Case Study Approach
To D/discourse Research

Combining theory, methodology, and methods into a coherent and logical research project is a matter of design. Thus, in terms of the overall logic of this particular study, I employed an ethnographic multiple case study design which subsequently defined the contours and boundaries of my project. Case study involves delimiting the object of study (i.e., the case) so that it becomes both an integrated and a (provisionally) bounded system. A case thus can be a "specific phenomenon" such as a program, an event, a person, a process, a classroom, an institution, or a social group (Merriam 1997, 27),[13] and each case is investigated within its "real life context" by examining multiple sources of evidence (Yin 1994, 90–94). This approach to research can be used to identify and interpret—as far as possible—complex interrelationships among components or participants. Much the same can be said for ethnographic studies; however, ethnography and case study are not necessarily equivalent research approaches. Indeed, it would be misleading to suggest that identical degrees of specificity are enabled by both designs, or that both are motivated by the same kinds of research questions.

The term *ethnography* generally refers to "a range of possible procedures for structuring one's experience of a social situation and transforming that experience into a systematic account which renders the social practices of the situation into patterns through which social forms are constructed and maintained" (Simon and Dippo 1986, 201). Case study, by way of contrast, is not necessarily concerned with the culture or social practices of a group. Sharan Merriam, for example, describes case study as an "intensive, holistic description and analysis of a single entity, phenomenon, or social unit" (1997, 34; see also Lieberson 1992). Robert Stake (1995) likewise suggests case study is interested most in generating knowledge of the particular. Thomas Yin describes case study as "an empirical inquiry that investigates a contemporary phenomenon within its real-life context, especially when the boundaries between phenomenon and context are not clearly evident" (1994, 13). The "particularistic," "thickly descriptive,"[14] and "heuristic" properties of case study research (Merriam 1988, 11–16, 1997, 29–30) enable researchers to analyze and interpret aspects of everyday lived experiences while keeping a keen eye fixed on larger sociohistorical and political events and practices.

At this point, it is useful to emulate Merriam (1997) and identify what case studies are *not*. Casework, case method, case records, and case history are not synonyms for case study, despite some researchers' conflation of these categories (e.g., Stake 1985). To clarify, casework denotes programs developed to address maladjustment or abnormality. Case method is a teaching strategy whereby patient or client "cases" are presented to students as problem-solving exercises. A case record, on the other hand, documents a patient's progress or one's dealings with a client. Finally, case history is concerned mostly with contextualizing a phenomenon, and involves tracing the history of a person, group, institution, or event. Thus, a case history may be one element of a case study report, or of other types of research designs (e.g., policy analysis), but is not necessarily a case study on its own.

The constraints inherent in the present study militated against full-blown ethnographic fieldwork. A comprehensive ethnography would have required much longer than the two weeks I felt were all I could ask each participant, their family, and their teachers to commit to this project. The intensiveness of case study design significantly compensates for such time restrictions (Lieberson 1992). Moreover, a multiple case study design can accommodate ethnographic methods of data collection and thus affords scope for the kind of detailed investigations and data required for investigating the usefulness or otherwise of conceptions of Discourse and discourse in understanding adolescents' everyday language and social practices. This proposal is backed by Thomas Yin, who notes that "the distinctive need for case studies arises out of a desire to understand complex social phenomena" (1989, 14). This desire writes the subtext of the present study.

Data Collection Design

Selecting case study participants. The four young people who participated in this study were drawn from a pilot study that surveyed 275 primary school students in the Brisbane region. Questionnaires and interviews (n = 36) focused on students' understanding of the social purposes of texts in response to the introduction of a new Queensland English syllabus grounded in genre theory approaches to language education (see Knobel and Lankshear 1995).

Four final year primary school students aged between 12 and 13 years were selected from the original pool for more detailed study; participant selection criteria were designed to maximize differences. These included: survey and interview responses given in the pilot study, gender, socioeconomic levels of the school community, school type, school size, teacher-rated language competence, and the like.[16] Summary profiles of each participant are presented in Table 1.2 below.

Table 1.2   **Case Study Participant Profile**

	Nicholas	Layla	Jacques	Hannah
Sex	Male	Female	Male	Female
Birth dates	October 24 1982	July 21 1982	August 1 1981	September 4 1982
Teacher-rated language competence	Well above average	Average	Well below average	Above average
School community SES[15]	Predominantly middle to upper middle class	Middle class	Broad representation of classes	Predominantly working to middle class
School location	Suburban	Urban	Suburban	Satellite city
School type	Lutheran	Catholic	State	State
Class size	26 students	30 students	28 students	54 students
Class type	Year 7, male teacher, single room	Year 6/7 composite, male teacher,	Year 7, female teacher, single room	Year 7, one male and one female teacher, double room

Data collection tools and techniques. Data were collected towards the end of 1994. Each participant was observed over a two week period (see Table 1.3), and seasonal practices were factored into analyses and interpretations (e.g., end-of-year testing, concert practices). The components of my data collection design included peripheral participant observation of case study participants and others, fieldnotes, journalistic notes, audiotaping, conversations, semistructured interviews, case study participant and researcher journals, and personal profile questionnaires.

Data were collected by means of audiotaping language lessons and general interactions as they arose, by archiving written texts produced or collected by research subjects, and by gathering or listing written and other language-related artifacts within research sites. Participant data were augmented by a minimum of two hour-long interviews with each participant's classroom teacher, informal discussions with other teachers in each

Table 1.3   Observation Timetable (1994)

Sept./Oct.	October				Oct./Nov.
26th - 2nd Holidays	3rd -9th	10th -16th Nicholas	17th -23rd Nicholas	24th -30th Layla	31st - 6th Layla

November			Nov./Dec.	December
7th -13th Jacques	14th -20th Jacques	21st -27th Hannah	28th - 4th Hannah	5th -11th School ends

participant's school, and informal conversations with each participant, their parents, and other family members and friends. Each participant was observed engaging in a range of language practices in and across various school and out-of-school contexts. Time-wise, data pertaining to each case study participant were collected intensively over a two week period, comprising for each participant at the very least: eight school days of observation, and ten hours of out-of-school observation. Altogether, this provided me with at least forty hours of observational data per case study participant. This multiplicity of information sources, tools, and methods enabled me to gather detailed and complex data about my case study participants and their language understandings and uses. Specific methods and tools are documented in Table 1.4.

Data were collected over as wide a range of sites and contexts as possible. This was done deliberately in order to map the possible range of participants' language and social practices for comparing with public assumptions about young people's language and literacy abilities and the "need" for setting language and literacy standards in primary education. School-based sites and contexts for data collection included lessons conducted by the regular classroom teacher or by specialized others (e.g., second language instruction, music lessons, relieving teachers), lessons conducted outside the regular classroom (e.g., physical education, mathematics, drama), in the playground (e.g., basketball courts, sports ovals), in church (e.g., for devotions, mass, graduation ceremonies), and in assembly areas (e.g., halls, asphalt tracts) for events like religious devotions, school announcements, concert rehearsals and the like. Out-of-school sites and contexts included participants' homes (e.g., watching television or videos,

Table 1.4   **Data Collection Profile**

	Participant	Teacher	Other
General out-of-school observation	• 8-12 hours observation • Fieldnotes • Audiotaping • Conversations		• Observation • Fieldnotes • Audiotaping • Conversations
General classroom observation	• 35-40 hours observation • Fieldnotes • Audiotaping • Conversation	• 35-40 hours observation • Informal discussion	
Interview	• 3 half-hour semistructured interviews	• 2 one-hour semistructured interviews	• Informal discussion
Lessons	• 2 language lessons	• 2 language lessons	
Language journal and self-selected audiotaping	• Journal: One week duration, written and audiotaped • Audiotaped events		
Audiotaped language lesson	• By case study participant from a range of contexts • By researcher: from a range of contexts	• By researcher lesson plans, teaching notes, resources, etc. books, videos, etc.	• By researcher: notes, lists, newspapers, magazines,

playing one-on-one basketball, talking with family members, doing homework, playing Nintendo or computer games, swimming in the pool), music lessons, drama lessons, rollerskating, basketball competition games, shopping centers (e.g., buying new school shoes, getting groceries), church, and Sunday school. My participation in these events was always negotiated with participants and other people present.

Each two-week period of observations ran consecutively. This compact time frame for collecting data about each case study participant's language and social practices can be justified in three ways. First, long-term intrusiveness of the research process and the commitment required of each participant, their family, teacher, and class was lessened by an intensive approach. This was a wise decision. All of the participants and their families led busy lives, and a long-term study may have seriously jeopardized the project. Second, the intensive time-frame was designed to maximize participants' motivation to cooperate in the research process. This proved successful in that none of the participants dropped out of the project, and each continues to contribute to the study even though my official fieldwork has long finished. Third, and to reiterate earlier claims, the multiple case study design lends itself to intensive periods of data collection which ameliorates to a large extent institutional constraints imposed on this study.

Trustworthiness and communicative validity strategies. Before finishing with this section on research design it is useful to identify the strategies used to maximize the trustworthiness and validity of claims and interpretations made later on behalf of this study. Historically, validity and reliability have been seminal constructs in evaluating the accuracy and generalizability of case study findings. Such measures and benchmarks traditionally employ a correspondence theory of truth in constructing their evaluative criteria. That is, validity is declared when findings are believed to demonstrate direct correspondence between test results and some external—often universally construed—criteria (Kvale 1994). These evaluative measures are predicated on assumptions that the phenomenon under study can be precisely contained or controlled and measured. However, direct challenges to these assumptions have been mounted by theoretical and research work (particularly work published during the past two decades) that subscribes to sociocultural interpretations of everyday life and the research process.[17] This ongoing body of work questions the claim, among many others, that there is only one fixed reality that is "discovered" by means of investigation and measurement. This challenges the very foundations upon which researchers who are interested in measuring language and social practice in order to arrive at some single truth build their validity and reliability claims.

For example, the present case study design does not assume that adolescents' everyday lives are measurable. Neither will findings be generalized, nor will they contribute to building a universally applicable theory from a claimed representative sample of research subjects. Instead, the ethnographic multiple case study design for the present study was chosen for the scope it affords in *maximizing* variables, rather than minimizing them as required for positivist research. I am not interested in presenting *typical* cases, but *telling* cases that can be used to investigate theoretical propositions and social relationships from a particular theoretical stance (Bloome, Sheridan, and Street 1993). This renders meaningless the traditional social science evaluative criteria pertaining to validity. This is not to suggest, however, that some form of verification of claims and interpretations is no longer necessary. Indeed the process may be even more demanding than that required for positivist research. The present study employs a number of strategies for maximizing communicative validity and the overall trustworthiness of the study.

Communicative validity reconfigures traditional constructions of internal and external validity in terms of verifying the research *process* in relation to everyday practices (Carspecken 1996, 59). This is in contrast to claims of "final product control" by researchers who hold fast to traditional validity measures. The main goal of communicative validity processes is to present the reader with trustworthy interpretations and evidence. Patti Lather (1991, 69), for example, describes this kind of validity in terms of a "click of recognition," a "yes, of course." Likewise, Phil Carspecken (1996, 19) speaks of "cultural recognition" as a significant reader act in the validation process. Steinar Kvale (1994, 7) conceives aspects of validation in terms of a dialogue among the researcher and participants, between the research report and the reader, and among various readers and discussants as well. Thus, communicative validity claims are built on the premise that there are multiple truths and multiple ways of knowing. Accordingly, validity claims have more to do with the soundness of the argument put forward than with the truth of statements (cf. Carspecken 1996, 55). Deliberate strategies used to enhance the communicative validity of the present study include: cross-examination of multiple sources of evidence, member checks, and description of the research methodology (which includes researcher self-reflexivity). These strategies are not necessarily "visible" in reporting, but nevertheless enabled a range of complementary insights into data analysis and interpretation in this study.

Evaluation of the trustworthiness of ethnographic case study data and interpretations relies on "the credibility of portrayals of constructed realities" (Kincheloe and McLaren 1994, 151). Much of this credibility depends on the perceived overall coherence of the researcher's question(s), theoretical framing, and data collection and analysis designs (cf. Harris 1979; Guba and Lincoln 1988; Lather 1991, 1993). In addition, Joe Kincheloe and Peter McLaren, among others, extend the criteria involved in ascertaining credibility to include what they term "anticipatory accommodation" (1994, 151). This kind of accommodation is embodied in the reader's familiarity with similar studies, research terrain, theoretical framings, and such like. In effect, the trustworthiness of a study can be claimed by a researcher, but ultimately can only be verified by readers.

ORGANIZATION AND OVERVIEW OF CHAPTERS

This book is organized into eight chapters. This first chapter broadly signals the parameters of my investigation of four young adolescents' everyday language and social practices. The second chapter acts as a launch pad for subsequent chapters by establishing a methodological frame for examining relationships among school learning and these four students' everyday lives. Chapters 3 through 6 present "snapshots" and discussions of each case study participant, and chapter 7 summarizes study findings in terms of the effectiveness or otherwise of bringing together Gee's theory of D/discourses and Green's event mapping techniques in language and literacy research. Chapter 8 shifts discussion to wider terrain and interrogates current "initiatives" in language education in light of findings from the four case studies.

Endnotes

1. For example, my partner and I book all our overseas accommodations using internet-based accommodations brokering services, purchase difficult-to-get books from an on-line bookstore, check currency exchange rates and weather around the world, access a swag of electronic journals that are easy to search and require no storage facilities on our part, and the like. All this and more from the comfort of our PC desktop computers at home.

2. The term *life chances* is used in this book as a shorthand way of describing opportunities for enjoying and participating maximally in everyday life in ways that obtain a visible quality of life for a person or group. Concomitantly, the *everyday* is used in terms of Ludwig Wittgenstein's conceptions of ordinary language, socially constituted meanings, and forms of life. That is to say, the everyday "is simply what I do" (1953, P217, 226; also de Certeau 1984). NB: The *P* in citations of Wittgenstein's work refers to the numbered paragraphs in Part A of *Philosophical Investigations* (1953) where he makes the point being referenced. Part B of his book is written more conventionally and only page number references need be used.

3. Throughout this book, references to *language* assume English language, and *language education* is used as a shorthand expression for English language and literacy education in primary schools.

4. As an aside, *social practice* is defined in this book as a "regular patterning of actions" (Lemke 1995a, 102). This patterning is not an arbitrary constellation, but is socially constituted over time by repeated and recognized ways of doing things. Social practices are caught up dynamically in their own processes and contribute to traditions and conventionalized ways of doing things (cf., de Certeau 1984, xiv; Wittgenstein 1953, P198). Thus, the meaning of a social practice is conferred by the shared purposes, values, beliefs, and so forth of those people participating—and not participating—in it. Social practices are always in indissoluble relationship with political, economic, moral, and cultural interests, and language is fully implicated in all of these.

5. Interestingly, earlier drafts of this goal also included "able to communicate."

6. The national English curriculum statement and profile is designed to "provide a framework for curriculum development in each area of learning" (Curriculum Corporation 1994, 1). These documents define the curriculum area, identify and describe key components in language and literacy education, and outline a sequence for developing language and literacy knowledge and skills. In addition, each Australian state has its own English syllabus which sets out theoretical approaches and content to be covered in English education in that state. Relationships among the forthcoming benchmark procedures, the national English statement and profile, and each state syllabus are unclear at present.

7. See also: *A Nation at Risk: The Imperative for Education Reform* (National Commission on Excellence in Education 1983), *Goals 2000: Educate America Act* (United States Congress 1994), and *America's Technology Literacy Challenge* (Winters 1996).

8. An excellent counter-argument to claims made by Hirsch is provided by Donaldo Macedo in *Literacies of Power: What Americans Are Not Allowed to Know* (1994). Joe Kincheloe, Shirley Steinberg, and Aaron Gresson provide an unequaled critique of *The Bell Curve* in their edited collection, *Measured Lies: The Bell Curve Examined* (1996).

9. The term *citizen* is used as a trope for describing the ways in which people are constituted by the interactive webs of relations of which they are a part. Being a citizen in this sense also includes along one dimension a raft of responsibilities for others, and along another dimension rights to opportunities for accessing and maintaining an acceptable quality of life.

10. See, for example: Anderson and Irvine 1993; Aronowitz and DiFazio 1994; Cook-Gumperz 1993; Cummins and Sayers 1995; Gee 1994b; Gee, Hull, and Lankshear 1996; Giroux et al. 1996; Macedo 1993, 1994; Reich 1992.

11. Reference to *Discourse* always assumes simultaneous reference to its concomitant *discourse*. At times, this interrelationship is emphasized by the form *D/discourses*, while at other times the distinction between them is emphasized by means of printing the initial letter in a bold font (e.g., **d**iscourse).

12. See, for example: Bleicher 1993; Bloome 1989; Bloome and Egan-Robertson 1993; Floriani 1993; Green 1990; Green and Meyer 1991; Green and Wallat 1981; Green, Weade, and Graham 1988; Heras 1993; Lin 1993; Putney 1996; Santa Barbara Classroom Discourse Group 1996; Yeager, Floriani, and Green 1997; and collections of papers in: Green and Harker eds. 1988.

13. The phenomena investigated in this study are complex, indeed, and involve more than drawing only on sense perceptions as allowed by conventional conceptions of "phenomenon." I am also interested, for example, in the networks of relations constituting a social group that are not necessarily visible to the eye. Such networks are interpreted from patterns of acting, speaking, dressing, gesturing, and so forth. Therefore, throughout this book, phenomena are not only material, but also cultural and social.

14. All descriptions in case studies—indeed, in any research—are products of researcher interpretation (cf. Brodkey 1992; Emerson, Fretz, and Shaw 1996, 11–12). Thus, description and interpretation cannot be clearly differentiated, as though a researcher can be alternatively studiously naive and analytically interpretive. Rather, the distinction between "description" and "interpretation" is more a matter of degree, ranging across moments of little explicit analysis and theorising through to explicit and rigorous analysis and theorizing of data.

15. Ethnicity was originally included as an aspect of the selection criteria, but was discarded after reflecting on my lack of cultural knowledge and experiences in cultures other than white Australian (e.g., Aboriginal, Torres Strait Islander, Taiwanese, Malaysian, Chinese mainland, Maori). This was exacerbated by a dearth of published sociolinguistic studies of Australian schoolchildren researched from these other perspectives.

16. Socioeconomic status (SES) descriptors are based on observations and discussions with officials within each Education system, with teachers, and with case study participants' parents.

17. See, for example: Athanases and Heath 1995; Baker 1991a, 1991b; Brodkey 1992; Carspecken 1996; Clough 1992; Coffey and Atkinson 1996; Delamont 1992; Delgado-Gaitan 1993; Haraway 1991; Heath 1993; Jones 1993; Kincheloe and McLaren 1994; Lather 1991, 1993; McLaren and Giarelli 1995; Roman 1992, 1996; Simon and Dippo 1986; Walkerdine 1988.

CHAPTER TWO

Researching D/discourses

Education reform ideals and initiatives are always hotly contested topics. Standards debates are raging publicly where debate is allowed or invited, but elsewhere—as in Australia—national and state level literacy and numeracy benchmarks seem to have become a matter of course in response to media catcalls over "falling literacy standards" and parliamentary appeals for national "literacy excellence." Pushes for curriculum reform, as with anything to do with public institutions, are always grounded in the interests of particular social groups, but are not necessarily for the benefit of all social groups. Colin Lankshear (1997c, 1) compellingly problematizes educational reform moves, and his analysis succinctly frames what follows in the remainder of this book:

> Educational reform, specifically, plays out around values, purposes, conceptions, and practices of teaching and learning within formal public institutional settings. Hence, to investigate meanings of literacy within the latest round of educational reform discourse is to ask what we are currently being "mobilized" to understand, become committed to, and enact through our practice in the name of "literacy"—where forces of mobilization include public policy documents, formal reports and commentaries, curriculum and syllabus statements, speeches, articles in the mass media, as well as legislated/formally required routines and procedures which regulate and shape up what we do and be as literate subjects. It is to ask what we are being rallied and directed to *become* as teachers and learners of text production, transmission, and reception/retrieval, and what we are enlisted to *make literacy* into as lived conceptions and practices within public domains [original emphases].

One contribution to understanding what is at stake in language and literacy education reform moves is to analyze aspects of young people's "already in place" literacy practices in school and other contexts, and how these compare with official expectations and predictions. This chapter is therefore deliberately self-conscious and aims at developing one way of theorizing and interpreting relationships among discourses and configurations of social practices, and hence, among the individual and the social. Although there is a swag of theoretical literature available that advances relationships between discourses and social practices,[1] I have found that the evidence used to support these relationships is generally confined to textual analysis at the level of utterances or text types. There is certainly room for developing replicable and valid ways of analyzing and displaying evidence in support of complex interrelationships at the nexus of theory and claims about discourse and social practice.

As indicated in chapter 1, James Paul Gee's polymorphic conception of D/discourses offers one of the best theoretical explications of relationships among discourses and social practices presently available. In addition, analytic strategies developed originally by Judith Green, and contributed to by the Santa Barbara Classroom Discourse Group and their associates, offer effective ways of exploring complex relationships among group members, discourses, and actions that are largely unavailable in other analytic approaches. The somewhat hybrid approach I develop here is also used to critique research practices that solely focus on micro-analyses of discourse and attempt to extrapolate—unproblematically—findings to wider social contexts. However, in order to support claims that Gee's and Green's work can be interwoven in theoretically coherent and mutually amplifying ways, it is necessary to begin with a brief historical tour of sociolinguistics.

SOCIOLINGUISTICS: ALL FOR ONE, AND ONE FOR ALL?

Sociolinguistics has a fertile, multidisciplinary history comprising theories and research approaches from disciplines such as: philosophy of language, anthropology, sociology, linguistics, history, and politics. According to Dell Hymes (1974, 195), whose work has been seminal in developing socio-linguistics as a recognized field of endeavor,

[t]he term "sociolinguistics" means many things to many people, and of course no one has a patent on its definition. Indeed not everyone whose work is called "sociolinguistic" is ready to accept the label, and those who do use the term include and emphasize different things.

Although Hymes was writing over twenty years ago, his observation remains pertinent. Some scholars regard such ambiguity as a hindrance and work towards unifying the plethora of approaches to sociolinguistic investigation into a single, seamless discipline.[2] That is not the aim of this book, which intends capitalizing on recently configured and/or emerging sociolinguistic approaches that are concerned with investigating and critiquing relationships among discourses, institutions, and social practices that enable or disable access to a range of goods and services.

Historically, a number of distinct approaches to researching language use and social practice can be identified within the broad scope of sociolinguistics. These include, among others: speech act analysis, variation studies, conversation analysis, ethnomethodology, interactional sociolinguistics, pragmatics, ethnography of communication, and critical discourse analysis. Boundaries delimiting each approach are, of course, fluid and overlapping; however, provisional distinctions between them are useful for my present purposes. These different approaches to sociolinguistic research can be identified according to their particular emphases fashioned from distinctive configurations of sociocultural worldviews, theories about social and language practices, a recognizable community of scholars, a body of reported research studies, and a set of research methods. Hymes, for example, identified three salient orientations within what was then the burgeoning field of sociolinguistics (1974, 195), and that bear directly on current approaches to researching language and social practices. These orientations, in turn, aim at: (i) the social as well as the linguistic; (ii) socially realistic linguistics; or (iii) socially constituted linguistics.

(i) A research orientation that focuses on the social as well as the linguistic is most interested in social problems involving language, but does not challenge traditional linguistic theories. This orientation is concerned more with practical applications of linguistics to social phenomena than with theoretical development (e.g., intensive, short course approaches to teaching "survival" English to immigrants).

Thus, within this orientation, language is assumed to be a fixed and autonomous system that can be used to ameliorate social problems.

(ii) Socially realistic linguistics refers generally to work that "extends and challenges existing linguistics with data from the speech community" (Hymes 1974, 196). Much of this work focuses on linguistic variation (e.g., Labov 1972, 1989), and on identifying direct correlations between—rather than dynamic interrelationships among—linguistic data and social data. Although this orientation is "system based" (cf. Milroy 1992, 356), it is grounded in a view that the rules of linguistic variation are socially and linguistically patterned, rather than belonging to a fixed system of language governed by rules inherent in the system. Thus, according to this orientation, the rules of linguistic variation can be identified by studying speech communities.

(iii) Socially constituted linguistics is characterized by the assumption that "social function gives form to the ways in which linguistic features are encountered in actual life" (Hymes 1974, 196). This challenges and moves beyond conceptions of socially realistic and traditional linguistics to posit *theories of language* that are grounded firmly in social meaning and action, rather than in grammar and speech rules.[3]

Hymes's distinctions can be used to map current sociolinguistic terrain and prove helpful in justifying the methodology of a study. Indeed, the third sociolinguistic orientation identified by Hymes contributes directly to identifying and shaping the theoretical framing of the present study. However, for my purposes, Hymes's third orientation is made more usefully complex by including the assumption that ways of speaking have a dynamic and co-constitutive effect on social practice. In any research endeavor, positing vibrant and mutually informing relationships among language and social practices more fully captures the complexities of everyday life (cf. Gee 1996a; Lemke 1995a, 106).

The investigation of socially constituted linguistics is a well-established project in a range of current sociolinguistic approaches to language research. Each of these approaches is constructed from a set of generally recognized assumptions about language and social practice. These assumptions include:

- human language interactions are patterned and governed by social practices or conventions;
- language has social functions;
- patterns of language use and purpose signify membership in particular social groups;
- systems of meanings vary across cultural and social groups, time, and context;
- language use and social practices change over time;
- language and knowledge are interrelated.

Researchers claiming to be interested in language as a social practice (i.e., Hymes's third orientation) often emphasize different aspects of these baseline assumptions. For example, critical discourse analysts foreground in their research uneven relationships among individuals, groups, social practices, language uses, and access to social goods and services (e.g., Fairclough 1995; Kress 1985; van Dijk 1993).[4] Interactional sociolinguists instead focus on social cohesion brought about through shared, situated presuppositions pertaining to interaction conventions and the mutual recognition of these presuppositions (e.g., Brown and Levinson 1987; Goffman 1974; Gumperz 1972; Heritage 1984a, 1984b). Ethnographers of communication, as a third example, generally emphasize the cultural relativity of language practices, variation, and communicative competence (Cazden 1988; Hymes 1971, 1996). Of course, the boundaries between ethnography of communication, interactional sociolinguistics, and critical discourse analysis have been made more distinct in the present discussion than they are in practice. Indeed, many reputable researchers working at the intersection of language use and education have made effective use of particular syntheses of (aspects of) these three approaches in ways that have contributed significantly to advancing language research and understanding.[5] I count the work of James Paul Gee and Judith Green (with the Santa Barbara Classroom Discourse Group) as falling within this category.

Although both theorists acknowledge debts to the ethnography of communication and interactional sociolinguistics, each has taken up these approaches to discourse analysis and interpretation in distinctive and different ways. Green and her associates, for example, appear to be most interested in identifying and tracing the ways in which a classroom community "comes into being" by means of shared and consensual ways of speaking and acting. Gee draws on additional bodies of sociolinguistic theory such as critical linguistics, and other disciplines such as cognitive science and philosophy, in his investigations of discourse and social practice in relation to differentiated access to social goods and services. Nevertheless, despite these differences, there remain a number of family resemblances between Gee's theory of D/discourses and Green's research methodology that facilitate the construction of a coherent and effective research methodology. These family resemblances include, among others: emphasizing the importance of the interrelationships among the individual and social contexts, identifying what it means to be a member of a particular social group, and the role of patterns of language and social practice in constituting and coordinating being a "person of a certain type" (cf. Gee 1994a, 4; see also Green and Meyer 1991).

There are, of course, myriad other sociolinguistic approaches available that are motivated by interests in socially constituted, and constituting, linguistics, including: speech act theory, variation studies, conversation studies, pragmatics, and ethnomethodology. In general, these approaches posit linear relations between social phenomena and language use, and emphasize data analysis at the level of utterance and turn taking, text types, and grammar (commonly identified as "micro level analysis"; cf. Erickson 1996). However, these approaches do not provide satisfactory explanations of the complex, mutually constituting, and historical-political relationships among language use and social practice. Neither do these approaches generally include possibilities for speakers or interactants to claim multiple and simultaneous identities and purposes. Indeed, researchers often are left stranded on a thin rope bridge as they try to provide evidence from their data for claims about language use and about social practice made from a particular theoretical and methodological position. One way of addressing this long-established problem is to begin with an analysis of "discourse" and how it might be used as an analytic and interpretive concept in sociolinguistic research. Consequently, the next section aims at building on current understandings of discourse as a concept in language research, rather than adding to the re-inventions upon re-inventions that are currently populating the field. At the same time, the following discussion also makes the case for using Gee's theory of D/discourses in tandem with Green's analytic approach to discourse and ethnographic data.

Rethinking the Construction of the Individual and the Social

Prior to the mid 1960s, anthropologists had long been interested in studying the ways in which cultural groups used language; however, such studies generally ignored language as a culturally constituted—and constituting—phenomenon. On the other hand, linguists during this time were ignoring performance in relation to language analysis, focusing instead on theoretical notions of competence (i.e., grammatical knowledge) which abstracted language from contexts of use and its functions. During the latter half of the 1960s, Hymes began drawing attention to the need for analyzing and theorizing "the interaction of language and social life" that encompassed "the multiple relations between linguistic means and social meaning" (1972, 39). Hymes's goal was to more fully understand the diversity and variety of language forms and functions, and to demonstrate sensitivity towards the ways in which these forms and functions are part of social and cultural meanings.

Hymes was thus among the first theorists to draw explicit attention to fundamental disjunctions between anthropological and linguistic studies of language use. Subsequently, he developed a methodology—ethnography of communication, or the ethnography of speaking—designed to ameliorate such disjunctions by focusing on investigations of language use and function within wider frameworks of beliefs, actions, norms, and culture. However, despite the attempts of Hymes and others (e.g., Fishman 1972a, 1972b; Gumperz 1971, 1972, 1982a, ed. 1982b; Gumperz and Hymes eds. 1972) since the early 1970s to develop a "socially constituted linguistics," the theoretical and analytical relationship between discourse and social practice is still a contentious issue for many sociolinguistic theorists and commentators.[6]

While well-recognized, this issue is often debated in terms of speakers and contextual principles (e.g., Fasold 1990; Heritage 1984b). However, it appears that a focus on speakers and contextual principles occurs at the expense of analyzing speakers in relation to larger social, historical, political, and economic contexts. Thus, it transpires that the emphasis in these debates is usually on the "speaking individual" (cf. Lemke 1995a, 10; Pennycook

1994, 25–26), who is often conceived as having a coherent and unchanging social identity.[7] In addition, within these debates, proffered evidence of relationships among speakers and among speakers and social practices is inferred often from their (spoken) interactions alone (cf. Milroy 1992; Erickson 1996).

Nevertheless, sociolinguistic researchers interested in exploring and analyzing complex interrelationships among language and social practices readily embrace the challenge of bringing together in theoretically coherent ways analyses of language function and use (regarded as both structural and social) and social practices. For example, John Bowers and Kate Iwi (1993) criticize binary constructions of the individual and the social within sociolinguistics.[8] Such constructions are often described in terms of micro and macro levels of analysis respectively. However, for Bowers and Iwi, and other like-minded sociolinguists, the macro/micro distinction is insufficient and often skewed in favor of one level of analysis at the expense of the other. Bowers and Iwi (1993, 360) propose instead that the individual and the social are conceptually symbiotic and complex:

> The individual and the social need to operate as a couplet so that you cannot eliminate one in the hope of promoting the other (so reductionisms of both an individual and holist flavor are always ultimately implausible) just as it is never satisfactory to theorize a stable relation between the two.

Indeed, as already mentioned, all too often in studies of language and social practice one level of analysis is sacrificed for the other. This is particularly the case when theorists and commentators attempt to infer in unidirectional ways the social, historical, and political from close textual or linguistic analyses of language use alone. To do so denies much of the complexity of relationships among language use and social practice.

Bowers and Iwi, among others, aim at constructing ways of rendering concepts of, and relationships among, society, discourse, and social relations in theoretically enabling ways. They are not calling for a grand synthesis of approaches, but rather, a reorientation to investigating and reporting the concept of society, and "how discourse should be studied and discursive phenomena accounted for" in any such investigations (1993, 362–363). To this end, they critique ostensive definitions of society, and opt for a performative definition instead; insofar that "a [version of] society comes into being in the way that it does *precisely* through the associations actors make as they recruit others to their definition of it," or are in turn—or simultaneously—recruited to others' performative definitions (364; original emphasis). This conception of society and, by extension, social practice, has significant implications for discourse analysis, and is discussed in more detail below.

Discourses about "Discourse"

Discourse, as indicated above, is a key concept in attempting to reconfigure traditional theoretical treatment of the individual and the social in language research. However, like the term *sociolinguistics*, discourse is not the exclusive property of any one discipline within or outside of sociolinguistics. Researchers focusing on micro level analyses of language generally use the term *discourse* to describe (types of) verbal interactions or utterance sequences between speakers and listeners. Conversation analysts, for example, emphasize the sequential structures in conversation, and focus on describing and interpreting the mechanics of conversation as interpreted by means of transcripts (e.g., adjacency pairs, repairs, turns, overlaps, intervals, stretches, gaps, aspiration).[9] Analyzing these constructs subsequently provides "a basis through which social order (including a sense of 'context') is constructed" (Schiffrin 1994, 12). Conversation analysts, however, pay scant attention to social relations and to social identities, contexts, and so forth beyond the analyzed moment (Erickson 1996; Taylor and Cameron 1987). The majority of conversation analysts therefore focus most on speaking individuals as constructed by their transcribed speech, and only gesture toward social analyses and interpretations.

Gunther Kress (1985, 6) challenges analyses of speaking individuals that are made to stand simultaneously for larger social analyses, and calls for accounts of language that accommodate a range of language types and functions.

> An explanation for differing modes and forms of speaking can only be given when we look at the phenomenon from a linguistic *and* social perspective. Then we find that these speakers share membership in a particular social institution, with its practices, its values, its meanings, its demands, prohibitions, and permissions. We also begin to get an

explanation for the *kind* of language that is being used, that is the kinds of texts that have currency and prominence in that community, and the forms, contents and functions of those texts [original emphases].

Kress draws attention to the multiplicity of discourses in social practice, and problematizes claims that language is only indexical to social phenomena. For Kress—as with Bowers and Iwi—discourses, social practices, and social institutions are mutually constituting; one dimension cannot be studied properly without studying the others. Kress's analytic stance, particularly in his early work, underscores the politicized nature of discourse studies that attempt to analyze some of the complex interrelationships between discourse and social practice in everyday life.

Researchers working at the intersection of discourse and language education and who claim agendas similar to Kress and to Bowers and Iwi— I include myself among them—believe that worthwhile investigations of discourses are simultaneously investigations of social and material contexts.[10] Bowers, Iwi, and Kress are generally identified as "critical discourse analysts," and it seems that much of the recent impetus for reconfiguring discourse analysis to account for complexity and multiplicity grew out of critical discourse analysis approaches to researching "language in use." For example, Norman Fairclough is a critical discourse analyst who works with principally European traditions of discourse analysis (e.g., Pecheux 1982). He also draws heavily on Michael Halliday's (e.g., 1978, 1985) original functional linguistic system of analysis, and Michel Foucault's (e.g., 1972) "orders of discourse" to describe discourse-context relationships by means of analyzing three-way interrelationships among texts, interactions (including processes of production and interpretation), and contexts (including social conditions of production and interpretation). However, and despite Fairclough's explicit differentiation between levels of discourse analysis, his published work emphasizes textual analysis of language functions and uses, from which he extrapolates to larger social practices (cf. Fairclough 1989, 1992, 1995). Moreover, Fairclough couches contextual levels of analysis largely in terms of singular, linguistically constructed ideologies rather than in terms of individuals constituted as members of historically construed and multiple social groups operating within and across myriad institutions. Fairclough, however, is not alone in emphasizing texts over social practice.

Kress, particularly in his earlier work, draws on the theory of critical linguistics he helped to develop and posits direct relationships between ideology, institutions, social practices, and discourses (e.g., Kress 1985, 1988; Hodge and Kress 1988). However, much of this work has focused on printed texts or institutionalized roles in specialized (usually adult) interactions (e.g., political speeches; newspaper articles; discussions between a councillor and a tax payer, or between an admissions officer and a potential student). Overall, his work appears to imply direct, causal relations between discourse and social practices; that is, if the discourse—and particularly the linguistic construction of texts—is changed, then (inequitable) social practices will also change (for the better). For example, Kress (1988, 127) claims,

> [t]he structures of power are ubiquitous, and may appear monolithic. And yet... there is always the possibility of using such power as is available to the participants to *their* ends. The more awareness we have of the effects and meanings of linguistic form, the greater our possibility of using them for our purposes [original emphasis].

However, interrelationships among discourses, social practices, group membership, and social institutions are far more complex than this suggests.

Teuwen van Dijk (e.g., 1993, 1996), working principally from a neo-Marxist theoretical framing, also regards the fundamental project of critical discourse analysis as contributing to our understanding of "social problems such as dominance and inequality" (1993, 254). He champions explicit sociopolitical stances in critical discourse research; however, he also promotes a bifurcated distinction between the "dominating" and the "dominated." This often constructs a single social identity for the individual, and implies that the dominated are powerless to change their circumstances for the better without the intervention of experts (i.e., critical discourse analysts). Like Kress, van Dijk proposes straightforward social interventions by means of actively changing discourses. He suggests, for example, "that one of the social resources on which power and dominance are based is the privileged access to discourse and communication" (255–256). This also includes access to corresponding social roles. This claim is explained, for instance, by means of parliamentary discourse on ethnic affairs, and how language choices are used to further discredit already powerless groups (265–279). Indeed, van Dijk appears to presuppose that power is always the province of those who hold (institutional) authority. I propose, however, that transformed and newly emerging discourses indicate that the foundations for such assumptions are not necessarily as obvious or as straightforward as van Dijk suggests. This claim is addressed in following chapters.

Jay Lemke (1995a), working in North America with theories of critical linguistics and social semiotics, is similarly concerned with interrelationships among discourses, power, and social practice. However, as with others discussed above, Lemke demonstrates his own theory about the relationships among discourse and social practices primarily by means of analyzing published texts or transcriptions of oral interactions (e.g., 37–79). For example, Lemke investigates a "discourse of the moral majority," and a "discourse of gay rights" (45–57) using texts published by each group. Each text is analyzed according to the kinds of meanings constructed and assumptions made within the text. The results of such analyses are extrapolated to particular sets of social practices and worldviews identified by Lemke (e.g., 41). Despite Lemke's concern for focusing on various dimensions of the individual and the social in discourse analysis, he, too, tends to favor close textual analysis.

Michel Foucault (e.g., 1972), although not technically a critical discourse analyst, has had a seminal influence in this area of study. His theory of language use is not explicitly adopted within the theoretical framing of the present study; however, his work has nevertheless been influential. His theory of orders of discourses lays useful terrain for exploring ways of drawing (temporary and always contestable) boundaries around discourses. In addition, his historical and political contextualization of discourse analysis is an exemplary guide for interpreting patterns of language use and social action, and social constructions of individual subjectivities. However, Foucault's theoretical focus is on social systems and structures (e.g., systems of power and regulation, institutions) and he appears to propose that assumptions and claims can be made about social practices based on analyses of these systems and structures rather than on analyses of the practices themselves.[11]

This discussion of different theorists' approaches to (critical) discourse analysis is not meant to posit their approaches as antithetical to the theoretical framing of the present study, or to deny the contribution of these and similar scholars' work in broadening our understanding of language and social practice (cf. applications of critical discourse analysis methods to feminist research concerns; see, among others: Cameron 1985, ed. 1990; Smith 1990; Tannen 1994). Indeed, aspects of their discourse and social analysis work are used to critique and contribute to the conception of discourses taken up in this study. Nevertheless, this brief tour serves two purposes. First, it presents a representative—but by no means exhaustive—sample of theoretical positions and research foci in critical discourse analysis as manifested in Europe, Australia, and the United States in the 1970s through to the mid 1990s. Also represented are various configurations of the lines of influence impinging historically on critical discourse analysis: Marxist theories, neo-Marxist theories, theories of discursive orders, and critical linguistics (cf. discussion in van Dijk 1993). Second, this discussion suggests that although there is a recognized need for reconfiguring approaches to conceptualizing and studying the individual in relation with the social, there remains much work to be done in developing ways of displaying and reporting evidence in support of claims and interpretations pertaining to "ways of speaking" and "being in the world."

In relation to the present task, constructing discourse as "socially constituted and constituting" moves analysis at the level of the sentence or text to include analysis of (richly contextualized) language and social practices. Such analyses entail investigating the ways in which various social groups and their discourses are accorded different degrees of social legitimacy and power. Therefore, gathering detailed information about four adolescents' language and social practices can establish fruitful ground from which to examine and critique assumptions documented in school reform agendas that pertain to (at least some) young people's language and literacy use in school and elsewhere. Admittedly, however, defining discourse as "socially constituted and constituting" gives little indication of the theoretical and analytical details incumbent in adopting this orientation.

From the range of interpretations and approaches available, James Paul Gee's (e.g., 1993a, 1996a) conception of D/discourse usefully encompasses ways of speaking and ways of being in the world. Gee, more so than Fairclough, Kress, van Dijk, and those akin to them, focuses on discourse, identity-formation, and meaning-making within and across a range of contexts, social practices, social groups, and institutions. Gee situates discourse in co-constitutive and coordinating associations with social identities, social networks, and everyday social practices. Indeed, it seems to me in light of the choices available, his theory of D/discourse offers one of the best available explications of the interrelationship among the individual and social. This is not to claim, however, that Gee's theory is complete and unassailable. The following section summarizes and critiques Gee's conceptions of discourses in order to identify areas of strength and fragility in his theory in relation to the present study. This discussion also shapes and informs the ways in which Green and her colleagues' approaches to data analysis are employed in the present study.

DISCOURSES

Gee, as indicated in chapter 1, usefully differentiates between two dimensions of discourse: **D**iscourse (with an upper-case *D*), and **d**iscourse (with a lower-case *d*). **D**iscourse describes

> a socially accepted association among ways of using language, other symbolic expressions, and artifacts, of thinking, feeling, believing, valuing and acting that can be used to identify oneself as a member of a socially meaningful group or "social network" (Gee 1996a, 131).

According to Gee, these "socially accepted associations" delineate one **D**iscourse from another, although the boundaries are always blurred and fluid. His conception of **d**iscourse bears closer resemblance to micro sociolinguistic definitions of language use. Gee (1990, 103) defines **d**iscourse as

> any stretch of language (spoken, written, signed) which "hangs together" to make sense to some community of people who use that language... [M]aking sense is always a social and variable matter: what makes sense to one community of people may not make sense to another.

Thus, "discourse" is concerned with meaning making and language use. Gee's distinction between dimensions of discourse provides useful analytic constructs for analyzing language use and social practices in terms of individuals, social groups, and larger patterns of social history and convention. Gee has written at length about his still-in-the-making theory of language and social practice, and in what follows, I aim at an overview of his key concepts and their interrelationships, rather than claim an exhaustive presentation of his theory.

Discourses: Forms of Life

Gee likens Discourses to "forms of life" in the manner of Ludwig Wittgenstein (1953, 1958). Forms of life, for Gee, are composed of particular sets of values, beliefs, activities, conventions, words, ways of speaking, interpretations, and bodily positions, along with material props and socially identifiable roles, that together constitute a particular—and recognized—social identity (Gee 1992/3, 13–14). Indeed, forms of life are tied to social action and to the public nature of language, and they have a material, observable presence. Thus, examining language use, as the present study proposes, entails investigating forms of life, and vice versa (see Wittgenstein 1953, P19). For Gee (1992/3, 1993a), forms of life are overlapping and fluid, and an individual is not necessarily (indeed, is rarely) confined to a single form, or Discourse. There are innumerable Discourses and each Discourse constitutes (patterned) opportunities for people to *be*, and to display being, a particular kind of person (Gee 1996a, 12). This is not to say that Discourses are ultimately idiosyncratic and individualistic. Indeed, this would render the concept meaningless. Discourses share mutually constituting relationships with social (and language) practices, and, just as there can be no such thing as a truly private language (cf. Wittgenstein 1953, P243–312), neither, I believe, can there be a truly "private" Discourse.

Social identities, in Gee's terms, are not fixed and unchanging, but are provisional and repeatedly negotiated in "actual contexts of situations," practices, and histories (Gee 1996a, 131). Thus, it is within and through Discourses "that we make clear to ourselves and others *who* we are and *what* we are doing at a given time and place" (129; original emphases). For example, in my own case, being a student, a Netgrrrl, a teacher, a friend, a Lutheran, a researcher, a daughter, a wife, and so forth, are all different and identifiable—but not necessarily mutually exclusive—identities within various Discourses. Each display comes with certain recognized ways of acting and speaking, all of which are part of subscribing to a particular configuration of Discourses. Moreover, each social identity is constantly negotiated according to context, other people present, my own purposes, memberships in other Discourses, and innumerable social and historical forces that shape, enable, and constrain the routines and conventional habits of being a particular kind of person (cf. Gee 1993a, 1996b).

In addition, membership in a Discourse may be an explicit decision and an assiduously practised identity such as being a sailboarder or gourmet chef, it may be forced upon one as with certain student identities, or one may be born into—as it were—a particular socially recognized group and/or identity.[12] Again, taking an example from my own life, I worked long and hard at becoming a member of the sailboarder Discourse. This involved reading all the "right" kinds of magazines, talking about sailboarding in all the right ways, buying all the right kinds of sailing gear and costumes, and sailing in all the right places. This required much effort and outlay on my part.

On the other hand, I was born into the Lutheran Discourse, which was entirely invisible to me for many years. This Discourse involved attending church and youth groups regularly, wearing particular kinds of clothes to these events, reading certain books, engaging in family devotions and prayers, valuing particular acts and thoughts over others, and even assuming for a long while that was how life out-of-school was for everybody. In retrospect, being a member of this Discourse needed seemingly little effort or thought in relation to appropriate or acceptable actions, forms of interactions, and props. Gee discusses these differences in membership in terms of primary and secondary Discourses, and acquisition and learning. Both pairs of concepts are discussed later.

Gee (1993b, 344) also proposes that it is possible to be a member of conflicting Discourses, even when such memberships may appear contradictory.

> People can be members of many, even conflicting Discourses, can give relatively pure or mixed performances within their Discourses in different contexts, can borrow from one another, can confuse them, can give them up, actively resist them, or take overt pride in them.

What may seem paradoxical at first is actually usefully enabling. Unlike other sociolinguists' treatment of individuals that assigns a singular and fixed identity to their research participants, Gee's theory enables the exploration of multiple social identities and subjectivities. Moreover, he usefully maintains these identities and subjectivities in relationship with social practices, language uses, and social institutions that promote and constrain them. This assists with interpreting what often appears to be contradictory memberships in Discourses enacted in adolescents' lives; such as between displays of concurrent membership in academic and streetcorner Discourses (cf. McLaren 1993).

Social identities are also constituted in relationship with sub-Discourses. These sub-Discourses bear identifiable family resemblances to their "parent" or "model" Discourse(s). "Model" Discourse is used in the sense of Gee's "cultural models." He uses these "models" to explain how things "are generally thought to be" by various sets of social groups (cf. Gee 1996a, 17). Usually, these models are generalized ideas and concepts, and rarely describe something that is actually enacted or made material. For example, "being a student" is both a concept and a practice. Thus, most people recognize what the term *student* means; however, there are many ways of being a student (e.g., private school student, state school student, problem student) that are socially recognizable, overlapping, and characterized by certain sets of practices, props, language uses, and meanings. Distinguishing between a parent or model Discourse (often institutionally defined) and its implicated sub-Discourses enables complex analysis and interpretation of everyday language and social practices. The concept of "sub-Discourses" is by no means unique to Gee, which suggests that others have also found similar categorical distinctions useful.[13] Moreover, Gee appears to draw an interpretive line at one level of sub-Discourse; there are no sub-sub-Discourses in his writings. This effectively heads off accusations of endless and useless reductionism, and Gee's restraint is maintained in the present study.[14] This is not to say, however, that the analytic usefulness of sub-Discourse categories will not be scrutinized in the course of remaining chapters.

Enmeshed with matters of social identity and subjectivity are matters of sense or *meaning*. All meaning and meaning-making, for Gee, occurs within or among Discourses; indeed, it is impossible, according to Gee, to ever make meaning outside of a Discourse (cf. Wittgenstein 1958, 167–85). That is, Discourses are constituted by particular and *shared* sets of values, beliefs, expectations, ways of speaking, and practices. Every Discourse thus provides a standpoint or position from which to put forward certain concepts, views, and values at the expense of others (Gee 1992b, 111). To be regarded as a *full* member or an "insider," one must be seen to hold and act unquestioningly upon these values, beliefs, perspectives, ways of speaking and thinking, and so forth, and be recognized as doing so.[15] Furthermore, most Discourses, especially powerful ones, are resistant to fundamental internal criticism and self-scrutiny that threaten its members' worldviews and values. Indeed, as mentioned above, any viewpoints that seriously undermine a Discourse necessarily define one as an outsider (Gee 1991b, 4). Thus, the nature of Discourses and their socially constituted meaning systems exclude outsider viewpoints because "the Discourse itself defines what counts as acceptable [and unacceptable] criticism" (Gee 1991b, 4). This is not to say that one must always be either "in" or "not in" a Discourse; there are degrees of flexibility available to individuals and groups. Indeed, this is how Discourses are negotiated and changed over time. However, such degrees of flexibility are still subject to the norms and values of the Discourse and its members. This point is taken up again later.

A Discourse can never be neutral, and members will always value or privilege particular meanings over others. Indeed, within networks of social groups some Discourses are accorded more power—and hence, access to social goods and services—for their members, than others. Such power accrues historically, socially, and politically. For example, white, middle class, Eurocentric Discourses have long dominated education in Australia, to the detriment of other Discourses, especially Aboriginal Discourses. Christine Walton (1993), for example, studied young Northern Territory Aboriginal children learning to write in an urban English-medium program by means of process writing and literature-based models of teaching. She found these teaching approaches assumed all students came to school with the same "literate cultural background"; that is, they had all read the same kinds of children's books in the same kinds of ways. This was certainly not the case for any of the Aboriginal students participating in the study, whose everyday lives were grounded deeply in rich oral, kinesthetic, and symbolic traditions. These students were labeled "failures" in their first year of government schooling.

Thus, Discourses are always ideological. Ideology, as Gee acknowledges, is a highly contested term. Gee defines ideology as "a social theory which involves generalizations (beliefs, claims) about the way(s) in which goods [and services] are distributed in society" (1992a, 12). "Goods" in Gee's sense pertain to anything that is deemed socially beneficial to have, experience, or lay legitimate claim to. Society, then, is construed as "any and all groupings of people who share beliefs about what counts as 'goods' " (Gee 1996a, 21). Goods, practices, social institutions, and so forth can also be accorded a range of interpretations, or can be coded in multiple ways. That is, the same practices, objects, people, settings, and the terms used to define them can be associated with many different Discourses but may mean different things within these Discourses. This is where a theory of "discourse" becomes significant.

discourses and Their Relationships with Discourses

To reiterate, Gee refers to discourses as the "language bits" of Discourses. This short-hand definition signals a symbiotic relationship between language use and forms of life. Wittgenstein theorizes this relationship in terms of language games. He uses this notion to "bring into prominence the fact that the *speaking* of language is part of an activity, or a form of life" (1953, P23; original emphasis). For Wittgenstein, language is not a fixed, autonomous system of denotative labels, but a series of socially negotiated and conventional ways of conveying particular and agreed-upon meanings designed to achieve particular social purposes. This is a key to understanding Gee's conception of discourse and its relationship with Discourse. In addition, Kress proffers useful insights into the relationship between discourses and their co-constitutive sets of social practice and institutions. These relations, for Kress (1985, 7), are systematic and potentially enabling or disabling:

> A discourse provides a set of possible statements about a given area, and organises and gives structure to the manner in which a particular topic, object, process is to be talked about. In that it provides description, rules, permissions and prohibitions of social and individual action.

Kress's description of discourse is consonant with Gee's shorthand definition, and emphasizes the normalizing and normalized role discourse plays in forms of life. discourses are also indissolubly interrelated with social identities. Although Kress talks about "subject positions" and "speakers" in relation to discourses, he sees them primarily as "established through the operation of discourses in texts" (1985, 37). Gee, on the other hand, links language use explicitly with displays of status and/or solidarity (e.g., Gee 1996a, 91). Accordingly, investigating language practices necessarily involves, among other things, analyzing patterns of language use, forms of life, memberships in social groups and institutions, and the historical construction of all these. It also generates possibilities for a far more complex rendering of the relationships among individuals, social groups, and institutions than Kress offers, and is best explained by way of Gee's distinction between primary and secondary Discourses.

Primary and Secondary Discourses

For Gee (1991a, 7), a person is born or initially socialized into her primary Discourse. This birthright comprises "our socio-culturally determined way of using our native language in face-to-face communication with intimates (intimates are people with whom we share a great deal of knowledge because of a great deal of contact and similar experiences)." Primary Discourses enculturate new members into being a member of a particular family or family grouping within a particular sociocultural setting. This cultural apprenticeship provides and shapes new members' ways of speaking, habitual ways of acting, views, values, beliefs, experiences, and their "first" social identity (Gee 1991a, 7, 1992b, 108). There is often very little choice involved in becoming a member of a particular primary Discourse. Indeed, according to Gee, primary Discourses "form our initial taken-for-granted understandings of *who* we are and *who* people 'like us' are, as well as what sorts of things ('people like us') do, value, and believe when we are not 'in Public' " (1996a, 137; also Lankshear 1997a: 66–70).

Secondary Discourses socialize people and groups within various institutions outside each person's immediate family group. Secondary Discourses are therefore more "public" than primary Discourses, and require members to act in ways that are strongly conventionalized and that are often under surveillance (cf. Foucault 1972, 3–20). Secondary Discourses require communication with nonintimates (or with intimates who must be treated as nonintimates within the rules of the Discourse; for example, interacting with a teacher who is also one's mother or father). These Discourses are "developed in association with and by having access to and practice with... secondary institutions (such as schools, workplaces, stores, government offices, businesses, or churches)" (Gee 1991a, 8). And each secondary institution comprises numerous and varied Discourses that build on—to different degrees—the (largely acquired) language and social practices of primary Discourses.

The boundary lines among primary and secondary Discourses are diffuse, however, and open to constant (re)negotiation and change. Nevertheless, distinguishing between these two categories of Discourse types provides an invaluable means of explaining, for example, how it is that some students are able to achieve, among other things, success in school more readily than others. A key component in this explanation is Gee's distinction between *acquisition* and *learning*.

Acquisition and learning. Gee draws on the language work of Stephen Krashen (e.g., 1982, 1985) and others to define acquisition as "a process of acquiring something subconsciously by exposure to models and a process of trial and error, without a process of formal teaching" (Gee 1991b, 5). Acquisition, for Gee, occurs in settings that are meaningful and functional, and acquirers are aware or know that they need to obtain particular things in order to operate effectively in such settings and to be recognized as belonging to a particular social group. First languages and conventional ways of using them, for example, are acquired in this way. "Learning" is more conscious and formal than acquisition. It involves direct and explicit teaching (not necessarily by an institutionally recognized teacher). Gee defines teaching as a process of "explanation and analysis, that is, breaking down the thing to be learned into its analytic parts" (Gee 1991a, 5). Learning is tied directly to attaining some degree of "metaknowledge" about what is being learned. Gee explains this by reference to apprentices who learn both the theory and practice of their trade from an expert. They also learn particular ways of talking about their tools, materials, and craft (cf. Lave and Wenger 1991). Furthermore, in Gee's terms, apprentices must have metaknowledge of how to "do" their craft before they are able to talk about what they do and why, and need to display this metaknowledge before they can be considered to have mastered their craft.

The distinction between acquisition and learning does not stop here for Gee. Acquirers *perform* more effectively than learners. Their knowledge of the practice, or Discourse, is "naturalized" and automatic.

However, meanings, knowledge, and practices acquired by means of a person's primary Discourse are rarely analyzed or critiqued, and thus remain largely invisible to that person (e.g., being born a Lutheran) until membership in one or more secondary Discourses provides alternative ideological stances and viewpoints. Learners, however, *know* more about what they have learned than those who have acquired it (e.g., compare second language learners with native speakers). Learners are forced to examine, analyze, compare, and evaluate whatever it is they are learning. For example, walking is an action that is rarely analyzed by those who have acquired the skills needed for walking. The mechanics, or analytic elements, become important, however, if one finds it necessary to learn how to walk, and how to talk about walking, after a serious accident or illness. Nevertheless, despite hours of analysis and practice, very rarely does walking become as natural seeming or looking as it was prior to the accident. Metaknowledge of walking, in these cases, helps unlock possibilities for masterly performance, but rarely enables expert or fluent performance.

Learning and acquisition, despite aforementioned differences, are not mutually exclusive processes. Indeed, acquisition generally precedes some form of learning, just as guided participation within an apprenticeship generally precedes overt teaching (cf. Gee 1996a, 139). Full membership in a secondary Discourse, although often assisted by acquired knowledge and performance, relies heavily on learning and metaknowledge (Gee 1991a, 9, 1992b, 25; cf. Lave and Wenger 1991). However, the contribution of acquired and learned knowledge to mastery of secondary Discourses differs from person to person, group to group, and so on. Knowledge and practices acquired in a person's primary Discourse and that are useful and valued in secondary Discourses usually mean that this person will have less to learn in order to master these secondary Discourses than other people who, by dint of the "distance" between their primary and these secondary Discourses, acquire much less (and therefore need to *learn* much more).

This unevenness is eloquently and graphically portrayed in research work done by Shirley Brice Heath (e.g., 1983). Heath's landmark study of three communities—black working class, white working class, and white middle class respectively—showed how the primary Discourses of the working class communities were not valued (i.e., practiced) generally within the secondary Discourses of the local school. Indeed, children from working class communities found many school practices unfamiliar and alienating. These children were often regarded as academically poor students, despite the rich language, literacy, and numeracy practices evinced in their primary Discourses. The primary Discourses of children from the middle class community, however, bore a strong family resemblance to many aspects of the secondary Discourses of the school. School for these children was a relatively seamless—and successful—extension of their home practices.

Gee (1989, 15) explains family resemblances among many primary and secondary Discourses by means of a filtering process, whereby aspects of one Discourse are transferred to, or made to mean differently by, another (Gee 1989, 15). Filtering, in the sense that it is used here, signals the seepage and cross-fertilization that characterizes the constitution of Discourses in relationship with other Discourses. Thus, boundaries between primary and secondary Discourses are always unstable and fluid, and aspects of secondary Discourses can be acquired and practiced at the same time as primary Discourses are being acquired. For example, the kinds of labeling rituals that occur in certain types of families (e.g., "What's that?" "A dog") make the common practice of labeling items in the year 1 classroom a recognizable and seemingly natural event. This is not the case for all year 1 children, however (cf. Heath 1983; Walton 1993). Furthermore, it is logical to suggest that the "amount" of secondary Discourses seeping into a person's primary Discourse will have direct bearing on the degree to which they become fluent in these secondary Discourses. In addition, Gee proposes that membership in secondary Discourses can influence a person's primary Discourse in ways that have diverse effects on it and that "(re)shape it in various ways" (Gee 1996a, 141). However, changes within and to Discourses are not necessarily simple or clear-cut events. Performances that shift the history of a Discourse (and its affiliated social groups and institutions) must be similar to earlier, conventionalized performances in order to be socially sanctioned and acceptable within the Discourse. Yet, each of these new performances "has the capacity to be just 'new' enough to change what counts as a recognizable performance in the future" (Gee 1992b, 109). Thus, institutions and their secondary Discourses are simultaneously complex, conventionalized, and changing.

These interrelationships between primary and secondary Discourses have important implications for the present study in that they provide interpretive ground from which to launch investigations of possible dissonances and resonances between school and out-of-school language and social practices, and larger social and historical contexts. In turn, this may inform debates about language and literacy standards by identifying and examining the kinds of literacies learned and acquired out of school by four different adolescents, compared with the kinds of literacies learned or acquired *in* school, and how these shape up in terms of options and possibilities for their future adult lives. Admittedly, the often symbiotic relationship between primary and secondary Discourses makes it difficult for a relative stranger or outsider to confidently trace all the seepages and cross-fertilizations that coordinate the primary and secondary Discourses of particular groups of people and individuals within groups. Nevertheless, as indicated above, distinguishing between primary and secondary Discourses enables more complex interpretations of students' language and social practices in school and out-of-school than is usually the case in educational research. Therefore, concepts of primary and secondary Discourses are employed—albeit provisionally—as useful interpretive devices for analyzing the language and social practices of the four adolescents discussed in later chapters. Finally, and despite filtering effects and often strong family resemblances, secondary and primary Discourses never match exactly. The degree of similarity or difference between them directly affects the amount of tension or ease that will be experienced in moving between primary and secondary Discourses. Generally, the closer the match between the two, the less will be the force of conflict or tension encountered in negotiating membership in both. The inverse also applies.

Examining aspects of the four participating students' primary Discourses (as far as they can be confidently identified) and their memberships in secondary Discourses thus helps with interpreting their everyday language and social practices. This comes with a reminder to look for aspects of primary Discourses that may not be valued currently within schools, but may be valued beyond mainstream schooling.[16]

D/discourses, Social Groups, and Social Institutions

Discussion of primary and secondary Discourses is incomplete without reference to social institutions and social groups. For Gee, "Discourses are always embedded in a medley of social institutions" (1992b, 108). However, the interrelationships among Discourses, institutions, and groups are complex and differ, for example, from Kress's proposition that each institution has only one discourse (cf. Kress 1985, 6–7). Social institutions, such as families, schools, workplaces, stores, government offices, businesses, sports clubs, churches, welfare groups, and religious orders, to name only a few, are normalizing social structures in most techno-industrial countries. Each social institution is characterized by a particular, but not necessarily immutable, configuration of Discourses (and sub-Discourses).

These configurations, in Gee's terms, are brought about by "coordinations" (Gee 1997), whereby the components of Discourses (e.g., people, places, objects, and ways of thinking, speaking, and acting) are constituted and synchronized by history, conventions, and other social forces (Gee 1996a, 183). Such traditions and conventions shape and delimit what can and cannot be said—and by extension, what can and cannot be done—while remaining open to degrees of revision and change in the present (Gee 1992b, 109). This renders each institution recognizable or distinct from other institutions, and each is, to various degrees, a product of Discourses that have become conventionalized and normalized/normalizing over time. Furthermore, social groups may lie wholly within an institution, or may intersect with any number of recognized institutions or other social spaces (e.g., rave parties or email-based discussion lists). Thus, social groups also coordinate and are coordinated by the Discourses to which they lay claim (or that lay claim to them).

Gee's notion of coordination adds an explicitly dynamic dimension to relational terms such as "co-constitutive" and "mutually constituting" that suits my quest for maintaining complexities pertaining to the four study participants' everyday lives. Likewise, school reform pushes and standards debates can also be interrogated against the background of their institutional and discursive constitution.

Relationships Among D/discourses

To reiterate, Discourses are normative. That is, characteristic ways of speaking, acting, valuing, and interacting are rewarded, ignored, or censured by members, who, in turn, hold true to the values and conventions of the Discourse. In addition, Discourses—like social institutions—extend beyond the lives of their members and are defined in part by their relationships with other Discourses. As Gee (1993c, 3) evocatively explains,

> Discourses jostle up against each other, fight and conspire together, influence and change each other; they make us, and we make them—though they have usually started before we got on the scene and continue long after we have left.

In addition, I am convinced that it is not Gee's intention to suggest that Discourses have a life of their own entirely separate from their members as some have suggested (e.g., Barton 1994, 57). Instead, close reading of Gee's work from 1989 to 1997 suggests that the issue here is really one of stylistics: Gee strives to use maximally accessible language to explain sophisticated concepts and ideas.

Throughout his published work, Gee vividly describes the ebb and flow of forms of life that are constituted by groups and networks of individuals, but that also extend beyond them. This characteristic of Discourses is embodied in, for example, the jostling and jockeying between feminist Discourses and patriarchal Discourses in certain societies. These Discourses are both larger than and extend beyond the sum of their members and their sub-Discourses respectively. They both coalesce in particular texts, and ways of speaking, acting, and thinking that are socially recognized as "belonging" to one or the other of these two Discourses (rarely both). The collocations of identities, practices, and props that characterize, say, feminist and patriarchal Discourses are not random, and do not occur in social and historical vacuums (cf. Haraway 1991, 183–202). Thus, Discourses are subject to shifts and variations on a moment-by-moment basis due to the fluidity of members' identities and the pull of historical and social events. Accordingly, it seems likely that Discourses can be identified by cataloguing and interpreting patterns (or coordinations) of observable social practices, identities, props, values, beliefs, conventions, words, ways of speaking and thinking, and so on, occurring over time. "Observable" in this sense is broadened to include those things people say they value and believe, cross-examined in light of the ways in which they act and speak.

Of course, I have made a conscious decision to employ Gee's theory of D/discourses as one possible way of reading the everyday lives of four adolescents. Thus, it may be that I am disposed to *see* D/discourses by reading the gathered evidence in those terms. This is a risk in any research that attempts to translate a theory into practice. Nevertheless, I believe there is important and useful work to be done here, and proof of the effectiveness of Gee's theory does not stand or fall on whether D/discourses can or cannot be identified. Rather, its effectiveness lies in *how useful* such work turns out to be. Gee's conception of D/discourse, however, is not without its problems. He has been criticized for positing deterministic models of language socialization, and for theoretical and methodological inadequacy.

Determinism, Individualism, and Overinterpretation: What Some Critics Are Saying

Critics have questioned the sufficiency of Gee's theoretical conception of D/discourses and subsequent implications for language education or social action suggested by his theory. Such criticisms variously accuse Gee of: determinism, overemphasizing individualism, and overinterpretation. Lisa Delpit, for example, considers Gee's conception of Discourse a "dangerous kind of determinism" (1993, 286, 1995, 153–166) whereby "people who have not been born into dominant Discourses will find it exceedingly difficult, if not impossible, to acquire such a Discourse" (1993, 286; cf. Cazden 1993). She takes Gee to task for suggesting that such people will never be able to perform fluently within powerful secondary Discourses. Delpit further criticizes Gee's Discourse theory for appearing to predestine people to success or failure according to their primary Discourse. She reminds Gee that most African-Americans and other marginalized people who have become successful—according to mainstream criteria—have acquired a Discourse other than the one into which they were born.

Turning to Gee's own exegesis of Discourses, two points can be made in response. First, Gee's definition of "fluency" entails incognizant expert performance; this kind of fluency is only ever acquired. Learning another Discourse, for Gee, is much more consciously analytical and tied intimately to metalevel understanding of the Discourse and its coordinating practices, values, and roles or dispositions. However, and this is the point Delpit appears to overlook, acquisition and learning are not necessarily mutually exclusive; indeed, these processes are often mutually enhancing. The example Gee gives is learning to drive a car (1992b, 113). For Gee, learning initially occurred in relation to mastering the instrumentalities of driving and the rules of the road through instruction. Thereafter, driving expertise was acquired through experience and practice. Thus, it is quite feasible for marginalized others to "acquire" powerful Discourses, but this will usually require some learning initially. Second, the degree to which these nonprimary Discourses are mastered is not solely dependent on individual effort as Delpit appears to suggest in her claims that powerful Discourses can be successfully taught in schools (1993, 268). Such mastery is always confounded or enhanced by the degree of best fit between one's primary Discourse and the secondary Discourse being mastered. Degrees of distance between Discourses are functions of the Discourses themselves, and of the enculturating effects of the social groups who lay claim to these Discourses. Learning and acquiring a secondary Discourse that is quite different from one's primary Discourse is far more complex and fraught with troubles than Delpit appears to believe.

Gee responds to Delpit's criticisms with the observation that "the entire history of Discourses is a history of struggle, contestation, and change." He acknowledges that nonmainstream people often win this struggle and "for better or worse, they become a new mainstream center of social power" (1996a, 137). He urges everyone, especially those who are currently marginalized, to never concede defeat in the face of mainstream and powerful Discourses. Indeed, Gee (150) champions Discourse analyses that enable people to see

> the multiple ways in which language becomes meaningful only within Discourses and how language-within-Discourses is always and everywhere value-laden and political, in the broad sense of political where it means involving human relationships where power and social goods are at stake.

In addition, Gee emphasizes the gatekeeping functions of many patterns of social and language practices. Oversimplifying access to powerful Discourses risks perpetuating equality myths in schools and beyond (cf. Graff 1987; Lankshear 1997a).

Jay Lemke (1995a, 16) locates Gee's work at the intersection of cultural anthropology and cognitive psychology and agrees with Gee's distinction between discourse and Discourse. However, Lemke criticizes

Gee for explaining Discourses in terms of "identity kits." Lemke interprets this as tying D/discourses to roles played by individuals, "rather than to activities and systems of social practices involving many participants." For Lemke, failure to account for systems of social practice emphasizes the individual and employs a mentalist interpretive framework that overlooks the ways in which the "mind" is "brought into being through the discourses and practices of a community" (1995, 16).

However, Gee's later work, particularly *Social Mind* (1992b), clearly locates the individual (and her mind) within complex networks of social and experiential associations and constitutive relations. Moreover, Gee's latest descriptions of D/discourses are couched more in terms of coordinations than identity kits. That is, Discourse elements such as "people—ways of thinking, feeling, valuing, acting, interacting, dressing, gesturing, moving, and being—places, activities, institutions, objects, tools, language, and other symbols" coordinate and are coordinated by (i.e., become synchronized with) other elements within (and outside) the Discourse (Gee 1997, xiii). In Gee's terms, "[w]ithin such coordinations we humans become *recognizable* to ourselves and to others and *recognize* ourselves, other people, and things as meaningful in distinctive ways" (xiii; original emphases). Thus, Gee's conception of coordinations suggests a dynamic social theory—and not a mentalist model—of discursive interaction and Discourse constitution.

Nevertheless, a methodological problem remains. That is, how to identify and analyze the individual—and the individual's multiple social identities—in ways that (i) avoid decontextualizing interpretations from social practices, institutions, and groups, and (ii) enable the individual to be the focus of inquiry despite the complex networks of Discourse and social group membership that coordinate her. These problems are raised rightly by Lemke and resonate with Adrian Bennett's (1993) criticisms of Gee's methodology. Bennett accuses Gee of failing to demonstrate "how 'language is embedded in the larger framework of social relationships and social institutions'" (1993, 575, citing Gee 1990, 137). In addition, Bennett claims Gee "tears his language samples out of their social contexts, treating them as texts that express or reflect the mental worlds of the speakers who produced them" and then proceeds to "overinterpret these samples" (575).

For example, Bennett criticizes Gee's (1990) interpretation of a white middle-class girl's enacted story reading for being both decontextualized and overinterpreted. He claims that instead of speculating on the young girl's story in terms of an extant literary culture (e.g., sympathetic fallacy device), Gee's purposes would have been served better by asking—and answering—questions such as: "How did she come to invent this story in this way? What were the local circumstances of its production? What has been her experience with stories in the past? What functions do the 'reading' of the story play in her relationships to the people around her? And how do we investigate the influence on the little girl's subsequent life that this kind of discourse will have?" (Bennett 1993, 575). Bennett (574) summarizes these questions in the form of two general methodological problems he sees in Gee's approach to D/discourse analysis: (i) how to evaluate specific interpretations of meaning, and (ii) how to evaluate the role or significance of the discourse [sic] under analysis in the lives of the people who produce it.

Although Bennett's general interpretation of Gee's theory of D/discourse is grounded seemingly in limited reading of Gee's work (e.g., Bennett's refusal to engage with Gee's conception of Discourse, and his promotion of interactional sociolinguistics instead as the best available methodology for investigating discourse), his criticisms regarding Gee's interpretive methodology hold some water. Gee's design and methods for analyzing and interpreting Discourses are, at best, sketchy. Interpretive evidence and substantiation of Discourse interpretations rarely are provided explicitly in Gee's papers. His methods for analyzing discourses, however, are far more readily identified and audited (see especially Gee 1991b, 1993b, 1996a, 90–121; Gee, Michaels, and O'Connor 1992). Thus, interpretive links between discourses and Discourses appear to be forged in Gee's wide reading and authorial craft. Such methodological invisibility is not unique to Gee and is certainly not cause enough to dismiss Gee's conception and application of D/discourse as Bennett appears to have done.[17] Gee himself is candid about the need for more research work in redressing such criticisms, and invites others to add empirically to his theoretical framing (cf. 1990, 189). This book aims to contribute directly to this growing body of work.

In response to Bennett's first methodological problem regarding how to evaluate specific interpretations of meaning-making I aim to use event mapping techniques to substantiate D/discourse interpretations. At the same time, this strategy will also speak to the decontextualization problems raised by Lemke (1995a). Addressing Bennett's second methodological problem involves evaluating the significance of the Discourse in people's lives and requires detailed and contextualized analyses of individuals' social and language practices over time.

Given the time constraints of the present study, this kind of work—as indicated in chapter 1—is done best by means of an ethnographic multiple case study research design. This, in turn, provides thick data for examining the empirical usefulness of D/discourse in interpreting the everyday lives and language practices of four adolescents. Findings from this study will make original contributions to understanding what is at stake in setting and subscribing to language and literacy education standards or benchmarks.

DATA ANALYSIS AND THE SANTA BARBARA CLASSROOM DISCOURSE GROUP

Key Concepts

The role that Judith Green and the Santa Barbara Classroom Discourse Group's techniques of mapping events and patterns of language takes in the present study was sketched in chapter 1. The group's theoretical positions and research program have a strong track record in the field and grew out of classroom research and data analysis methods originally developed by Judith Green in the 1970s (e.g., Green 1977).[18] These methods synthesize key aspects of ethnography of communication and interactional sociolinguistics, and apply them in innovative ways to investigations of classroom contexts. Key concepts in this approach include: culture, social group, participation and meaning-making, and membership. These concepts have much in common with other sociocultural approaches to language, including aspects of Gee's theory of D/discourses.

Culture is described by Green and her associates in terms of recurring patterns of social action and negotiation that are common to a particular group. Being a member of a particular culture is explicated in terms of obtaining the knowledge needed to participate effectively and appropriately in this culture and associated social group(s); this constitutes a situated definition of culture. In addition, culture and social action appear to be indissolubly related; that is, social action is viewed as culturally patterned and what members of a social group come to know, understand, expect, produce, and do is learned from participating in and observing how members participate in the everyday events that make up the life of the social group (Green and Meyer 1991, 143).

Social groups are defined as affiliations of people that occur over time and are organized around patterns of practice that are meaningful for members. In addition, participation in each social group influences and is influenced by memberships in other groups (Bloome and Egan-Robertson 1993). Thus, a person's membership and participation in social groups constructs a set of "norms and expectations for how everyday life is 'supposed to be' and about what 'counts' as appropriate and/or preferred action, knowledge or interactions in those groups" (Green and Meyer 1991, 143–144).

"Participation" is a repeated motif in this body of literature, and is tied explicitly to social action and the ways in which people appear to be making sense of interactions in particular contexts. For example, the Santa Barbara Classroom Discourse Group's research regularly focuses on how "words and actions come to mean in the classroom, and how the words one hears come to reflect [or produce] a world of action common to members of that classroom" (Putney 1996, 128). For Green and her colleagues, meaning is negotiated by way of social interactions on both a moment-by-moment basis and within the patterns of interaction that are established over time (cf. Floriani 1993, 243). Thus, the meaning of an action or interaction within an event is not analyzed in terms of content, but rather in terms of the event's relationships with other events, socially negotiated roles, and patterns of practices recognized and accepted by the group. As such, meaning is never stable or singular, and language and actions are regarded as always inherently dialogical (Bloome and Egan-Robertson 1993, 309).

Membership in social groups is another key concept in Green and her colleagues' approaches to research, and is defined as a person's status in relation to a social group, and the terms of reference for each group are negotiated by members (i.e., "participation" is more closely aligned with social action). Thus, according to Green and her colleagues, membership in a social group is ascertained by observing individual and group participation in events. This becomes especially visible when "frame clashes" occur. For example, "individual members may 'breach' a norm, adopt an inappropriate role, or communicate in ways that are not clear [i.e., recognizable] to others" (Green and Meyer 1991, 145). These clashes in frames of reference make visible to the researcher the often unspoken expectations, assumptions, values, beliefs, and so forth of a group.

An Approach to Data Analysis

One particular strength of Green and her colleagues' approach to analyzing language use and social practice lies in the possibilities it creates for analyzing the social construction of identities. These possibilities are established by means of various levels of analysis (Green and Wallat 1981, 164). The three levels or degrees of scope most pertinent to present purposes are: event mapping, interaction units, and message units.[19] These categories are interdependent, and are not demarcated in a strict, linear progression from most broad to most focused. Thus, although I present each category separately, using them to analyze data requires a recursive process. To reiterate, the Santa Barbara Classroom Discourse Group defines an event as a "bounded activity around a particular topic on a given [school] day (e.g., spelling, writing workshop, reading period, math)." Thus, event mapping is the graphic "transcription or representation of an event, a cycle of activity (a series of intertextually tied events), or a segment of history constructed by the actors" (1995, n.p.). The Group uses event maps to examine contexts as constructed by participants, and claims that event mapping makes it possible to examine

> a variety of aspects of social life including: what aspects of social life are basically stable and which are variable, to compare demands for participation within and across days, to identify current events, to identify cycles of activity, to locate intertextual relationships among events, and to identify patterns of social interaction (n.p.).

By examining these aspects of social life, these researchers aim at interpreting the dynamics of social groups, participation, membership, and so forth. For example, event mapping can be used in, say, a grade 7 classroom lesson on the North American Civil War to trace the ways in which this war is construed in this particular classroom, the formation of student-student groups and their relationship with the teacher-student group, the construction of authority of text reproduction, and the "negotiation of ignorance" (Bloome 1989, 86), insofar as these things are visible to the researcher. Event maps can be organized in a number of ways, but each researcher generally aims at a broad interpretation of events and patterns of interaction (see, for example, Table 2.1 below).

Table 2.1   An Example of an Event Map

Event, Subevent, and Time	Actors	Actions and Topics
Before school (8:05–8:20) Entry		Researchers entered the room at 8:05
	Teacher	Organises materials at the front
	Students	Enter
	Teacher	Mentions "sit down wherever you want to sit"
STAR (8:20–8:35) Openings (8:20–8:24)	Teacher	Schoolbell rings Briefly introduces herself and the class "English 7"
		Explains video cameras and researchers in the classroom
		Passes out STAR booklets to each student and explains their functions in STAR program (as note taking and idea taking)
		Mentions and compares DARE in elementary schools
Citizenship policy and class rules (8:24–8:30)	Teacher	Establishes citizenship policies in class
		Indicates class rules (written on an overhead projector) etc.

(Source: Lin 1993, 376)

Another strength of event mapping is that it enables the researcher to trace patterns of (and variations in) language and social practices within and across events over time. This also serves to organize data for easy reference and cross-examination purposes, which, in turn, strengthens the trustworthiness of interpretations. Interaction units within and across events also play a significant role in this approach to data analysis. Interaction units are defined as a "series of interpersonally related message units that implicate each other" (Bloome and Egan-Robertson 1993, 314). Examples of interaction units generally include question-answer and question-answer-evaluation sequences in classrooms. There are of course any number of possible configurations. As with events, interaction units are identified by means of contextual cues, prosodic features of the discourse, and by shifts in content or body positions.

An example of this, borrowed from LeAnn Putney (1996, 132), is provided in Table 2.2 over the page, which demonstrates one possible way of representing patterns of interaction within events.

Message units also play a significant role in analyzing what it means to participate in a certain social practice, or to be a member of a particular social group. A message unit represents a "minimal unit of conversational meaning" as interpreted by the researcher, who draws on contextual and prosodic cues to identify these units (Green and Wallat 1981, 196). Message units are grounded on the premise that meaning is constituted by social negotiations within a particular context and by (shared or clashing) histories of interactions (see Table 2.2).

A message unit is not necessarily recognizable semantically, but is nevertheless socially recognizable as a "bit of information" (Santa Barbara Classroom Discourse Group 1995, n.p.). Therefore, message units are research constructs and are based on contextual analysis; that is, "a post-hoc description [i.e., interpretation] in terms of what has happened previously in the event" (Bloome and Egan-Robertson 1993, 314; see also Green and Wallat 1981). Message units, however, are always ultimately subject to the researcher's interpretations of meanings being made and the contextualization cues that facilitate meaning-making in each interaction (e.g., the source of the message, the context, its possible purposes, or relationships with other message units). Therefore, the kind of information carried by message units is not solely content-based, but extends

Table 2.2 Interaction and Message Units

Sequence units	Interaction units	Actors	Dialogue in message units and action units
Establishing topic		TM	001 okay
	Bringing in prior knowledge		002 remember
			003 what does this kind of a classroom structure
	Recalling definition from prior day		004 what kind of a classroom structure
	Seeking a name of the class type	St	005 are we working around?
	Naming the type of class	St	006 seminar
		TM	007 a seminar
Shaping a particular way of being literate	Framing a condition for seminar	Sts	008 and what does a seminar depend upon?
		St	009 working in groups
			010 us
	Defining practices of student	TM	011 you, exactly
			012 student input
			013 you are it
			014 what you have to say about the topic
			015 you are it
	Defining practices of teacher		016 I'm not lecturing and saying
			017 now all these wonderful people up on
			018 you know, elsewhere
			019 have all these things to say about this

(Source: Putney 1996, 132)

to information conveyed about the social group, effective participation, the context, expectations, and cultural knowledge. Message units do not necessarily occur in chronologically ordered sequences, but rely on webs of links to previous, present, and future events, patterns of practice, expectations, and so forth.

I have drawn on the approaches demonstrated in these examples, along with others employed by Green and her colleagues, in tracing links among message units and interaction units, and in mapping patterns of events and social practices over time in my own data. However, in doing so, a number of modifications were made to the received theoretical concepts of this group in order to develop an analytic approach that enabled me to investigate a range of D/discourses in the everyday lives of four young people.

DISCOURSES AND EVENT MAPPING

If indeed, and I believe they do, Discourses comprise patterns of "ways of talking, acting, valuing, and believing, as well as the spaces and material 'props' the group uses to carry out its practices" (Gee 1992b, 107), then these patterns must surely be identifiable and able to be traced in some way. I am convinced that Green and the Santa Barbara Classroom Discourse Group's approach to data analysis—with some modifications—can be employed for such purposes. These modifications involve expanding the notion of membership as promoted by this group to include membership in sets of practices, values, beliefs, ways of speaking that extend beyond the immediate social group to include membership in a range of Discourses. Discourses are conceived as more broadly distributed than the conceptions of culture, social group, and membership proposed by Green and her associates.

Moreover, framing this research largely in terms of Gee's theory of D/discourses secures a wider focus on the individual and the social than would be possible using Green and her colleagues' approach alone. Indeed, this framing obtains a critical edge for Green and her associates' approach to data analysis that is often underplayed in the published work of the Santa Barbara Classroom Discourse Group.[20] Thus, in the present study, membership is not only analyzed in terms of *observable* group participation, but also in terms of (conscious and/or unconscious) alignment with—and being aligned by—"words, deeds, values, thoughts, beliefs, things, places, and times so as to recognize and get recognized as a *person of a certain type*" (Gee 1994a, 4; original emphasis). It is also possible to be a person of many different types. I propose, therefore, that mapping patterns of language and social practice enables me to make certain claims about social group and Discourse membership.

In addition, I deliberately extend the reach of an event as defined by the Santa Barbara Classroom Discourse Group to include possibilities for examining patterned or divergent ways of acting, talking, valuing, believing, meaning, dressing, gesturing, glancing, body positioning, role taking, and other ways of indicating membership in one or more (overlapping) Discourses. Accordingly, I define an event as: a set of social practices (including roles and props) and language uses demarcated by shifts in activity, time, location, physical presence or absence, and/or language. In addition, an event may bear more than one meaning (i.e., can be multiply coded). Consequently, interpretations of events need to be carefully cross-examined in order to establish the trustworthiness of claims made on their behalf.

An example of what this "looks" like and how it "works" is provided in the next section.

Case Study Data Analysis: An Example

Reporting ethnographic and sociolinguistic research is demanding. It requires the writer to be rigorous in reporting findings, but at the same time be able to spin a good yarn. Consequently, in reporting the present study much of the fine-grained analysis of spoken texts has been inevitably erased. As a result, I use this section to present an overview and sample of my approach to analyzing data. This sample stands in the stead of repeating this process over and over again in following chapters.

Each two-week period of observations was event-mapped at the level of language use and social action (cf. Green and Meyer 1991, 146). Event mapping, to restate points made earlier, entails identifying sets of social practices (including roles and props) and language uses that are demarcated by shifts in activity, time, location, physical presence or absence, and language (e.g., theme, topic, tenor, type). Therefore, I found it useful to include as many interaction units and sequences as possible within each map. Interaction units, as already defined, are subsets of events and constituted by particular patterns of language and social practices.[21] For example, interactions between an academically successful student and a teacher are generally qualitatively different to interactions between an academically struggling student and a teacher, or among different groups of classmates.[23] In addition, sequences of interaction units can be used to analyze how certain practices come to be established and maintained (Putney 1996, 133). This kind of analysis is demonstrated in Table 2.3 below.

Mapping observed events enabled me to analyze data in terms of panoramic views of each participant's everyday life, zoom in on fine details within and across events, then pan out again to the larger picture I was constructing of each participant's language uses and social practices (cf. Fetterman 1989, 47). Interview data, artifacts, journal entries, and the like were also indexed to each map. Fine-grained investigations were conducted primarily on detailed transcripts of interactions, and interaction and message units were employed in analyzing discourse practices. At this point, I was most interested in examining how meanings and patterns were constructed and negotiated interactively, rather than in grammatical structures of interaction.

For example, Nicholas and his mates regularly engaged in what I called "Rubber Wars." The following segment of an interaction unit is delineated by my introduction of the topic and Nicholas's shift to another topic following his recount of the history of this practice. Message units are also indicated within this segment of transcript, and marked by the start of each new line. Message units, in this case, were identified largely by means of prosody cues (e.g., falling or rising intonations, pauses, self-corrections) and context cues (e.g., the authority of Mrs. Ross). This is not to suggest that the message units as I have presented them here are predetermined in this interaction; rather, this is how I have chosen to represent them, based on analysis of the content and meaning(s) of what he was telling me, prosody markers, and the context of the conversation as well as the contexts of the original events (see Table 2.4 on page 61).

Nicholas's explanation of his group's shift from using rubber bands to rubber bits probably says much more than he consciously intended. Indeed,

> [s]peakers do not just "say what they mean" and get it over with. They lay out information in a way that fits with their viewpoint on the information and the interaction. They are always communicating much more than the literal message (Gee 1996a, 96).

Table 2.3 A Sample Event Map: Nicholas

Monday 10 November, 1994 (Day 1)

Time	Event	Actors, actions, and interactions
10.55	Language lesson	• Ter instructs Sts to organize themselves into 3 groups and begin their respective activities: library lesson, grammar textbook exercises, and basal reader work – N takes out textbook and shares with Rajiv • Ter explains grammar task – N throws a piece of rubber at Stuart, scores a hit and makes an "impact" noise – N asks Ter if he can write in pen in the textbook. Ter replies that it must be done in pencil. Two boys move to lend N a pencil and are reprimanded – N clarifies task with Ter
11.10		• N begins working – Ann asks N how many words his short story is: N: "614" Kylie: "Oh, did you count them?" N: "No, I used the word count on the computer," etc.

Wednesday 12 November (Day 3)

Time	Event	Actors, actions, and interactions
10.55	Language lesson	• N and Tim flick rubber bands at each other while waiting for the lesson to begin. N "low fives" with Rajiv, who offered his hand first • Ter instructs Sts to move into their English groups – N walks over to the computer and discusses a number of disks with Kylie
11.00		• N sits at the computer with Chris and begins typing: "Athletics Day." – He starts typing the body of his report, then rolls his eyes and mutters, "I hate this computer."
11.02		– N discovers he has keyed his text into the "heading" space and has run out of room. He tries to "select" what's he's written, but the program won't let him. He mutters: "Can you believe this stuff?" and deletes what he has written, etc.

Key: Ter = Teacher   St(s) = Student(s)   N = Nicholas   • = sub-event   - = particular actions and interactions within a sub-event

Everyday Literacies 61

Table 2.4   Analyzing Message Units Within an Interaction Unit: A Sample[23]

(Monday, October 10, 1994. 4:40 p.m. Day 1 of observations)
EVENT: PLAYING COMPUTER GAMES.
SUB-EVENT: *I ask Nicholas about the bits of rubber I'd seen thrown around in class earlier today.*

Nicholas	Yeah,
	normally we..
	uhm,
	do use rubber bands ((laughs))
Michele	Really?
Nicholas	((Laughs)) Yeah,
	and we fling them around in **class**.
	Except Mrs Ross ((the vice-principal)),
	and uhm she,
	she told the—
	I mean,
	talked to us about it
	and that we'd better not do it
	anymore
	((laughs))
Michele	Oh yeah.
	So now
	it's bits of rubber
Nicholas	((Laughs))
	I've got a lot
	in my desk now.
	((Laughter))
	Building up

Organizing this segment of Nicholas's discourse into message units enabled me to identify the ways in which he aligned himself with a particular group (e.g., we, us) that engages in overt physical action (e.g., fling, building), in tension with—in this instance—authority (e.g., "Except Mrs Ross... talked to us," "we'd better not do it any more," "I've got a lot in my desk now—laughter—Building up"). Analyzing the sequence of message units is also important, especially in terms of interpreting the function(s) of utterances and speech events (cf. Schiffrin 1994, 356).

In the present example, the sequence of message units provides me with supporting evidence for my interpretation that Nicholas is signaling solidarity with his mates in the face of institutional authority by means of his laughter and comments on his growing arsenal of rubber bits. Message units can also be mapped according to themes (cf. Bloome and Egan-Robertson 1993, 314; Schiffrin 1994, 28). I have used this technique in the present example to identify and trace how Nicholas and his mates publicly construct borderline subversive behavior by substituting bits of rubber for the banned rubber bands (see Table 2.5).

Accordingly, mapping message units can be used to interpret the thematic organization of Nicholas's explanation. In stripped-down terms, his discourse theme comprises: doing→told not to→still doing, only differently. Interestingly, following only the letter of the law turned out to be a regular feature of Nicholas and his mates' language and actions in school.

Interaction and message units can be interpreted from a number of angles, depending on the researcher's purpose. Hence, in order to make additional interpretive sense within and among interaction and message units, I also chose to investigate elements of prosody, cohesive devices, and sequencing, interaction or discourse organization, contextualization and intertexuality signals, and thematic organization.[24] Although it is extremely difficult to capture the intonation, emphases, pronunciation, and rate of discourse in transcriptions, certain expressive elements in Nicholas's explanation give it force beyond the actual words he uses. For example, Nicholas's voice falls in pitch at the end of: "I've got a lot in my desk now." His falling intonation brings closure to this set of messages, and emphasizes the significance of his ongoing borderline subversive behavior, indicated by his penultimate message unit comprising laughter,[25] and his final message unit: "Building up."

Nicholas also uses laughter to tie message units together and to help develop the theme of his explanation (i.e., his group of mates has found a way around constraints on behavior imposed by institutional authority). Words such as "normally," "and," and "yeah" also assist in fashioning cohesive ties among his message units. His use of "except" marks a significant event that occurred in relation to the history of these Rubber Wars;

Everyday Literacies 63

Table 2.5   Themes Conveyed by Message Units

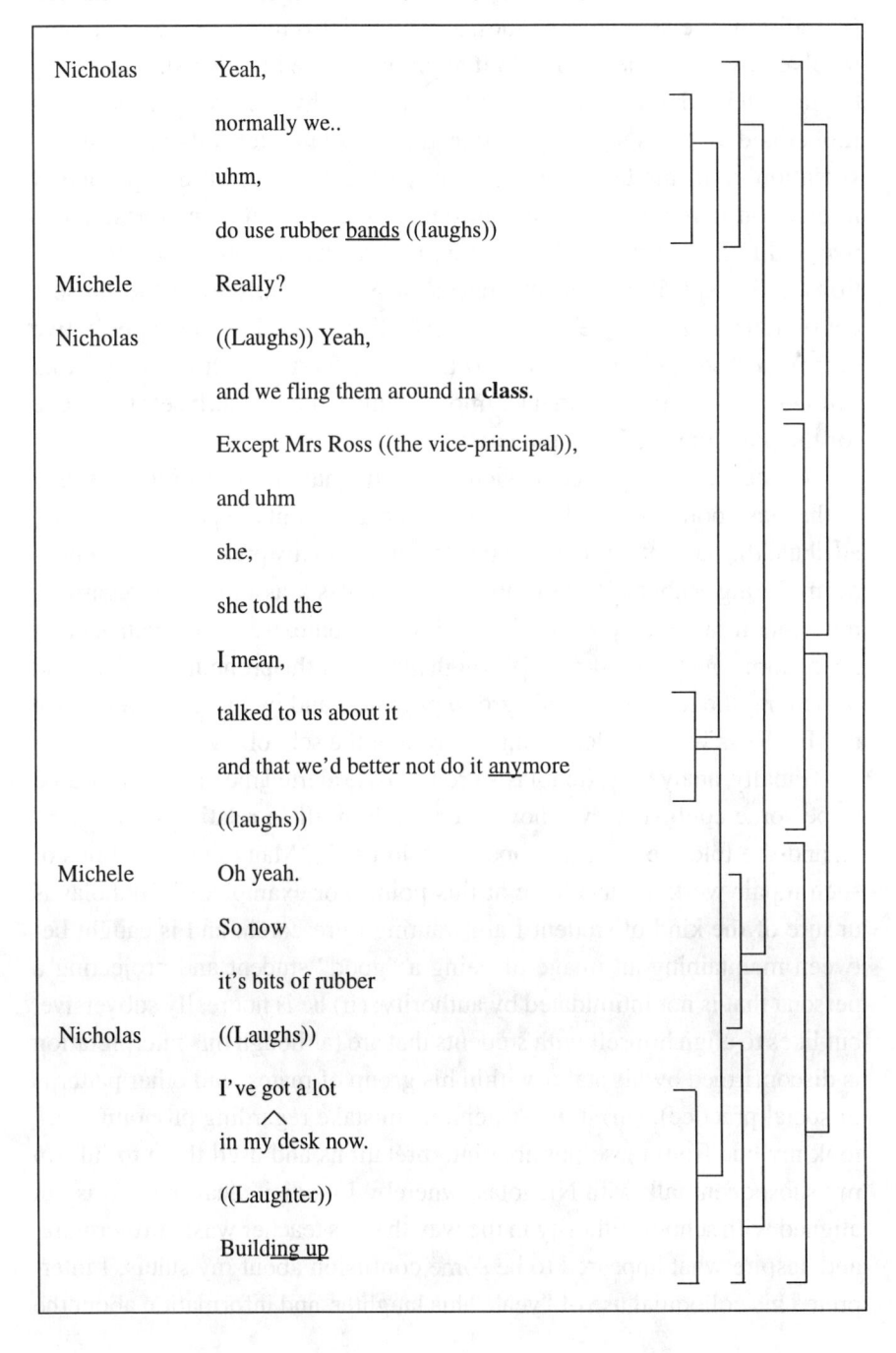

Nicholas	Yeah,
	normally we..
	uhm,
	do use rubber <u>bands</u> ((laughs))
Michele	Really?
Nicholas	((Laughs)) Yeah,
	and we fling them around in **class**.
	Except Mrs Ross ((the vice-principal)),
	and uhm
	she,
	she told the
	I mean,
	talked to us about it
	and that we'd better not do it <u>any</u>more
	((laughs))
Michele	Oh yeah.
	So now
	it's bits of rubber
Nicholas	((Laughs))
	I've got a lot
	in my desk now.
	((Laughter))
	Build<u>ing up</u>

an event that resulted in a modified arsenal, but little change in behavior. In addition, the sequence of message units introduced by "except" and resolved by "we'd better not do it anymore" is tied to his explanation by his laughter, which effectively cues me into why the group uses bits of rubber and answers my original question. His laughter following my observation confirms this interpretation. Thus, cohesion in this particular interaction is more a result of discourse organization than cohesive ties *per se*. In particular, Nicholas distinguishes between ongoing sets of actions and a specific event by means of a tense shift from the present continuous to the simple past (i.e., perfective). His shift to the perfective occurs at "except" and returns to the imperfective with the laugh that follows "we'd better not do it anymore." This temporal shift sets the scene for the punchline to his explanation.

Context is downplayed in Nicholas's explanation, with references only to the classroom and his desk tying his message units to particular sites. I attribute this lack of direct reference to context to my presence in the classroom during Rubber War events, and Nicholas's assumptions regarding my general familiarity with school staff and contexts. His discourse casts me as someone "in-the-know" through his use of the pronoun "we" instead of naming the members of his group of mates, and by his direct reference to Mrs. Ross without identifying her role in the school.

Finally, analyzing Nicholas's pronoun use alerted me to what appeared to be some confusion over how to define himself in relation to me (e.g., "...and she told the—I mean, and she told us..."). Many interpretations of such repair work are available at this point. For example: (i) Nicholas is unsure of the kind of student I am wanting to research, and is caught between maintaining an image of being a "good" student and projecting a persona that is not intimidated by authority; (ii) he is not really subversive, but likes to align himself with students that are (although this interpretation is disconfirmed by his status within his group of mates, and other patterns of social practice); (iii) it was a genuine mistake regarding pronoun use. I took my cue from these possible interpretations and used them to inform my subsequent talk with Nicholas, whereby I made it clear that I was not aligned with school authority in the way that his teacher was. Furthermore, and despite what appeared to be some confusion about my status, I interpreted his colloquial use of "yeah," his laughter, and information about the arsenal in his desk as ways of signaling that I was being recruited as an insider or as a co-conspirator.

This brief analysis of a sample of Nicholas's discourse is not intended to be exhaustive or posited as the only set of interpretations possible. There are many more analytic opportunities offered by this text (e.g., discussing the phrasal rather than clausal or sentential organization of discourse). Indeed, such analyses are always *post facto*, and are very often shaped by (provisional) hunches and analyses made on the run during data collection. Nevertheless, the particular analytic strategies outlined above produced what I believe to be trustworthy and useful evidence in support of my interpretations and discussions.

CONCLUSION

There are three key claims underpinning the present study. First, I argue that Gee's theory of D/discourses can be made to do effective "work" in language and education research. That is, **D**iscourse and **d**iscourse distinctions, and their substantive definitions, provide useful interpretations of relationships among individuals, groups, language uses, and social practices. These distinctions, I propose, can be used effectively as interpretive devices in language and literacy research. Thus, my study aims to make an original contribution to Gee's theory of D/discourses by employing Green's data mapping techniques to substantiate D/discourse interpretations in ways that are theoretically and methodologically trustworthy. Second, this study aims to examine and discuss the degree of fit between in-school and out-of-school practices and social purposes as enacted by the four participants. Third, I propose that interpretations afforded by analyzing the D/discourses in the everyday lives of four adolescents will contribute valuable information and understandings for comparison with assumptions that seem to undergird benchmarking procedures in Australia and elsewhere. In addition, the insights afforded from these four cases, while not generalizable, will be used in the final chapter to inform suggestions for possible ways of enhancing language and literacy pedagogy and teacher education in Queensland and beyond.

Endnotes

1. See, for example: Barton 1994; Baynham 1995; Erickson 1992, 1996; Fairclough 1995, 1996; Fishman 1972a, 1972b; Goffman 1967; Gumperz 1982a, ed. 1982b; Halliday 1978; Heritage 1984b; Kress 1985, 1987, 1988; Kress and Hodge 1979; Lemke 1995a; Martin 1992; Milroy and Milroy 1985; and van Dijk 1996.

2. See, for example: Fasold 1990, 1992; Milroy 1992; and summarized discussions in: Figueroa 1994; Hymes 1996; Pennycook 1994; Schiffrin 1994; Taylor and Cameron 1987.

3. Hymes (1974, 196) proposed that linguistics is actually a theory of grammar, rather than a theory of language, and that a theory of language necessarily encompasses much more than grammar alone.

4. Just as there are many theoretical possibilities and scholarly communities within sociolinguistics, so too are configurations of critical discourse analysis many and varied. However, all of these approaches share foundational assumptions regarding the nonneutrality of language and complex and uneven relations among language, power, social practices, and institutions. They can thus be grouped for present purposes under a general discipline heading.

5. See, for example, among many others: Cazden 1988; Collins and Michaels 1986; Cook-Gumperz ed. 1986, 1993; Green and Yeager 1995; Heath 1983; Hull and Rose 1994; Myers 1992; and O'Connor and Michaels 1993.

6. See, for example: Fairclough 1992, 1995; Fasold 1992; Hymes 1996; Milroy and Milroy 1985; Milroy 1992; Pennycook 1994; Smith 1990; and van Dijk 1996.

7. For example, Ralph Fasold (1992, 352) conceptualizes "speaker" in terms of a set of principles whereby people talk with each other in order to communicate ideas and information, as well as to "present their permanent social identities to [others] and to negotiate their momentary relationship with the people they are talking to."

8. Bowers and Iwi use "the individual" and "the social" as shorthand formulations of complex, multidimensional, and dynamic interrela-

tionships that are historically, biologically, economically, and politically circumscribed (1993, 361). So do I.

9. Transcripts themselves are always already interpretations. See, for example, discussions in: Baker 1991b, 1996; Fairclough 1992; Green, Franquiz, and Dixon 1997; Kantor, Green, Bradley, and Lin 1992; Morine-Dershimer 1985; Ochs 1979; and Psathas and Anderson 1990.

10. See, for example, among many others: Anderson and Irvine 1993; Cazden 1988; Cook-Gumperz ed. 1986, 1993; Delgado-Gaitan 1990, 1993; Gee 1989, 1993b; Gee, Michaels, and O'Connor 1992; Giroux 1993, 1995; Gutierrez 1993; Gutierrez, Rymes, and Larson 1995; Gutierrez and Stone 1997; Heath 1983; Heath and McLaughlin 1994; Hull and Rose 1994; Kress 1988; Lemke 1995a; Michaels 1986; Moll 1992; Moraes 1996; Shuman 1993; Steedman 1981; Street 1984; Weiler 1995; Walkerdine 1985, 1990.

11. For critiques of Foucault's theoretical assumptions about relationships among the individual and social systems, structures, and practices, see for example: de Certeau 1984, 46; Fairclough 1992, 57; Haraway 1991, 236; Moraes 1996, 99; Smith 1990, 79, 108.

12. Describing the ways of being *in* a Discourse is constrained by the language available. Discourses can seem to be reified by using such terms as *inhabit* and *use*, and by interpreting these terms instrumentally. However, inhabiting a place can be interpreted dynamically; one always shapes and changes—and is shaped and changed by—where one lives, even if only in small ways. Additionally, to *use* something suggests human agency; to deny such possibilities is too pessimistic. The active and optimistic interpretations of these terms are assumed throughout this book.

13. See, for example: Kress 1985, 7; Fairclough 1995, 12–13; Foucault 1972, 26.

14. An alternative interpretation of endless subdivisions is offered by McNeill and Freiberger (1993, 82–100). They suggest that nested and dynamically interrelated layers of sub-categories open up the complexities of language and everyday life for detailed examination.

68   *Everyday Literacies*

15. Of course, some Discourses, such as those aligned with feminism or literary criticism, for example, value debate and critique in relation to certain *other* Discourses. Nevertheless, members need to be seen to value and engage in such practices. Voicing internal criticism, as evinced by recent feminist debates here in Australia, marks one as no longer a full member of a particular Discourse.

16. These aspects include, for example: ray tracing with computer-generated graphics, artistic or playful uses of language, entrepreneurial acumen, the ability to construct a logical and persuasive oral argument outside traditional debating teams, and so on.

17. See Green and Dixon (1993) and Hymes (1996, 90–104) for illuminating discussions of methodological invisibility in academic writing.

18. See, for example, among many others: Bleicher 1993; Bloome 1989; Bloome and Egan-Robertson 1993; Bloome and Theodorou 1988; Green and Meyer 1991; Green and Harker eds. 1988; Green and Wallat 1981; Green, Weade, and Graham 1988; Kantor, Green, Bradley, and Lin 1992; Lin 1993; Putney 1996; Santa Barbara Classroom Discourse Group 1992, 1994, 1995.

19. Other analytic categories within this approach include: sequence units, cycles of activity, and action units. Although these categories have important functions to play in a full-blown microanalysis of events, I found that these categories either did not add significant information to interpretations in the present study (e.g., sequence units, cycles of activity), or were not suited to my data (e.g., action unit analysis requires video data).

20. The term *critical* is used here in terms of critiquing interrelationships among the individual and the social, and evaluating opportunities for accessing social goods and services that accrue for the individual and her affiliated social and cultural groups (cf. Lankshear 1997a).

21. These patterns are also "patterns within patterns" in the manner of Chinese boxes, entailing a series of smaller and smaller conversationally or interpersonally related units of analysis. In order to avoid *reductio ad absurdum*, a line is drawn at the smallest unit that still holds meaning.

22. See, for example: Delpit 1995; Jones 1986; Lesko 1988; McLaren 1993; and Walker 1988.

23. *Transcription conventions:*

,	running pause	-	a break in utterance flow
__	rising intonation	∧	rising and falling intonation
.	pause (0.1 sec)	(( ))	context markers

24. See, among many others: Gee 1996a; Hatch 1992; Hymes 1996; and the Santa Barbara Classroom Discourse Group 1995.

25. Indeed, the role of laughter as a message unit is an area worth further investigation. I found that all four study participants used laughter to convey myriad messages; for example, signaling jokes, indicating guesses, showing delight or appreciation, to cover embarrassment or bewilderment, to cue others into the interaction, as an opening and a closing, to demonstrate solidarity, as self-sufficient replies, and so forth (cf. Hatch 1992, 42).

CHAPTER THREE

Nicholas

REPORTING EMPHASES

All case study reporting is necessarily incomplete. Reporting everything observed, heard, or collected is unmanageable for writers and readers, and decisions must be made about what to include and what to leave out or save for other venues. The following case studies (chapters 3 to 6) do not claim to be tidy and encyclopedic; neither do they masquerade "as a whole, when in fact they are but a part—a slice of life" (Guba and Lincoln 1981, 377, cited in Merriam 1988, 33). Although there are no hard and fast rules for deciding what to emphasize in ethnographic case study reports, some set of criteria is usually imposed on the data and explicitly focuses reporting (cf. Carspecken 1996, 173; Coffey 1996, 69). Consequently, I have chosen to focus on the various ways in which constructions of "being a student" are enacted by participants, and on at least one other aspect of their everyday lives that appeared to be significant.[1]

In addition, a recurring criticism of case study research is that data are often invisible in reporting (cf. Fine 1993, 269; Stenhouse 1985, 270). I have attempted to address such criticisms by incorporating "snapshots" of events, segments of transcripts, and samples of fieldnotes directly into my discussion of Nicholas, Jacques, Layla, and Hannah (see also Table 3.1).

Table 3.1   Key to Codes Used in Reporting

[	Indicates overlapping utterances
(( )) or [ ]	Provides additional context details
....	Indicates a pause (one dot equals 0.1 of a second)
xxxx	Inaudible utterance

Indented sections in reported snapshots indicate undercurrents of action and interaction.

From the range of reporting strategies available, narrative approaches enable rich descriptions of events and practices and seem best suited for presenting D/discourse analyses.

A Narrative Approach to Reporting

Narrative approaches to case study reporting yield useful exposition tactics, including: scene-by-scene, characterization, and point of view strategies (Zeller 1995, 79). Scene-by-scene reporting usually produces a chronologically sequenced analysis and account of events. Scenes—or key events—are, in a sense, representations of social activity and can convey a "wealth of meaning" (Fetterman 1989, 93). Using them as reporting devices provisionally partitions data into manageable chunks that can be analyzed as part of a larger whole. This approach is very like snapping a photograph, which holds still a moment in time for detailed scrutiny, and is always already interpreted through (and by) the lens of the photographer/researcher. Analyses of details in snapshots can be examined in relation to wider contexts or to other events at other times (past, present, and even future in some instances) provided there is sufficient and trustworthy evidence to support wider-reaching claims. An important variation on this approach foregrounds a significant scene or key event, which is then analyzed and discussed (Stake 1995, 128).

Character descriptions, or characterizations, are achieved by reporting the researcher's impressions of the participant's character, appearance, attitudes, apparent motivations, interactions with others, ways of speaking, and so forth (Zeller 1995, 80). Characterization aims at bringing participants to "life" on the page. Characterizations need not be chronologically linear, and can be interwoven with snapshots of events that are organized around themes rather than times (e.g., a characterization may be composed from any number of instances of family talk around the dinner table and is used to provide accumulated evidence for interpreting that family's interactional patterns). This strategy can also be used to help contextualize claims, all the while recognizing that characterizations are far from neutral in their construction. Point of view reporting does not attempt to lay claim to positions inside the mind of a research participant. Rather, this strategy is concerned with the technical management of point of view (Zeller 1995, 80; Carspecken 1996, 48–49). Thus, point of view considerations assist drawing boundaries around what is and is not reported, and helps establish the "analytic periphery" of findings and claims (Yin 1989, 147).

In summary, combining point of view strategies with snapshots of events and characterization strategies enables me to focus on study participants as fully implicated in a network of relations with people, objects, and other phenomena (e.g., institutions, technology, youth culture). In particular, snapshots of events variously represent recurring patterns in the everyday lives of study participants, comprise unique or startling events, or are a combination of both. These snapshots and their accompanying analyses become terrain for interrogating the usefulness of D/discourse distinctions for interpreting each participant's everyday language and social practices in school and out-of-school contexts.

NICHOLAS

Nicholas (aged 12 years at the time of the study) is tall for his age, with the lanky build of a basketball player. His short brown hair is cut stylishly, and he likes to dress fashionably, but comfortably, away from school. His smile is ready and engaging, and his manner open and friendly—indeed, talking with him is often a humorous event as he brings his keen sense of irony and quick wit to bear on the conversation. In addition, one is struck time and again by his energy; just watching him in action is quite exhausting.

He lives with his family in a predominantly white upper middle-class suburb on the western edge of Brisbane. His mother, Debra, teaches business principles at a nearby independent secondary school, and his father, Russell, works long hours as a project manager responsible for coordinating interior designers for construction companies. Both Debra and Russell are very active in their Uniting Church; Russell is a church elder and Debra runs a Sunday group for young teenagers with the help of Nicholas's older brother, Joshua (18 years). Joshua is in his final year of schooling and hopes to enroll in a computer science degree program at a Brisbane university next year. Nicholas also has two older sisters, Jacinta (16 years) and Elyse (14 years). Jacinta would like to work in sports medicine, but fears her final marks will not be "good enough" and may opt to study to be a physiotherapist. Elyse would like to work as a teacher or in an office somewhere, but "not as a secretary." After reading John Grisham's *The Client* and visiting the Queensland Parliamentary offices as part of a school excursion, Nicholas is considering becoming a lawyer, or someone else who "makes a lot of money." Nicholas, his sisters, and his brother are encouraged by Debra and Russell to participate in a range of activities outside school. Nicholas, for example, regularly attends church, Sunday school and up to four church-related youth groups, plays competition basketball, has regular piano lessons, and has a paper run.

Family life appears close and loving. At the time of the study, Nicholas identifies his family as the most precious thing in his life. Nicholas appears to share a warm and loving relationship with his parents. He and his mother enjoy a particularly close relationship and regularly read the same books for relaxation, go "halves" in buying music compact discs, and work collaboratively on school homework and projects. His father's long working days meant that Russell's time at home fell largely outside observation periods. However, when opportunities arose to observe Nicholas and Russell interacting (e.g., at church, at basketball competition games), they evinced an affectionate and comfortable relationship with each other as demonstrated by chatting about a basketball game during half-time, talking together after church, as enacted in Russell's commitment to managing Nicholas's basketball team, and the like. In terms of interpersonal relationships within Nicholas's family, discussion and democratic negotiation are a key dimension. For example, each family member was involved directly in deciding which house to buy when they moved to Brisbane from Melbourne five years ago.

Nicholas is popular with students and teachers from all grades at the large Lutheran primary school he attends. He is often called on by school friends to mediate disputes concerning, for example, technical points in basketball rules or who should be on whose team. Nicholas's teachers often ask him to carry out a variety of tasks calling for responsible and reliable behavior, including, for example, tutoring year 1 students in reading, or relaying messages to other teachers.

Nicholas's classroom is square-shaped, with banks of large windows along parallel walls. This makes the room light-filled and airy, although not airy enough to dispel the already heavy heat of late October. The classroom is organized along traditional lines; the teacher's desk is at the front of the room at right angles to the chalkboard, and students' desks are arranged in serried rows. The seating arrangement is girl-boy-girl-boy,

Everyday Literacies 75

although Nicholas explains that this is a relatively recent arrangement caused by everyone talking too much in class with their friends. Nicholas sits in the back row near the double door leading to the open verandah outside. However, he is given to roaming the room during self-directed work times and chatting with his mates, or with Mr. Lasseter (with whom he appears to enjoy a friendly relationship).

His teacher rates Nicholas's language and literacy skills as "well above average." Nicholas himself is keen to be seen doing well at school. For example:

> (Tuesday 18 October 1994, 12:10 p.m. Day 9 of observations)
> EVENT: MATH
> SUBEVENT: *Mental math sums*
> Mr. Lasseter tells students to start working on their mental math problems. Nicholas finishes and takes out *The Client* and begins reading. He marks his work as Mr. Lasseter reads out the answers. When finished, Nicholas calls out: "Mr. Lasseter, I got one hundred percent!" His teacher nods and tells students to take out their math textbooks.

A number of themes or forms of life can be identified within this all too brief characterization of Nicholas. These include, among many others, being a member of a particular family, a member of a church, a successful student, a mate, and a basketball player. Nicholas lives out or enacts these various memberships and social identities in complex and dynamic ways, and with varying degrees of apparent seamlessness or disjunction. Some of these complexities are explored in the following two snapshots.

SNAPSHOT 1: A SLICE OF NICHOLAS'S CLASSROOM LIFE

> (Monday 10 October 1994, 9:20 a.m. Day 1 of observations)
> EVENT: LANGUAGE LESSON
> SUBEVENT 1: *Spelling*
> Mr. Lasseter asks students to call out their pretest spelling scores, and begins recording them in a notebook. Nicholas delivers his score—nineteen

out of twenty—in a loud voice, then asks Mr. Lasseter whether he had fixed up his score from last week, which had been recorded incorrectly. The students continue working on the spelling exercises in their English textbook.

Nicholas chats about the spelling list and definitions with Tim sitting in the row in front, then with Rajiv who sits two desks over.

SUBEVENTS 2 and 3: *Writing task and "Rubber War."*

Nicholas completes his spelling activities and begins working on a writing task. His best friend, Stuart, stops by Nicholas's desk on the way to the rubbish bin and says, "Y'know, it's supposed to be a short story," gesturing towards Nicholas's writing. "It *is* a short story," Nicholas insists, and they discuss how long a short story should be. Stuart is called over to see the teacher, then returns with his writing book and leans on the empty desk beside Nicholas and rubs out something in his book.

James throws a small piece of rubber at Stuart, who looks up and pulls a face.

Nicholas begins reading some of his written text to Stuart, who is again called over to see Mr. Lasseter. From across the room, Mr. Lasseter asks Nicholas if he has finished his book review and placed it in his writing folder. Nicholas calls out "Yep," then says more quietly, "Yeeesss, Mr. Lasseter" in an exaggerated voice. The teacher turns to talk with a student.

Nicholas swings around in his seat and hurls a piece of rubber into James's chest. James retrieves the piece and throws it, hitting Nicholas in the back of his head. Nicholas rubs his head and grins, then pitches another piece of rubber across the room at Stuart. James, Rajiv, and Tim join in.

(9:50 a.m.) Mr. Lasseter finishes speaking with the student and tells everyone to take out their social studies books.

Quantification of work in teacher-class interactions and in Nicholas's in-class dealings with his peers is a repeated pattern in this classroom. This is despite Mr. Lasseter's exhortations to his students that "All you've got to do is improve yourself. No one's better than anybody else." However, over sixteen teacher references to tests and test scores were recorded during the eight days of in-class observations. Although this could be a product of the time of year in which observations were conducted (i.e., close to the end of the school year), this emphasis was not so apparent in other classes observed later in October and in November of the same year. This emphasis on scores in Mr. Lasseter's class seemed to permeate male students' in-class interactions in particular, and they were observed regularly comparing test scores and assignment marks. Various interpretations can be made with regard to Nicholas's practice of quantifying his work and focusing on accuracy over content, and it would be easy to label such activity as competitively motivated alone. However, this interpretation is complicated by other evidence which suggests Nicholas understands some of the pitfalls resident in accentuating quantity over quality, and indeed, he can be quite scathing with regard to the quality and value of some school tasks he is set regularly to complete:

> (Monday 10 October 1994, 5:10 p.m. Day 1 of observations)
> EVENT: DOING HOMEWORK
> Nicholas sits at the kitchen table and tells me he has to work on the *English Magic* [textbook] exercises set for spelling homework. He laughs dryly and says there's no point to doing them. I ask him what he had learned from the literal and figurative language exercises he had done in class today and he replies, "Nothing. It was just a time filler." Debra interjects from the laundry, "Why is that? Why do students say they don't learn anything? I hear it all the time from my kids." Spelling is a waste of time, too, according to Nicholas. He has to rewrite all of his spelling words twice—even though he only got one wrong in his pretest this morning. He shows me the work set in *English Magic* and explains that instead of writing the sentence given in the book and filling in the missing word from his spelling list, all he has to do is write the word. Other work also requires only one-word answers (e.g., "Write verbs from these nouns: composer, conductor"). He explains that this is no way to learn spelling: "Writing a word instead of a whole sentence doesn't give you the meaning of the word, and if you can write the word, then you already know its meaning, so what's the point?"

In relation to learning, Nicholas appears to be distinguishing between "meaningful activity" and "doing school." The former appears to be, for him, tied to learning, whereas the latter is more closely aligned with doing as the teacher says. Nicholas also demonstrates a metalevel understanding of what kinds of student performances are valued by his teacher. Thus, for Nicholas, being a "good" student in year 7 involves "getting things right," knowing the exact answers, filling in the blanks, and producing a teacher-set amount of work.

However, my observations also suggest that Nicholas has acquired (in Gee's sense) an understanding that successful learning requires much more than these kinds of display. Such acquisition occurs through being immersed in effective student practices that have become an organic part of home life for Nicholas. These practices are modeled by his brother and sisters as they complete their own school assignments—and complete them very successfully by all accounts. Even more noticeably, the ways in which Debra works on school tasks with Nicholas at home involve explicit modeling and demonstration of effective student practices. For me, these complex overlappings between Nicholas's primary and secondary Discourses have significant educational and economic implications for his life chances beyond primary school. This is explored more tellingly in relation to snapshot 2 (see p. 86).

"Yes, Mr. Lasseter": Being a Student and Being Successful

I propose that Nicholas embodies a particular "student Discourse" at school that is constituted in part by the institutional—and therefore, cultural, social, and normative—role of primary schools in Queensland. He wears the regulation school uniform, he sits at a desk for the greater part of each school day engaging in (usually) teacher-set tasks, and his body, ways of speaking, and actions are regulated by clocks, bells, other people, and sometimes by himself. Nicholas is also a member of a particular modulation of the institutionally constituted student Discourse that is specific to his class. That is, particular configurations—or coordinations—of his teacher's Discourse memberships, the school's alignment with Lutheran Discourses and with the institutionalized student Discourse, and so on, coalesce within a particular social group: Nicholas's class. Thus, for Nicholas, it appears that being a member of the student Discourse as constituted and enacted within his classroom (i.e., a student sub-Discourse) requires him to focus on accuracy and quantity of work, to conduct himself as an independent and fast worker, to show respect for the teacher and the teacher's knowledge, and to sit or behave as though he is attending to the lesson at hand.

Membership in this student sub-Discourse is played out in Nicholas's student discourses, as well. He demonstrates adroit understanding of how to speak in class in ways that show him to be a successful student. He participates actively in class discussions (but only when he has the answer, or has what he—and not necessarily his teacher—considers to be a relevant anecdote), asks the teacher to clarify points that are unclear for the rest of the class, reminds the teacher about formats for writing in different subject areas, talks with peers about work progress and scores, displays for his classmates high scores on tests and positive teacher feedback on work submitted, and so on. Nicholas's mastery of successful student discourse in this class is reinforced by Mr. Lasseter, who repeatedly takes up and extends Nicholas's contributions to discussions and other class work. Thus, in a sense, Nicholas is also used by his teacher as a "class model" of effective student discourse.

However, Nicholas's understanding of and participation in other student Discourses is indicated by his ability to distinguish between "meaningful activity" and "doing school." Observing his brother and sisters completing their school-set tasks and engaging in collaborative practices around schoolwork at home—along with the language used to talk about language, learning, and work quality with his mother—have shown him ways of being a successful student other than the student Discourse enacted in his class. This home version of being a successful student can be interpreted as another modulation of the institutionally constituted student Discourse operating in Australia and described above. Although much could be said here about the implications of Nicholas's access to at least two versions of a student Discourse, there is more to be said first about the Discourses coordinating Nicholas at school. Indeed, Nicholas's membership in a particular student sub-Discourse is not the only form of life Nicholas lays claim to at school, and the student Discourse he enacts in class is thrown into high relief at times by his membership in a same-age group of males attending the same school.

BEING A MATE

Schooling, for Nicholas, is borne mostly with a kind of patient endurance, made conspicuous by regularly sliding down in his chair and resting his head on the chair-back, yawning, humming, scribbling aimlessly in his workbooks, fiddling with objects and so forth during teacher-to-whole-class talk times. This alternates with regular borderline displays of subversive behavior during individual work periods or during intervals between curriculum subject changes. Such behavior marks him as a member of a particular group of male friends—his mates—and largely manifests itself in a range of softly violent (and competitive) ways of acting, speaking, and maintaining relationships. For example, the Rubber Wars observed on the first day of school-based fieldwork were a regular feature of in-class behavior for Nicholas and his mates. In subsequent conversations Nicholas described how they began with rubber bands as ammunition until reprimanded by the vice principal. Now they use bits of rubber (see chapter 2, pp. 60–63, for a related transcript segment). The boys also hand wrestled each other, which comprised trying to twist an opponent's hand and arm until he begged for mercy. Hand wrestling occurred mostly in class behind chair backs, while standing in line, or while the teacher was engaged elsewhere in the classroom.

Another repeated form of soft violence was enacted in "High and Low Fives." This comprised hitting an opponent's open palm as hard as possible with your own, and vice versa. The first person to submit was the loser. Nicholas claimed it hurt "really bad," but he never surrendered. Afterwards, the lads liked to compare the redness of their hands. In all cases, these ways of interacting involved displays of physical prowess, courage, and competition, rather than quick-wittedness, intelligence, world knowledge, and other characteristics pertaining to the student Discourse promoted in Nicholas's class. In addition, boys on the outer edge of this group of mates were seen offering their open palms repeatedly in High and Low Fives interactions, or putting out their hand for a wrestling bout. This can be interpreted as overt efforts towards becoming full members of this group by challenging insiders, or by acting as a foil for letting full members display their strength (and in this way become tolerated by the group of mates, if not accepted). In any case, there are identifiable norms, values, ways of speaking, and certain practices operating to include some boys and exclude others. For example, Nicholas describes in his language journal an interactional pattern that arose while playing basketball at school:[3]

> (Wednesday 12 October 1994. Day 3 of research participation)
> Playing basketball with Steve and Josh. I was playing, and when we do a really good move we say: "That's the move!" It doesn't really make sense, it just means "that's good." When someone hits a reject we say: "Get that out of here" or "Get that out of my house." We say it because we think it's good and it looks good and people think you're pretty good after that.

Lingo such as this and accompanying exaggerated actions—like, running flat out for the ball, missing it, and continuing to run across the court and then up the mesh fence around the outside edge of the court—were successfully initiated only by insiders, and never by outsiders. Sharing this insider lingo remained a constant feature of interactions among this group of mates throughout the observation period. However, the actual phrases and words varied in durability of take-up, with many having only a fleeting currency before being replaced with something else. For example, the turns of phrase recorded by Nicholas above lasted only three days before being replaced with "cricketing speak"; for example, "No dings or you're out!" and "C'mon, gimme some spin."[4] This, too, served to shift the boundaries of what counted as being an insider for this group. These shifting linguistic signals support theorists' claims that discourse is more than an autonomous system; it is fully implicated in actions and social systems.[5]

These ways of acting and speaking demonstrated by Nicholas and his mates were not confined to out-of-class contexts, and affected in-class interactions in ways that sometimes conflicted with the student D/discourse expected by their teacher. Their interactions in class included cough codes for attracting attention or for signaling a rendezvous at the rubbish bin, throwing objects, and passing notes, to name only a few. For example:

> (Monday 10 October 1994, 4:40 p.m. Day 1 of observations)
> EVENT: PLAYING COMPUTER GAMES (audiotaped)
> SUBEVENT: *Talking about school*
> Nicholas describes how they throw things at each other in class. He confesses that he and his mates are "pretty bad," but explains that they don't

> get into too much trouble as they write notes to each other all the time. He recounts how one day they sent about 22 pages of writing amongst themselves without the teacher seeming to know. I ask whether they were able to get any school work done, and Nicholas tells me they did, when they had time. He comments on how they sometimes get a bit behind in their work due to passing these notes.

Thus, "being a mate" for Nicholas comprises maintaining relationships with his male friends, and includes among other things: borderline subversion of school ways of doing things (e.g., cough codes, the Rubber Wars, parodying polite behavior, note passing), participating in ritualized interactions (e.g., High and Low Fiving, playing basketball, oral word plays), displaying physical strength and sporting prowess, sharing basketball expertise and knowledge about the game and professional North American teams, (usually) demonstrating loyalty to his group of mates particularly in the face of authority, maintaining boundaries between inner circle mates and others, and not appearing too academically oriented. The overtly competitive nature of many of these mates' interactions is discussed later in relation to their talk about school work.

Occasionally, however, Nicholas's membership in the group of mates ran up against other, seemingly stronger values which resulted in a temporary breakdown of relationships. For example, on the fourth day of observations, relations between Nicholas and Stuart were obviously strained. When Nicholas was asked about it that afternoon at home, he described how he and Stuart had a falling out over a "foot violation" Stuart called against an outsider while playing basketball before school. Nicholas challenged Stuart's call by saying that it was not deliberate and therefore, technically, wasn't a violation. Things came to a head late in the school day (after observations had ceased) when Stuart provoked Nicholas with a rubber band and they began fist-fighting in earnest while Mr. Lasseter was out of the classroom. They were still fighting when he returned and both were dispatched to the vice-principal's office where they were reprimanded, banned from playing basketball at school for a month, and ordered to write a letter of apology to Mr. Lasseter for their behavior.

Nicholas's membership in this group of mates can be interpreted by means of a number of coordinating and overlapping Discourses, including: North American sport Discourses (garnered from television, magazines, mates, computer games), mateship Discourses (e.g., those promoted by Australian-produced television and other media images),[6] and institutionalized Discourses of "caring for others" (valued and authorized by the school and church, and by family expectations regarding friendship and being a friend).

"Yessss, Mr. Lasseter": Being a Member of a Group of Mates

Gee's theory of D/discourses enables shifts in interpretive orientations within the theoretical framing of a study. Hence, analysis of Nicholas's in-class student Discourse is made more detailed and complex by juxtaposing it with analyses of Nicholas's membership in a particular group of mates at school. This is not to suggest that these orientations are the only positions available. However, teasing out Nicholas's various and embodied ways of being a student and being a mate helps unravel some of the complexities that comprise Nicholas's language practices at school. In the recent past, studies of young Australian males at school have tended to conflate "being a student" and "being a mate," or have focused only on one of these forms of life (see, for example, Macpherson 1983; Walker 1988). This oversimplifies data analysis and narrows the range of interpretive possibilities.

On the other hand, a theory of Discourses enables me to "see" that Nicholas lays claim to more than one social identity. For example, what I first interpreted as an eagerness in Nicholas to be seen as a successful student in the eyes of his teacher and peers was revised in light of his subtle—and not so subtle—parodying of the student Discourse promoted in his classroom. This was noticed after a week of observing and analyzing Nicholas's relationships with his mates and other school friends. Nicholas's parodic play with language and actions in class suggests he has mastered the *form* of the student Discourse authorized by his teacher. That is, Nicholas parodies this Discourse in ways that are recognizable by others—especially his mates—and displays metalevel knowledge and understanding of the student sub-Discourse coordinating his class. Thus, Nicholas knows that he can couch a knowledgeable and correct answer in language that threatens to subvert class undertakings. For example:

> (Wednesday 19 October, 11:20 a.m. Day 9 of observations)
> EVENT: LANGUAGE LESSON
> SUBEVENT: Reading session using basal readers
> Mr. Lasseter ((to the reading group)): "What's a 'lookout'?"
> Nicholas: "It's a thing where you stand... and all the seagulls poo on it."
> Mr. Lasseter ((somewhat hurriedly)): "Thank you Nicholas."

These kinds of exchanges, which were regular occurrences in class, suggest to me that Nicholas engages in a complex process of being seen to take classroom work seriously enough to be recognized as a successful student, yet doing so in ways that do not alienate him from his group of mates. In addition, this also suggests that Nicholas appears to understand what kinds of knowledge displays enable access to success in the particular student Discourse operating in his class.

Analyzing ways of "being a student" in terms of D/discourses alerted me to numerous possible configurations of student forms of life in school and out-of-school; the same was found in analyzing mateship Discourses. "Mateship" is a recurring theme in studies of Australian male school students (see, for example, Macpherson 1983; Walker 1988), and studies of Australian males in general (see, for example, Buchbinder 1994; Connell 1995). Collectively, these studies offer various insights into aspects of mateship and suggest that the category label is a trope for describing a range of ways of belonging to a group of (usually male) friends. In Nicholas's case, however, his group of mates is never truly subversive in comparison with the kinds of mateship groups traditionally studied (cf. Willis 1977; McLaren 1993). Their collective behavior and ways of speaking appear tempered by the coordinating Discourses of the school, the school's alliance with the Lutheran Church locally and nationally, and so forth. Nevertheless, this group of boys remains distinct from other social groups within the school.

Nicholas himself talks about his "mates" and his "friends," linguistically emphasizing the relational distances between them. Nevertheless, Nicholas appears to value friendship and being a friend. He repeatedly demonstrated respect and care for others regardless of their social status at school, and always called for fair dealings, which at times—as we have seen—brought him into conflict with his mates. His care for others is demonstrated by the help he gives to Rajiv, a recently-arrived ESL student from India.

> (Wednesday 12 October 1994. Day 3 of research participation)
> **What happened:** Talking to Rajiv about how to do research [for a school project]. He had no idea of what to do and he was very hopeless at it but I didn't tell him that. I just said this is the way I do it and it works well for me. Then I helped him a bit and he got it, and his sentences were getting a lot better after that.

This example was recorded in Nicholas's language journal. Further examples of respect or care include: speaking respectfully with girls in his class, labeling items in English for the newly arrived Chinese-speaking boy, helping Rajiv to sort out a friendship dilemma at school, and defending year 1 students against older bullies. Such valuing of others also characterizes much of Nicholas's family and church life.

These foregoing analyses suggest that Nicholas is able to (usually) negotiate tensions set up by what are sometimes opposing Discourse practices. For example, he actively engaged in ritual exchanges and actions with his mates in class, yet seemed to know when to stop subversive behavior, or how far he could push Mr. Lasseter before being admonished. Indeed, Nicholas was rarely reprimanded as an individual by his teacher; only two minor instances of teacher-discipline directed at Nicholas were observed throughout the entire observation period. This was in marked contrast with the number of reprimands directed at his mates. This ability to shift competently between mateship and student sub-Discourses is confirmed by Mr. Lasseter: "Nicholas knows what's appropriate—when to muck around and have a bit of fun, like sometimes we have in here, and when maybe it's not so appropriate, and when it's time to be serious and things like that." This is consonant with James Macpherson's (1983, 49–64) distinction between "mucking around" and "stirring," where the former connotes high-spirited humor and exuberance, and the latter describes how students deliberately set out to antagonize their teacher. Mucking around appears to be more socially acceptable than stirring in Nicholas's class, and when interspersed with exemplary student behavior does not endanger success at school. Nicholas's overt displays of being a mate in class and during breaks seemed to secure high status within the dominant group of males, who never seemed to question his relative immunity to teacher discipline. At the same time, he is able to maintain his status as a high achieving student by knowing when to display knowledge and competence.

Moreover, the coordinating and constituting interrelationships among student Discourses and mateship Discourses, and Nicholas and his group overlapped in interesting ways. For example, Nicholas and Stuart regularly compared test scores and teacher comments on assignments. These kinds of actions can be interpreted as academically competitive and closely aligned with the student Discourse in that class; however, such events rarely seemed threatening for the boys and were generally accompanied by the laughter and verbal plays characterizing their mateship Discourse. Although interpretation of these overlaps can only be provisional, it seems that competition is valued by Nicholas and others in both Discourses and that academic achievement becomes a form of currency in the status stakes, provided mates show clearly that they do not take it too seriously. Once again, this underscores the dynamic and complex disposition and interpretation of Discourses, social identities and memberships. It also justifies calls from Gee and others for ethnographic approaches to researching D/discourse coordinations; such approaches are required to collect the kind of thick data needed as evidence for interpreting D/discourse memberships in people's everyday lives.

Below, the second snapshot revisits Nicholas's membership in at least two student sub-Discourses and enables exploration of aspects of Nicholas's in school and out-of-school language practices in terms of Gee's conceptions of primary and secondary Discourses.

SNAPSHOT 2: HOMEWORK

(Thursday 20 October 1994, 4:55 p.m. Day 10 of observations)
EVENT: DOING HOMEWORK
SUBEVENT: *Government project work for school on the Apple computer*

Earlier this afternoon, Nicholas's mum, Debra, keyed three subheadings into Nicholas's project text. She tells Nicholas to "flesh them out" using the reference texts he has brought home from school. Nicholas explains to me how she always checks that the text he writes isn't too similar to the original source, and sometimes changes words he has keyed in to ones he is more likely to use.

(5:09 p.m.) Nicholas sits at the computer and props a reference text against the front of the monitor behind his keyboard. He reads this book as he types, having learned to touch type when he was seven years old (he explains that Mum gave him a few cents every time he practiced touch typing and so he learned how to do it quite quickly).

(5:15 p.m.) Debra enters the study and begins reading Nicholas's keyed-in text. They discuss some on-screen changes, and she corrects his spelling of "definite." Debra suggests including a direct quote, and explains how to mark it off from the rest of his text by using quotation marks.

Debra	Why don't you just make that a direct quote?
Nicholas	What's that?
Debra	Where you copy something straight from the book.
Nicholas	Is that what you call it? How do you do that?
Debra	Just put it in quotation marks. Just put that... ((pointing to text on screen)) in quotation marks.
Nicholas	Do I write where it's from?
Debra	Mm-hm ((pause)). Do you use the Harvard method of bibliography, or not? Where you've got to put the brackets around—
Nicholas	Yeah, that's it. Yep.

They talk about the referencing conventions Elyse is using in her current project on Indonesia. Debra also suggests that Nicholas should be building his glossary as he goes along. She reads aloud some of Mr. Lasseter's assignment criteria and Nicholas shows her the reference book these criteria came from. This is the book he has propped against the monitor. Debra recommends he use a different book as his main reference source, reminding him that all his classmates will be using Mr. Lasseter's recommended text:

> | | |
> |---|---|
> | Debra | Start with that ((indicating second book)), all right? |
> | Nicholas | What about this "debate" stuff? |
> | Debra | Just leave that for the moment, all right. |
> | Nicholas | That's a bit hard. |
> | Debra | Well, it's not that it's hard, it's just you've got to have a notion.... So, use this as a reference, then, do like we did the other time, once you've used that ((indicating second book)), go back and fill in the gaps from your other material. |
>
> Debra tells Nicholas to finish the section on "Making Laws," then work on the "Debating" section. She tells him it should take about twenty minutes, and then he can stop.

Academic work is valued within Nicholas's family. Work spaces have been set aside for the children in the home. The formal dining room has been given over to an IBM computer, a desk, and a bookshelf holding textbooks and other reference materials. This is in addition to the study proper, which contains a late model Apple computer, more bookshelves holding student texts and materials, two filing cabinets, and another desk. Debra explains how this is still insufficient, especially given Joshua's plans for attending university next year. They are considering a desk and study space in the main bedroom downstairs, as it is too hot in the afternoons for Joshua to work in the bedroom he shares with Nicholas upstairs. Moreover, exchanges between Nicholas and Debra around Nicholas's schoolwork (like those above) were recorded regularly throughout the observation period. Indeed, Debra unintentionally confirmed this pattern of interaction, and emphasized the high priority given to the children's school work at home:

> (Thursday 20 October 1994, 4:57 p.m. Day 10 of observations)
> EVENT: NICHOLAS'S GOVERNMENT PROJECT
>
> | | |
> |---|---|
> | Debra | Oh! I just realized I've got Elyse's project on Indonesia, and I said to her I would do it yesterday! |
> | Michele | [You're doing it? |
> | Debra | [And I'm just sitting here and I haven't—I mean, she's done |

> it, I'm typing it up. Ohhh ((groaning)) I don't want to know about Indonesia ((laughter)). Last night I was looking at Joshua's essay, that was China—ancient Chinese and Indian families, the similarities and differences, and I'm thinking, I'm trying to get my poor head around this you know ((laughs)). Meanwhile, I'm burning an apricot loaf and.... ((laughter))[7]

Debra's involvement in her children's school work comprises more than simply ensuring they meet completion deadlines. As demonstrated in snapshot 2, Debra scaffolds metalevel ways of thinking and talking about their school work. This is exemplified in her identification of subheadings, her talk with Nicholas about them, references to previous collaborative project work, and her explanation that understanding is about having "some notion" of the content and concepts. In a very real sense, Debra is providing Nicholas with opportunities to learn through guided participation strategies (cf. Rogoff 1995; also Heath and McLaughlin 1994). Debra also models a contextualized metalanguage for talking about Nicholas's writing (for example, terms like: reference material, bibliography, glossary, paragraph, quote, and quotation marks).

Debra's experiential knowledge of what constitutes successful learning—an outcome of her insider knowledge of schooling gained from being a teacher herself—is brought to bear on her collaborative interactions with her children in relation to their school assignments. She makes explicit for them what it means to produce a successful assignment, and in so doing, how to go about being a successful student. In other words, Debra is apprenticing Nicholas—albeit somewhat unwillingly on his part—to an institutionally successful student sub-Discourse.

Debra's suggestion that Nicholas focus on a reference source other than the class textbook is telling evidence of this. Here she signals what is valued by schools in general, and therefore what usually counts as being a successful student. This includes: resourcefulness in going beyond what the teacher has provided, evidence of understanding, and originality of thinking. Additionally, she signals that being a successful student includes:

developing and following a logical assignment design, displaying evidence that assignment criteria have been met, and in relation to Nicholas's present assignment, emulating published expository texts.

Nicholas recognizes the value of meeting assignment criteria and of producing a polished, professional-looking text. However, he is keenly aware that Mr. Lasseter's assignment criteria are drawn directly from the class textbook: "I've got—what he's done, he's just copied out of this book. See look, 'Making Laws' and he's just put it all together." Judging from comments made to his mother when they began discussing his text to date, he appeared to have interpreted the task as a large "cloze exercise" whereby he was required simply to fill in text beneath his teacher's criteria-as-headings until the set word limit was reached. Indeed, at this stage of his assignment he seems more interested in constructing a glossary (his own idea), than in engaging with the concepts of government in Queensland. However, when pressed, he is able to deliver the "successful goods"—at least in the eyes of his teacher:

> (Teacher's assessment comments on returned assignment. December, 1994)
> An extremely pleasing effort, Nicholas. Information is clear and accurate, presentation is fine although a little more care with the cut and pasting would have completed it nicely[8]. A thorough, well thought out project.
> 48.5/50

Possible implications of Debra's and Mr. Lasseter's constructions of a successful student—and successful text production—are discussed later.

Other details visible in the second snapshot that warrant closer scrutiny pertain to Nicholas's technological literacy skills. Using computers appears to be a regular family practice. Each family member moves fluidly between the IBM and Apple computers, depending on their purposes (e.g., gaming, assignment writing, testing out new software, designing interiors, planning units of schoolwork). Nicholas, too, was able to talk about computers in knowledgeable ways. For example, at the time of observations his family was in the process of buying a new computer printer and he was able to explain, using technical terms, the benefits of laser over dot matrix and bubble jet printers. Debra tells how she has always encouraged her children to master computer technology; all of them touch type and are able to troubleshoot most programming problems they encounter. Indeed, she claims that parents and teachers cannot afford to ignore "computer literacy" any longer.

Nicholas is also part of a gaming network that shares software and gaming tips. For example, Nicholas was observed handing a computer disk to a friend at church, telling him that it was "wiped clean." When asked about this later, he explained that this friend was going to copy five computer games onto the disk for Nicholas, and Nicholas in turn was borrowing a popular computer adventure game from a school friend to pass on to this church friend. Members of this gaming network traveling to North America—where game software is a fraction of the cost it is here in Australia—are also enlisted as software buyers and new game scouts for the others. Snapshot 2 contrasts with Nicholas's access to computers at school, and with Mr. Lasseter's position regarding the role of computers in the classroom. There is no permanent computer in his classroom. The two year 7 classes at the school and the library share a single Apple computer and its small collection of software, which means that Nicholas's classroom houses the computer for only one-third of the school year. Students in Mr. Lasseter's class are rostered to use the computer in pairs for half an hour per week, and time spent at the computer has no direct educational relation with what is happening in the rest of the classroom. Most students spent their weekly half hours playing educational problem-solving games, like *Where in the World Is Carmen Sandiego?*, or publishing work they had handwritten in class. Mr. Lasseter rarely intervenes during computer sessions, and when he does it is usually to restore orderly behavior.

Not surprisingly, this sets in place significant tensions for Nicholas, who is often nonplussed by his teacher's refusal to let him use the computer to complete school tasks efficiently. For example:

(Tuesday 11 October 1994, 10:21 a.m. Day 2 of observations)
EVENT: SOCIAL STUDIES LESSON
SUBEVENT: *Discussing class work with Mr. Lasseter.*
Nicholas is standing by Mr. Lasseter at the front of the classroom, while his classmates work on a social studies task. Nicholas and Mr. Lasseter talk

> briefly about a handwritten draft of a report on the school's Athletics Day Carnival that Nicholas and Stuart have been asked to write for the end-of-year school magazine. Stuart appears beside Mr. Lasseter and all three discuss Nicholas's handwriting. Nicholas asks his teacher whether he could "do it on the computer and *then* handwrite it." Mr. Lasseter replies, "No," and Stuart contends, "But you must use the technology if it's there!" All three debate the merits of handwriting and technology.

For Nicholas, using word processors to complete his work not only obviated the need to write successive—and for him, tedious—rough drafts, but enabled him to craft his texts in ways that proved satisfying: "I hate writing it down 'cause then you can't change it and, y'know, it makes it a lot harder. I just read through it and delete the bits I don't like and put in better words."

Eventually, Mr. Lasseter relents and the following day finally agrees to let Nicholas word process the Athletics Day report at school. Indeed, perhaps the sharpest contrast between Nicholas's computer literacy practices in school and out-of-school occurs when snapshot 2 and the following subevent are juxtaposed.

> (Wednesday 12 October 1994, 11:00 a.m. Day 3 of observations)
> EVENT: ENGLISH LESSON
> SUBEVENT: *Nicholas sits at the class computer and works on his Athletics Day report.* He quickly becomes frustrated. "I hate this computer," he complains, rolling his eyes. The word processing program loaded onto the computer is designed for young children, and is very basic and inflexibly sequenced. It begins with commands for inputting "the heading," then moves to "the first paragraph," and so on. The default font on the screen is large and simple; very different from the sophisticated fonts on the computers in Nicholas's home. He begins composing his text, only to find he has been keying into the "heading space." He tries to select his text with the mouse in order to shift it to the "paragraph" section, but the program won't recognize the command. He quickly becomes frustrated—"Can you believe this stuff?"—and gives up on composing. He spends the next half hour keying

> "Athletics Day" into the heading space, in a variety of fonts, alternately enlarging and reducing the text. At the end of his allotted half hour on the computer, with the report not written, Nicholas asks for an extension. Mr. Lasseter is visibly displeased, but gives his consent.[9]

Accessing Different Ways of Being a Student

The second snapshot and the event presented above provide fruitful ground for exploring what Gee would call Nicholas's dynamic coordination by his primary and secondary Discourses (see especially Gee 1996a, 141–145). Debra's insider knowledge of the secondary Discourses constituting schooling and successful students is fused with ways of speaking and acting in this family when engaging with school-related tasks. This is especially evident in the student sub-Discourse Debra helps coordinate at home, wherein Nicholas is, to use Gee's concepts, both acquiring *and* learning how to be a successful school student. Thus, I am convinced that Nicholas is actually spending his time at school practicing—and mastering—much of what he already knows. Indeed, his classroom teacher provides signposts for this interpretation. For example, Mr. Lasseter readily identified the following about Nicholas: "The comprehension activities and things like that he does fairly well, so that's probably consolidation." Although Nicholas may have gained such understanding in previous classes, his expertise far outstrips that of his long-term classmates and suggests that factors other than school-based ones are at work here.

Students such as Rajiv, for example, appear to have very little time for practicing being a successful student; most of their energy seems to be consumed in trying to "crack the code" in the first place.[10] This becomes significant in light of the current English syllabus operating in Queensland (Department of Education, Queensland 1994). This syllabus is grounded in genre theory, and claims that knowing about and understanding genres enables members of cultural groups to function usefully and effectively in society. In addition, the syllabus proposes that this knowledge and understanding help to effect changes; "[p]eople who understand how genres work can be powerful instruments of critical review and change in any culture" (5). Thus, within this syllabus, as with much of the genre theory and education literature, utopian conceptions of genres as powerful—and empowering—instruments prevail and "change" is configured as always socially beneficial, or at least unproblematically functional for those involved.[11] However, if claims about direct relationships between language use and power as promoted by this syllabus and by genre theorists in general are to hold any water, advocacy of explicit approaches to text structures and linguistic functions will need to be coupled with, at the very least, ways of analyzing and critiquing what it means to be a successful student (or whatever) in a range of contexts.[12]

To reiterate, Debra constructs, models, and expects a different version of "being a successful student" from the one constructed in Nicholas's class at school. She focuses on the quality of the final product, and discusses the kinds of processes that enhance the quality of a written text with Nicholas. She shows Nicholas how to pace himself when completing independent research assignments, and encourages creativity and innovation in addressing assignment criteria. This can be interpreted as setting in place a student sub-Discourse for Nicholas that is likely to prove more enabling for him in the long run than a student sub-Discourse that values quantity and accuracy over quality and risk-taking.[13] Debra is also keenly attuned to changing times and the significance of being computer literate. She bemoans the fact that many teachers and parents seem unaware that "computers are a large part of children's lives." She emphasizes the importance of being computer literate by encouraging Nicholas to touch-type, providing her children with adult-level software, and promoting computer use at home for a range of educational and recreational purposes. Thus for Nicholas, using a word processor to produce a text is much more "natural" than using pen and paper. This conflicts with the teacher-orchestrated writing and computer experiences provided at school, and usually results in Nicholas avoiding writing at school whenever he can.

In addition, Debra provides opportunities for Nicholas to gain a metaperspective on schooling. She speaks openly about problems with schooling in present times, and encourages her children to question the purposefulness of some of the school tasks they are set to do (see, for example, Nicholas's comments about his English homework, p. 77). Both parents appear to value problem-solving abilities, independent thinking, and the capacity to make reasoned decisions. This contrasts with the kind of learning opportunities provided for Nicholas at school, which appear to promote single, correct answers for tasks and seem grounded in the assumption that students will comply unquestioningly with teacher directives (cf. the letter of apology to Mr. Lasseter as punishment for fighting). Indeed, looked at in this way, the rich and multifaceted apprenticeships Nicholas is experiencing out-of-school warrant more complex analysis than the apprentice-master configuration Gee employs. Barbara Rogoff (1995), for example, provides a more satisfying way of theorizing and describing "apprenticeship." Rogoff proposes three planes of analysis for interpreting relationships among learning, acquisition,[14] and sociocultural activity. These planes or dimensions comprise: apprenticeship, guided participation, and participatory appropriation. In everyday life, these three dimensions are mutually constitutive and interdependent.

Apprenticeship, in Rogoff's terms, operates within a community and institutional activity and describes "active individuals participating with others in culturally organized ways." Thus, the primary purpose of apprenticeship is to facilitate "mature participation in the activity by less experienced people" (Rogoff 1995, 142). For example, in Nicholas's case, he is being apprenticed among other things to a technological Discourse. Whether or not this is a deliberate choice on Nicholas's part is not important; rather, the point I am making is that Nicholas does indeed have ready access to a community of people who are interested in using technology, and in particular, computers. This community comprises relative experts (e.g., his mother and father) and peers with whom to explore the possibilities of the medium. Experts and peers are equally important features of Rogoff's conception of apprenticeship. For Rogoff, "peer" indicates status within a community or group, rather than a same-age cohort of people. Thus, the group "may involve peers who serve as resources and challenges for each other in exploring activity, along with experts (who, like peers, are still developing skill and understanding in the process of engaging in activities with others of varying experience)" (143). Investigating and interpreting sociocultural apprenticeships therefore focuses attention on the activity being mastered (and its concomitant skills, processes, and content knowledge) and its relationship with cultural and community practices, as well as with institutions.[15]

Guided participation comprises the "processes and systems of involvement between people as they communicate and coordinate efforts while participating in culturally valued activity" (Rogoff 1995, 143). Guided participation encompasses a range of social interactions including face-to-face, side-by-side (which is more frequent than the former in everyday life), and other arrangements whereby the activity does not require copresence. Accordingly, "guidance" in Rogoff's sense is afforded by cultural and social values (desirable or undesirable),[16] as well as by social partners who may be local or distant (1995, 142; also Rogoff 1984). For example, Nicholas's brother, Joshua, regularly shared technical information with Nicholas (e.g., discussing processing speeds, modem bandwidth), and Debra repeatedly encouraged Nicholas's technological participation in myriad ways (e.g., providing more-than-adequate hardware, bringing home software from school for review, paying him to learn to touch type, and discussing the family's computing needs with Nicholas and the others).

"Participatory appropriation," the third component of Rogoff's theory, refers to ongoing and dynamic engagement with learning through socially constituted activities which ultimately transform the learner. Rogoff uses this concept to describe "the process by which individuals transform their understanding of and responsibility for activities through their own participation" (1995, 150). For example, Nicholas appears to have appropriated a range of technological skills, knowledge, and processes. Indeed, I consider Nicholas to be a highly competent computer user. Among a plethora of abilities I saw demonstrated, he is able to create folders independently, make and retrieve files to work on, cut and paste text, play computer games with great dexterity, and discuss the benefits of using computers over pen and paper. In Rogoff's sense, "appropriation" is a process of "becoming" (1995, 142, 1990, 86–109). Nicholas is indeed well on his way to becoming a competent, mature user of computers. In addition, and as an aside, I am convinced that the process of appropriation may also transform the activity and what needs to be learned in some instances. This is consonant with Gee's interpretation of Discourse change (Gee 1992b, 109; see also chapter 2). Accordingly, Rogoff's conception of apprenticeship enables rich interpretive possibilities that move beyond traditional, dyadic conceptions of apprenticeship and mastery.

Finally, and from a pragmatic angle, it is virtually impossible to differentiate between what Gee would call Nicholas's primary Discourse, and the secondary Discourses that overlap with his family's shared form of life. Certainly for Nicholas, computers are very much an organic part of being a member of his family. Nevertheless, in terms of theoretical or heuristic applications, Gee's distinction between primary and secondary Discourses provide inroads into understanding how it is that students like Nicholas and Rajiv perform so differently in terms of school success, and how this will most probably impinge significantly on their respective future life chances.[17] If claims about symbolic-analytic processes and understandings made by current theorists and commentators working at the intersection of sociology, anthropology, technology, and education are taken seriously (e.g., Cummins and Sayers 1995; Reich 1992; Rheingold 1994), then it can be said that the student Discourse to which Nicholas is being apprenticed in his primary Discourse is potentially more powerful in the long term than the student Discourse privileged within his classroom.

A Brief Point About Literacy Standards and Education Outcomes

Being successful in Nicholas's case—and, I would argue, all students'—is to do with much more than being "good at language." Indeed, the Queensland English syllabus and the national literacy benchmarks, as two examples among many, promote cultural illusions by suggesting that language is (always for everybody) a powerful cultural and social instrument (e.g., see also Clinton 1997; Kemp 1997). Nicholas's case suggests that acquiring and learning how to use language effectively for a wide range of social purposes in present times may have, for some students, very little to do with what is currently happening in schools and everything to do with what is happening outside them. This, too, seems to be borne out in the case of Jacques presented in the next chapter.

Endnotes

1. Criteria employed in these decisions included: relevance to research aims and questions, trustworthiness and communicative validity of interpretations could be established, and reporting these foci would not breach ethical considerations accompanying all studies that delve into students' lives.

2. The language used to describe participants' actions is a case in point. For example, "laughed" or "chuckled" have different social connotations from "giggled."

3. Nicholas chose to audiotape his language journal. Transcriptions of his recordings are used throughout this chapter, and thus are already interpreted.

4. At this time, this group of mates and other male year 7 basketball players were banned from the basketball courts for fighting and turned to cricket for solace. The cause of the fight is discussed later.

5. See, for example, among many others: Carspecken 1996; Gee 1990; Hymes 1996; Heath 1983; Kress 1985; Lankshear 1997a; Moraes 1996; Smith 1990; Street 1984.

6. For example, television shows such as *Blue Heelers*, *Water Rats*, *Home and Away*, *Neighbours*, *The Footy Show*; advertisements for pies, beer, some cereals, even flavored milk; movies such as *Gallipoli*, *The Man from Snowy River*, *Mad Max*; and the like.

7. The mother of each case study participant was a remarkably significant and pervasive influence in each participant's life. This was intriguing as I had expected all four participants to be less attached to their mothers given each participant's age and so on. For me this suggests important terrain for future research work.

8. Nicholas had printed out his text, then cut it into sections which were glued into a sketch book along with pictures from a project pack and an information sheet.

9. Eight days later, 20 October, Nicholas produced this report on the Apple computer at home inside 8 minutes.

10. See: Heath 1983; Jones 1986; Levinson, Foley, and Holland eds. 1996; Walton 1993.

11. See, for example: Cope and Kalantzis eds. 1993; Cranny-Francis 1992; Martin 1992, 1993; Christie 1987, ed. 1990; Macken 1990; Martin, Christie, and Rothery 1987; Williams 1993.

12. This will also necessarily include critiques of what it means to be "empowered." See for example: Lankshear (1994, 1997a), and LeCompte and de Marrais (1992).

13. Compare Aronowitz and DiFazio 1994; Cummins and Sayers 1995; Jones 1986; Reich 1992.

14. The concept of *acquisition* is itself contested terrain. For example, Rogoff defines acquisition in terms of "transmission" or "internalization" rather than in terms of transformation (1995, 153). On the other hand, Gee's use of *acquisition* is aligned with dynamic, active (largely unconscious) transformation of an individual's understanding and practice (i.e., Rogoff's sense of *appropriation*). Consequently, in order to maintain consistent sense, I use the term *acquisition* in Gee's sense here.

15. See also: Heath and McLaughlin 1994; Lave and Wenger 1991; Rogoff 1990.

16. See Rogoff (1995, 161) for an interesting discussion of apprenticeships to, and guided participation in, sociocultural activities that are negatively valued by the larger social community (e.g., interpersonal violence, addictive behavior).

17. Compare Pierre Bourdieu's conception of cultural capital (e.g., 1977).

CHAPTER FOUR

Jacques

Jacques (13 years) has a stocky, outdoors look about him, a beaming smile, and an infectious laugh. He has short, light brown hair and clear blue eyes. He prefers to dress casually and mostly wears surf shirts and boardshorts at home. Jacques wears full uniform to the large State school he attends, but always manages to look somewhat disheveled in it. His two favorite items of clothing are his White Sox and Phoenix Sun baseball caps, and he wears either one of them at every opportunity. His talk is laced with hilarious witticisms, and parodies of people, situations, and remembered conversations. Jacques appears to be well liked, and everyone—including his teacher—calls him by his nickname: J.P. Despite this general acceptance, however, Jacques seems more at ease interacting with older people, females, and males who appear to be outside the core of boys making up the dominant group in his class. He rarely mixes with these boys, either in class or in the playground. Jacques's teacher, Ms. Bryant, confirms Jacques's outsider status in relation to this group, and observes that they appear to find Jacques's humor trying at times and usually exclude him from their sporting games. Indeed, Jacques's circle of friends appears to be small, and he identifies his younger cousins, Graeme and Jake, as his best friends.

Jacques's school was established in 1875 and is situated at the northern edge of Brisbane. The school population was traditionally working class but now varies dramatically in terms of socioeconomic status, owing in large part to recent and extensive luxury housing developments nearby. This has caused a boom in enrolments, but the school has little room for expanding existing infrastructure. Consequently, classroom space is limited and resources are stretched. Jacques's classroom is small, cramped, and congested with groups and rows of desks, storage cupboards, and shelves. There is little space for navigating one's way through the furniture. Even with the ceiling fans set to high, this ground-floor room is hot and airless.

In class, Jacques sits at a group of desks close to the chalkboard at the front of the room. He either moves restlessly in his chair, or sits motionless staring at the busy road that lies beyond the large bank of windows lining one wall of his classroom. By his own admission, he is easily distracted and often loses track of what is happening in class:

> (Monday 7 November 1994. 12:30 p.m. at school. Day 1 of observations)
> EVENT: INTERVIEW 1 (utterance 118)
> Jacques   I get distracted a lot, by other things y'know, if they're doing something better, I'd rather my attention's on them instead of on my work.

His desk work is usually accompanied by a "running meta(con)textual commentary"; that is (usually extended) asides about a task, class activity, or interaction, and/or context (cf. Floriani 1993). Such commentaries are often teasing or self-ironic, they generally pertain to his immediate context, and are usually accepted with good humor by others. For example:

> (Monday 14 November 1994, 9:50 a.m. Day 7 of observations)
> EVENT: LANGUAGE LESSON
> SUBEVENT: *Reading an information sheet on Balinese cultural customs*
> Ms Bryant tells the class to pair up and take turns reading the information sheet to each other. Jacques insists Sean read first. Sean struggles with some of the words and Jacques pats him encouragingly on the back saying, "You'll make it through. C'mon, you'll make it through."

Jacques rarely contributes voluntarily to lessons and is infrequently called upon by his teacher to furnish answers or information for the class. Even when working in groups, he usually waits for others to make suggestions, asks them for the answers, or simply copies what they have written. Much of his work remains incomplete, or mysteriously becomes "lost." His teacher, Ms. Bryant, rates him as "having great difficulty" with literacy. Jacques repeated year 1, and appears to have a history of school failure.

At least two themes or identities can be identified in this brief school-based characterization of Jacques. That is: being a low-achieving student, and being a joker. Although there are many other interpretive possibilities, both embody significant—and symbiotic forms—of life in Jacques's everyday school world. Snapshot 1 contextualizes these themes for the purposes of close interpretive work. Forms of life pertaining to Jacques's world beyond school are examined in the context of a second snapshot later.

SNAPSHOT 1: COMPARE AND CONTRAST

(Monday 14 November 1994, 9:47 a.m. Day 7 of observations)
EVENT: LANGUAGE LESSON

SUBEVENT 1: *Reading information sheet (pair work)*
Ms. Bryant tells students to take out their language books and explains that today they'll be working in pairs. She hands out a photocopied information sheet on Balinese customs to the students, along with an Open Compare and Contrast proforma. Ms. Bryant tells students to take turns reading.

Sean starts reading and Jacques mutters to me, "I hate reading. It's boring." Sean keeps reading and Jacques comments, "Boring, hey." "You're not wrong," replies Sean. "C'mon. Keep going," counters Jacques, and then pretends to fall into a deep sleep. They discuss Sean's recent trip "down the coast," and Jacques talks about accidentally knocking over a girl at rollerskating.

SUBEVENT 2: *Learning task (whole class)*
(9:50 a.m.) Jacques and Sean have read only three paragraphs when Ms. Bryant brings the class together again. She explains once more that she wants them to compare and contrast Balinese and Australian customs.

Jacques is reprimanded for pretending to give Sean electric shocks.
Ms. Bryant asks various children to read aloud consecutive paragraphs. She identifies things in common to both cultures, and points out things that differ.

> *(Snapshot 1 continued)*
>
> > Jacques and Sean share a running meta(con)textual commentary on proceedings (e.g., Ms. Bryant talks about baptism and Jacques declares softly: "Yeah, and Sean was dropped.")
>
> Ms. Bryant directs the class to complete the compare and contrast proforma, using information from the sheet and what they know about Australia.
>
> SUBEVENT 3: *Work task (pair work)*
> A student asks Ms. Bryant what they're supposed to write, and she tells him she's already told the class twice. Jacques turns to Sean and asks with a wide yawn: "What have we gotta write? She didn't even say." Sean doesn't seem to know and they ask Nikki, who tells them to write something about baptism. Jacques asks Ms. Bryant to clarify the task, claiming he couldn't hear what she was saying. Ms. Bryant explains again.
> (10:15 a.m.) Sean works on the proforma while Jacques sits and yawns, looks around, or fiddles with a pencil.

It became apparent right from the beginning of observations that Jacques is not enamored of school. He seems to be patiently enduring school until the time comes for him to leave in year 10. Jacques claims he has no intention of continuing his formal education into senior secondary levels, and openly declares that he "doesn't like school very much." When asked about his reading and writing practices Jacques closes down the conversation saying, "I'm like my dad. I'm not a pencil man."

WHO WANTS TO BE A DUMBO?

Jacques understands that children have to go to school, but seems to have only a vague notion as to the reason why. He suggests: "To learn I suppose," then adds, "So they don't grow up duds." Seated at his desk, Jacques punctuates class time with regular bouts of yawning, heavy sighing, feigning sleep, shifting in his chair, leaning his elbows and head on his desk, fidgeting with pens and water bottles, and watching events transpiring inside and outside the classroom. In short, he feels trapped:

> (Monday 7 November 1994, 12:47 p.m. Day 1 of observations)
> EVENT: INTERVIEW 1 (utterances 113–114)
> Michele   You said before that you didn't like school ... Why's that?
> Jacques   I don't know. I just don't like being in classrooms and stuff like that.

Jacques would much rather be outside playing or helping his dad than sitting in a classroom doing schoolwork. He feels the same about homework, which he rushes through in order to "get it over and done with." More specifically, Jacques declares emphatically that he's "not keen on language and that." He finds reading laborious and claims he rarely reads for recreation. He explains that if he finds a book "boring" he begins thinking of other things and nothing of what he is reading "sinks in," which means he has to start all over again the next night.

Jacques completes very little schoolwork unless constantly supervised, and has developed a range of elaborate strategies for avoiding schoolwork. These include: looking for items he seems to have misplaced, delegating tasks to others (especially to Sean), "helping" others instead of working (e.g., filling glue pots), "fixing Mum up" to collect resources, claiming he hadn't heard instructions, and spending time planning what to do.

Frequently, these avoidance strategies seem to be lampooning the school work he is set to do by his teacher. For example:

> (Wednesday 16 November 1994, 3:00 p.m. Day 9 of observations)
> EVENT: TEACHER INTERVIEW 2 (utterance 047)
> SUBEVENT: *Talking about Jacques assembling miniature books in which he writes ten-word stories about himself.*
> Ms. Bryant   I had a corner set up of ways to publish stories, and he would take—I used to fight with him, because he'd take *two days* to get the paper cut out and stapled. He was wasting time because he didn't want to write. Yet, he got a lot of approval from the rest of the class for those books. I can remember him reading them out, and they'd be laughing... so he continued writing them.

Teacher-set tasks appear to have little or no meaning for Jacques. When asked what he thought of his table group's seminar presentation about India, he cut the thread of questioning with a shrug of his shoulders saying, "Yeah, it was all right. A project is a project." Neither does he appear to make connections between the various literacy skills and processes his teacher develops explicitly in class and the literacy tasks she sets.

For example, Ms. Bryant models metacognitive strategies for her students and expects them to be utilized in assignment work. Large charts around the room encourage students to reflect on processes and performances. For example, one such chart listed: "What were you supposed to do? What did you do well? What would you do differently next time? Do you need any help?" Students are also equipped with a range of templates that are to be used to structure cognitive approaches to academic tasks, or to guide reflective thinking. For example, "KNL" column templates are used for listing what students *know*, what they *need* to know, and what they have *learned* about a topic or concept (see, for example, Berman 1993, 83). Ms. Bryant is also interested in left-brain/right-brain theories of effective learning, and students are encouraged to drink lots of water, work in naturally lighted areas, and participate in "brain gym" sessions (e.g., deep breathing exercises, a range of arm and eye movements that cross the body, and so forth. See Ward and Daley 1993). Jacques sighs deeply whenever the class engages in brain gym, but regularly uses the need to fill his water bottle as an excuse to escape the classroom.

Although Ms. Bryant refers repeatedly to, and demonstrates, the metacognitive strategies she aims to develop in her students, Jacques often does not recognize the templates or seem to understand the purpose of these strategies. For example, students worked on individual projects following the language lesson described in snapshot 1. One aspect of this assignment required them to complete an "open compare and contrast" for their chosen country. Jacques turned quizzically to Ms. Bryant and asked "What's a compare and contrast?" He seemed genuinely surprised when she glared at him and walked away.

Jacques frequently asks his teacher and classmates to clarify teacher-set tasks, or to bring him up to date as to where they are in a lesson. For example:

> (Monday 7 November 1994, 11:32–34 a.m. Day 1 of observations)
> Jacques   What do we need? ((asked three times following Ms. Bryant's explicit instructions))
> Jacques   I hate tests. Are we having a test?
> Jacques   Are we having a test here or in the Maths Challenge room? ((Teacher doesn't hear or ignores his questions))
> Jacques   What are we doing, Ms. Bryant? What page is it?
> Jacques   What are we doing, Ms. Bryant? Are we having a test?
> (11:38 a.m.) Ms. Bryant explains a new task and hands out sheets of graph paper. Jacques turns to Sean and asks, "What do we do with these?"

These frequently repeated requests for clarification or re-explanation suggest Jacques disengages from most academic-related events in class. This is underscored by the significant number of comments he makes throughout class time that have no bearing on the immediate task (e.g., in snapshot 1, recounting how he knocked over a girl while rollerskating).

Despite his constant calls for school task clarification, Jacques rarely asks for direct help with his schoolwork in class. This can be interpreted in at least two ways; he has not done the work, or he does not want to draw public attention to his academic troubles. Evidence collected during the observation period supports both interpretations, with the balance swaying towards the latter. Certainly, conversations with Jacques's mother, Monica, indicate that Jacques is fearful of appearing to be a "dumbo." Monica herself underscored Jacques's sensitivity when she vividly recalled his "extreme anxiety" brought about by having to go to school each day, and which usually manifested itself in tears, nightmares, and physical illnesses. This anxiety seems to have been rife since his first year of school. Jacques himself indicated a sensitivity towards being singled out as a low achiever by suggesting that, in general, teachers should not talk so much in class and "focus on other people" (i.e., not him):

> (Monday 7 November 1994, 12:45 p.m. Day 1 of observations)
> Jacques   Like, if, oh like the teacher asks, "Anyone doesn't understand?" and no one else puts up their hand, and you're sticking up like this ((raises his hand and mimes looking around with embarrassment)) the others say: "Dumbo over there, look at him!" ((mimes whispering to a friend and pointing)) and things like that.

When asked whether it would bother him if people thought he was a "dumbo," Jacques declared: "I don't care if they do, I just take it as a practical joke kind of thing ((smiles)). I just laugh at them." Jacques also appears to try and make others laugh whenever he can. Indeed, in contrast to his written work, Jacques is an accomplished speaker. His lively and engaging conversations and in-class commentaries are interwoven with theatrically told anecdotes and recounts. Such tales are exuberant productions and each storyline is carried by words, a repertoire of character voices, evocative sound effects, and exaggerated facial expressions. For example, Jacques's team won a swimming relay race during a physical education session, and he climbed out of the pool with exaggerated effort and loudly announced in a deep "sportscaster" voice: "A great swim by The Fish." He looked around with mock modesty then raised both hands above his head in a triumphant winner's salute. Everyone laughed.

There is an intriguing incongruity between Jacques's confession-like comments on being singled out as a dumbo, and his disavowal that this has any effect on him because he is able to laugh it off. Consequently, it is difficult to talk about Jacques as a student without addressing his use of humor and jocular actions in everyday school life and beyond.

OH JACQUES, HE'S A JOKER!

Punning, telling humorous anecdotes, using quirky turns of phrase, performing exaggerated reactions to his teacher's (and others') instructions,[1] and making others laugh are significant performance patterns in Jacques's everyday life. At school, he appears to use humor for at least two purposes: to deflect attention from his academic troubles, and/or as a ticket to general acceptance by his classmates. Both of these purposes are dynamically interrelated, as his teacher, Ms. Bryant, observes:

> (Wednesday 17 November 1994, 4:00 p.m. Day 9 of observations)
> EVENT: TEACHER INTERVIEW 2 (utterance 069)
> Ms. Bryant   Like everyone says, "Oh Jacques, he's a joker. Happy. He's always happy," and so I think he's learned that's a good way to be. I think—like all children, but some seem to need it more than others—he likes the approval. He doesn't want to seem to be the dumb one in the class. He would hate that.

Jacques's humor often features teasing play with language and contexts. For example, during group project time, Jacques's team was working on their India project. Eva showed me the cover for their written text and explained that Ben had drawn the illustration freehand. Jacques interrupted: "Did he get the hand free? Get it? *Free* hand." He laughed exaggeratedly in a cartoonlike manner. Everyone at the table groaned.

He also uses teasing banter to deflect attention away from—or perhaps to parody in self-ironic ways—his lack of application to a school task. This manifests itself in a range of ways, including: commands for partners to hurry up and complete the set work (while he sits and does nothing; see snapshot 1), making potentially incendiary comparisons (e.g., "Sean, you're nearly as good as Kylie"), and double-edged comments about classmates' knowledge and identity (e.g., during a German lesson to a German-born classmate: "Neuter. You'd know about *that*, Eva").

Public ridicule of academic tasks appears to be one way Jacques deals with his evaluation of himself as a (non)literate student. Given Jacques's comments about schooling, his subversion of the Writers's Center can also be interpreted as a refusal to engage in tasks that have little "real world" meaning for him. It may also be an attempt to align himself with the dominant group of male students in his class by refusing to comply with classroom writing conventions; most members of this in-crowd are far from being compliant students. It seems only when Jacques is behaving or using language in comical but risky ways that these boys notice him and accord him approval.

Additionally, Jacques's use of humor includes elements of parody for seemingly subversive purposes:

> (Wednesday 16 November 1994, 3:00 p.m. Day 9 of observations)
> EVENT: TEACHER INTERVIEW (utterance 012)
> SUBEVENT: *Talking about Jacques's literacy abilities.*
>
> Ms. Bryant   Jacques speaks very well and he can express his thoughts very accurately verbally. But it's a vicious cycle because he doesn't like to write—it's difficult because his spelling is poor. And for that reason he avoids writing; and I find that he tries not to take it seriously. He tries to make a joke of his writing in all his stories. In first term, all the children did general process writing, and he made these little books called "J.P.'s Stories." He made about six of them and the kids thought they were hilarious. But there was nothing in them; like, they might have had ten words at most in them. They were very, very childish.

NEGOTIATING IDENTITIES

Jacques's construction of being a student often clashes with his teacher's expectations. For him, as already noted, "being a student" requires patience and endurance until he reaches year 10 and can leave school. School learning has little or no connection with the "real" world for Jacques, and much of what he does in class seems pointless to him. His teacher, on the other hand, makes it explicit that she expects students to be organized, self-directed, hardworking, attentive ("You're not even facing the blackboard, J.P."), independent thinkers, task focused, to use higher order thinking skills, and to behave with maturity. Jacques rarely appears to satisfy the membership requirements of the particular student sub-Discourse orchestrated by Ms. Bryant.

Indeed, Jacques appears to manage as best he can by turning much of his schooling into an elaborate joke fest. His "small stories" are a telling example. Jacques's joker discourse seems simultaneously to act as a buffer against ridicule from his classmates over what he sees as his "school" inadequacies, and to generate classmates' appreciative laughter and feelings of inclusion. Thus, he does not fill the oft-cited role of class clown or buffoon intent on drawing attention to himself (cf. Vinnie in McLaren 1993, 161; Murph in Walker 1988, 45). Rather, Jacques appears to use humor to deflect or defuse attention, or to send himself up, usually by means of self-directed irony (cf. lending "encouragement" to Sean's reading), before someone else does. In addition, some students, like Sean, act as foils for Jacques's running meta(con)textual commentaries and teasing banter. However, these classmates customarily play a secondary or peripheral role to these commentaries (cf. the traditional "straight" player in comedy troupes). His style of humor, however, is not always met with enthusiasm from his classmates. This sometimes leads to relational ruptures, particularly when Jacques oversteps classmates' tolerance limits and becomes annoying rather than amusing.

Jacques clearly brings to his classroom relationships a particular discourse that appears to be coordinated by certain sets of worldviews and values. These values include: being able to laugh at yourself, not taking yourself or others too seriously, being able to defuse a potentially uncomfortable situation, and so forth. This joker discourse does not seem to have been acquired at school or within his classroom, although I cannot vouch for previous classes. Apart from Jacques, no other person in class produces this kind of discourse as a "natural-seeming" aspect of their interactions with peers, except when they are recruited by Jacques as foils to, or co-conspirators in, his meta(con)textual commentaries (cf. Jacques's interactions with Sean).

Despite the seeming idiosyncrasy of Jacques's joker discourse at school, it is possible nonetheless to make tentative interpretations about his use of this discourse. For example, I never observed Jacques recruiting male members of the in-crowd as material for his jokes and puns, unlike his conscription of other classmates. This suggests Jacques's use of humor in class may be implicated in expressing some degree of (limited) personal power in what is often for him an exceedingly powerless situation. In addition, I have deliberately used a lower case *d* in referring to Jacques's joker discourse. Although it is easy to identify this discourse as a well-established and practiced pattern of interaction in Jacques's repertoire, it is extremely difficult to talk about him as a "member of a joker Discourse" (i.e., Discourse with a large *D*). For example, his joker discourse is recognized (variously) by the audiences he recruits at school on a moment-by-moment basis, and is characterized by a number of patterns of practices (e.g., Jacques rapidly raising and lowering his eyebrows to let you know that he is "having you on," repeated audience responses such as "Yeah right, J.P.," or laughingly "Oh, J.P.!"). Nevertheless, as indicated above, his classmates do not take up this joker discourse and initiate joker interactions with Jacques or others, and as such, cannot be identified as members of a "joker Discourse." Indeed, it is difficult to confidently extrapolate the sets of social practices and beliefs that would constitute membership in such a Discourse (or any of its modulations) from the way he uses his joker discourse at school.

Thus, it seems that in order to be able to identify this discourse as a co-constitutive and dynamic element of a particular Discourse, I would need to observe—over time—Jacques interacting with others who actively engage in and generate the kind of joker discourse he employs. This strongly suggests that in order for a Discourse to be recognized or identified by an outsider, there needs to be some sort of explicit and observable demonstration of what it means to be a member of a social group that lays claim to the D/discourse. Observing a single member of a dispersed or inaccessible group renders interpretations of Discourses difficult.[2] In addition, a number of Discourses appear to be easier to identify with confidence than others. This suggests that some Discourses (e.g., particular student Discourses) may be more institutionally stable and perennial than others, and therefore more familiar, recognizable, and generally more researched by others (although not necessarily in terms of Discourses *per se*). Other Discourses may be more fluid and more easily changed than others, and therefore more difficult to pin down in terms of (relatively) enduring patterns of practice, values, beliefs, and so on.

Looking beyond school, I have a suspicion that Jacques's joker discourse may be a particular instantiation of his family's interactional patterns. Interactions among all of Jacques's family members are shot through with humorous language uses, quick banter, and exaggerated gestures and facial expressions. Being a member of Jacques's family includes having access to each others' exploits and turning them into hilarious anecdotes, being able to identify when someone is "having you on" and being able to play along in like manner, and sharing insider jokes. For example, while retelling the movie *Robin Hood: Prince of Thieves*, Jacques repeatedly referred to "Maid Marion" as "Maid Miriam." Monica laughed from the kitchen, saying "Miriam! That's my mother's name." "And we *don't* want to talk about that!" Gerard, Jacques's older brother, immediately responded with an exaggerated conspiratorial air and knowing nod. Jacques and Monica dissolved with laughter. This suggests that perhaps the joker discourse Jacques employs—and which appears to draw on established traditions of oral humor that celebrate "leg-pulling," self-directed irony, and clever banter—is an intrinsic part of, or has seeped into, his primary Discourse.[3] Jacques's joker discourse demonstrates masterful performance of complex and intertextual language patterns, but he seems unable to utilize these skills in his school tasks in ways that are academically successful. This suggests that Jacques may not have metalevel understanding of the complex language practices in which he is engaging, or the possibility of using these language capacities for other purposes. This interpretation would help explain the disparity between his oral language capabilities, and his reading and writing performances.

To sum up, the weight of collected and cross-examined evidence suggests that although Jacques may see some purpose in schooling (i.e., to stop people becoming "duds," which he regards as an important role) it holds very little personal significance for him out-of-school (apart from the anxiety it causes him). Conversely, I propose that being a joker at school plays a significant role in Jacques's life as, at the very least, a general coping strategy.

JACQUES'S EVERYDAY LIFE OUT-OF-SCHOOL

Jacques's life outside school contrasts dramatically with his life in school. As practicing Jehovah's Witnesses, Jacques and his family are closely involved with church outreach work in local communities. Jacques's father, Rod, owns a successful earthmoving business and is an Elder in the church. Jacques's mother, Monica, runs their home and is heavily involved in volunteer church work and other activities each day. His sister, Felice (19 years), works part-time for Monica's sister and brother-in-law (Graeme and Jake's parents) and is completing a diploma in business management.

She also teaches piano part-time at home. Jacques's brother, Gerard (16 years), attends a local state secondary school, is more academically inclined than Jacques, and is an avid rollerblader. Jacques's family lives in a large, well-kept home in an affluent area some little distance from the school. Their house is a sprawling, chocolate-colored brick home surrounded by lush lawns and gardens. The house is light and airy inside, with a large open-plan kitchen and living space giving onto a generous inground pool set beside the house. All three children have their own bedroom.

Family interactions are openly warm and loving, and they spend much time talking together as a family, usually after dinner each night. These times, Monica explains, include Bible readings and discussions with Jacques, Gerard, and Felice about "morality, problems they may be experiencing, or aspects of their personality they need to develop." For both Monica and Rod, it is important to "keep communication between parents and children open." Many of these values parallel conceptions of family and personal well-being promoted in the Jehovah's Witness literature. For example:

> (*The Watchtower: Announcing Jehovah's Kingdom.* May 1 1993, 7)
> A wealth of relevant, practical advice is found in the Bible. Principles related to cleanliness, industriousness, communication, sex, divorce, the paying of taxes, dealing with personal differences, and coping with poverty are just some of the aspects of life touched on in the Bible. Millions will testify that the difference between success and failure in their lives has depended on the degree to which they have applied Bible principles.

Continual self-development is a recurrent theme in both Monica's and Rod's talk, and is not necessarily tied to academic success (among other things). In Jacques's case, for example, they actively encourage his interest in his father's earthmoving business, and he is free to stay home from school camps and the like in order to spend time accompanying his father to work. They are confident that Jacques will do well in life, despite his experiences at school.

In addition to other religious activities (e.g., Bible study, witnessing), Jacques's family attends Theocratic School once a week, and Jacques is required to read and explain texts regularly to the assembly (often up to one hundred people). Theocratic School is held every Thursday night and runs for 90 minutes. Each session comprises two meetings. The first (45 minutes) focuses on developing public speaking and exegesis skills. The second (45 minutes) is devoted to enhancing aspects of ministry (i.e., witnessing). Reading, speaking, and exegesis is evaluated publicly by members of the Theocratic School, who use checklists and criteria from the Theocratic School literature to assess his performance (see also Beckford 1975).

At least two identities can be drawn from this brief characterization of Jacques: being a worker, and being a Jehovah's Witness. Myriad other identities could be interpreted from the data collected in relation to Jacques; however, those identified above constitute significant and coordinating elements in Jacques's everyday life. A second snapshot acts as a useful starting place for exploring these identities.

SNAPSHOT 2: AN AFFINITY WITH MACHINES

(Friday 18 November 1994, 5:00 p.m. Day 10 of observations)

Jacques sits in the driver's seat of Felice's Volkswagen, revving the engine. The car is parked on the street and Jacques has asked Felice if he can bring it into the carport. I sit—somewhat nervously—in the passenger seat. Jacques explains to me that the car is actually semi-automatic. He points out that it doesn't have a clutch, and demonstrates how to change gears. He eases the car into reverse, and in one fluid motion backs the car up the street (farther than actually necessary) and then forward into the driveway. He is very confident and competent.

His parents have come outside to watch, and we stand talking as Jacques continues to position Felice's car "just so" beneath the carport. Rod observes how some people have "an affinity with machines" and that Jacques is one of them. Rod describes how Jacques "learned" to drive unassisted when he was 7 years old; he and Rod were out "doing a job" and Rod simply told Jacques to bring the work vehicle closer. And he did. Monica and Rod explain how Jacques will most likely follow his father into the earthmoving business, although the final decision will be left to him. They describe how Jacques likes nothing better than to spend his school holidays working in his father's earthmoving business, where he drives heavy vehicles and, in Rod's words, "Works harder than a lot of twenty-year-olds I know."

Jacques's conversations at home and elsewhere—including school—are interwoven with references to work and being a worker. His talk about his father's business and machinery is couched usually in first person collective grammatical terms (i.e., we, ours), and distinctions between his father's experiences and Jacques's work roles are often blurred. For example, Jacques was discussing schooling experiences with a number of his classmates and observed: "A mate of mine at work—a mate of Dad's—dropped out of school in grade four." Later, Jacques declares his strong affiliation with this world of work by explaining to his classmates who were describing themselves variously as homeboys, surfers, and gamers: "I'm nothin.' I'm just a working man." Indeed, school only seems to make sense to him when he is able to relate it to his working life outside school. For example, when I asked him what "duds" were (see earlier), he defined them as people who don't know anything and identified that as a problem: "Because if you wanted some gravel to put on some road, well you gotta know how many square meters and all that stuff to put on."

Jacques's world of work is very much an adult world, where he is expected to assume adult responsibility for the jobs he is allotted. Indeed, when talk at school turns to hit songs and hip clothes, Jacques either does not join the conversation, or contributes comments—like the one above—that usually bring the discussion to an abrupt close. Alternatively, Jacques is able to talk in technical detail about all manner of machines and their workings, and is cognizant of legal aspects connected with this world. For example:

(Monday 7 November 1994, 12:45 p.m. Day 1 of observations)
EVENT: INTERVIEW 1 (utterances 001 to 006)

Michele	So what sort of things do you do when you do "work"?
Jacques	With my dad? Oh, shovel, I drive the machinery. There's this new thing out now, a new law, that if you drive machinery for seventy hours you can get your license for it.
Michele	Doesn't matter how old you are?
Jacques	Oh, yeah, well you can drive it for seventy hours, and then when you're seventeen you can get your license straight away.

Jacques also puts his knowledge of the business world and his skills as a worker to his own personal use. For example, with the help of his mother and brother, Jacques used his father's computer to compose a flier advertising "J.P.'s Mowing Service."

J.P.s
Mowing Service
- **Efficient, reliable service.**
- **Grass clippings removed.**
- **All edging done.**
- **First time lawn cut *FREE*!**
  (only regular customers)
- **For free quote Ph. 3543 3773**

He posted his flier in local letter boxes, and soon established a profitable weekend and summer holiday business. When asked about the language used in the flier, Jacques explained he had included "First time lawn cut free" in order to entice customers; or in his words, "So they all go, 'Oh yeah, this is great' ((mimes a double take)) Whhhhttttt!! ((grabs the flier)) 'What's that number again?!' " ((mimes dialing frantically)). The smaller font for "Only regular customers," too, complies with the genre of business fliers and emphasizes Jacques's metalevel understanding of the way things are done in the business world.

I'm Just a Workin' Man

Jacques's life out-of-school appears to be much more meaningful and purposeful for him than life in school. Additionally, it can be claimed with confidence that Jacques values being a particular kind of worker in the adult world of business. Such claims are grounded in regular patterns of reference to work and his parents' confirmation of his love of working. Applying Gee's theory of D/discourses to data collected about Jacques makes it possible to see that through his father and the family's earthmoving business Jacques has direct and physical access to a real-world business Discourse. Indeed, it can be said that Jacques is being apprenticed to this secondary Discourse in ways that promote acquisition—and therefore expert performance—more than learning (although this balance may change once Jacques begins working with his father full-time). This is aided and abetted by the imbrication—or coordination—of Jacques's primary Discourse and this secondary business Discourse, and there are many overlaps. For example, Rod's office is at home, Felice is studying a Diploma of Business Management part-time at a local university, and Jacques's uncle and aunt are extremely successful entrepreneurs.

Interpretations of Jacques's apprenticeship, as with Nicholas, are served more usefully by Rogoff's (1995) three-dimensional conception of apprenticeship, than by Gee's novice-expert dyad. Thus, Jacques can be said to be apprenticed to at least one potentially powerful Discourse (i.e., business), in which he has immediate and regular access to experts in the form of his father and relations. He is also provided with opportunities for guided participation by means of his father and his father's work associates, his sister, and his uncle and aunt's business (his father was in partnership with them a number of years ago, as well). Participatory appropriation is clearly demonstrated in Jacques's conception of, and action in relation to, his mowing business. The implications of such acquisition, learning, and supported practice opportunities for Jacques's life beyond school are enormous.

Many current economic and social theorists agree that the nature of work and the roles of workers are changing as modes of production and consumption change.[4] Economic success in the future, according to these writers, will depend at the very least on one's abilities to identify and solve problems, and to predict future life chances for oneself (and for others) based on analyzing the past and present. In their terms, expert performance in such analytic work requires metalevel understanding of consumers and business. Jacques, however, adds an important entrepreneurial dimension to these analyses.

Jacques may not master the kinds of "symbolic-analytic" work that Robert Reich (1992, 174) believes will characterize economically successful—and powerful—workers in the twenty-first century.[5] However, Jacques's increasing metalevel understanding of business enterprise and his ability to put these understandings to work in practical ways (cf. his lawn mowing business) will stand him in good stead with regard to economic prospects in the not-too-distant future.[6] Indeed, and despite technically failing primary school, Jacques seems confident—as do his parents—that he will be successful out-of-school.

The contrast is striking between Jacques's membership in at least one business sub-Discourse and the ways in which he is coordinated by student Discourses. As a "worker," Jacques engages in real-world tasks that are purposeful and meaningful for him. He is expected to conduct himself as an adult worker and is involved in various kinds of autonomous and team work. He has access to guided participation and opportunities for participatory appropriation, and has some understanding of the links between work and livelihood. Such opportunities and knowledge are obtained from observing and working with his father, from watching him ordering machine parts and other materials during the day, and seeing him balancing accounts at night. Unfortunately for Jacques, the expertise he has acquired out-of-school is not valued academically within his classroom. Even when opportunities arise for Jacques to demonstrate his mastery of the business Discourse—such as his thriving car sales business established during *Earn and Learn* sessions[7]—these opportunities are disregarded as an aspect of being a successful student by his classmates and teacher.

The Discourses of work and business, however, are not the only "adult" Discourses coordinating Jacques's social identities out-of-school. Being a Jehovah's Witness[8] involves Jacques in a range of complex language, literacy, and social practices, and includes a range of important and recognizable props.

JEHOVAH'S WITNESS

Jacques, as mentioned earlier, attends Theocratic School once a week with his family, and engages in a range of other church-related activities. Theocratic School has a dual purpose; it provides ministry training, and it acts as a forum for knowledge sharing (Watch Tower Bible and Tract Society of Pennsylvania 1971, 9). In Jacques's case specifically, this requires him to write an introduction and conclusion to a Bible reading which he then presents to the congregation. The introduction and conclusion usually tie the reading to current issues or to personal experiences in ways that help explain the meaning of the Bible text for everyday life. At the same time, Jacques has to work on "points of counsel" which are linked to ministry training. For example, at the time of observations his reading for December requires him to focus on Study 29: "Fluent, Conversational Delivery with Proper Pronunciation" (142–149). To reiterate, this particular aspect of Jacques's delivery is evaluated by a member of the congregation, who suggests areas requiring further attention. Monica helps Jacques prepare for these public presentations; they work together on writing the introduction and conclusion, and then Monica reads the text and Bible passage onto an audio tape for Jacques to read along with as he practices. Jacques also participates in family and congregation Bible reading and study sessions held regularly in members' homes.

Jacques's church commitments are very much part of an adult world, and Saturdays see him dressed in shirt, tie, and suit, and carrying a briefcase as he, his family, and others in his group go witnessing in their allotted "circuit." This work requires Jacques to be familiar with the literature they show to people (e.g., *The Watchtower*, *Awake!*) and involves Jacques in discussing with a range of people sophisticated concepts and understandings about personal values, religious beliefs, and contemporary social issues. Jacques gives some intimation of this in describing how they go about witnessing:

(Monday 7 October 1994, 12:52 p.m. Day 1 of observations)
EVENT: INTERVIEW 1 (utterance 298)
SUBEVENT: *Describing what he says when they go witnessing*
Jacques   "We're just calling today, to show you these magazines," and it depends what they have on the front of them. Some are, like, child abuse, some are to do with robbery and stuff like that. It all depends what's in *The Watchtower*. And *Awake!* is its partner kind of thing and you just, and you just open up the front page and show them inside it. If they buy one then you call back. Maybe if you see an article they like, or if they tell you what they like, then you just say "Oh yeah, that's an interesting one," kind of thing, and you might take them back a book.

Being a member of the Jehovah's Witnesses involves Jacques in a wide range of reading, writing, speaking, and listening practices. Although Jacques sometimes engages in these practices reluctantly, the amount of public and private reading, public speaking, and discussion he does in connection with being a Jehovah's Witness far outstrips his application to literacy activities at school. Unfortunately, few—if any—of Jacques's extremely proficient oral language practices and understandings appear to be allotted academic space or obtain him academic kudos at school. This is despite his teacher's recognition that he is a fluent speaker.

A Cultural Apprenticeship

Being a member of the Jehovah's Witnesses community is to be constituted and coordinated by a Discourse that has its boundaries and membership criteria clearly delineated in a body of literature and set of social practices. Interpreting Jacques's membership in this community requires more extensive observations of Jacques as a Jehovah's Witness and more extensive insider knowledge than I was able to obtain during the time I spent with this family. Accordingly, the following discussion focuses only on those language and literacy practices to which I had some access.

Bringing Rogoff's notions of apprenticeship, guided participation, and participatory appropriation to bear on Jacques's and his family's practices as active Jehovah's Witnesses, it is possible to claim that Jacques is being apprenticed to a range of literacy practices that will no doubt help him "improve in ability to gather, develop and present information logically to others" (Watch Tower Bible and Tract Society of Pennsylvania 1971, 9). At a surface level, these practices appear indistinguishable from school language and literacy practices.[9] However, in my opinion, Jacques will use these sets of practices to meet vastly different social purposes. In relation to becoming a Jehovah's Witness, Jacques is being apprenticed to a Discourse that, among many other things, values the ability to witness through speaking confidently, cogently, and persuasively. Although Jacques is learning the craft of speaking as a Jehovah's Witness explicitly through Theocratic School, he is also acquiring the ability to tell engaging stories, share humorous recounts and anecdotes that often have a "message" to them, and to construct persuasive verbal arguments as modeled by his parents, siblings, Graeme and Jake's family, and other church members. This differs from school literacy practices, where teaching in Jacques's class appears to focus on reading and writing for primarily school purposes.

Indeed, juxtaposing the "compare and contrast" lesson in snapshot 1 with Jacques's out-of-school oral language practices throws an intriguing disfluency into sharp relief. During the compare and contrast lesson, Jacques did not give the impression that he understood the purpose of the lesson. Indeed, his question about comparing and contrasting information in the following session confirms this, as seen earlier in this chapter. At home, however, Jacques is able to successfully compare and contrast phenomena in order to arrive at a position or decision. One example was recounted during our second interview, when he described in great detail what was similar about his and Graeme's new roller skates with regard to features and performance, what was different between them and how that impinged on prices, and how he had opted for the cheaper pair in case roller skating did not become a passion for him. Similar reasoning had worked effectively on his parents who subsidized his purchase after initially refusing to do so. However, his oral ability to "compare and contrast" seemingly had no currency in his school-based academic performance for either Jacques or his teacher.

Given that acquisition leads to expert performance—which in Jacques's case is already being enhanced through learning opportunities presented at Theocratic School—I predict with confidence that Jacques will be a fluent and persuasive public speaker and engaging conversationalist (regardless of his future relationship with the church). I also strongly suspect that this mastery will not be matched by his writing performance. The economic effects of these predicted outcomes for Jacques can only be speculated. However, Rod's business does not appear to require a great deal of written text production as much of his business is conducted either over the phone or in face-to-face encounters. Thus, the orality of the kind of work Jacques intends pursuing, coupled with his metalevel understandings of a business Discourse, indicates economic possibilities far beyond those that could be predicted from his school performance.

Indeed, from my observations, it seems that current language lessons at school have no bearing on the real world for Jacques. Even by year 6 Jacques was claiming he did not read or write out of school. The two weeks spent observing Jacques for this study confirm a rupture between what Jacques is doing in school and the kinds of adult D/discourses he is being apprenticed to out-of-school. Thus it seems that it will be his out-of-school social practices, and not his in-school practices, that may prove most valuable to him in his adult life.

Endnotes

1. For example: looks of intense pain or horror, rapidly raising and lowering his eye brows Groucho Marx-style, freezing as though stunned by what he is hearing, and so forth.

2. This also has significant implications for using D/discourse as an analytic device in research when participants do not overtly engage in conversations or physical action. This is addressed more explicitly in chapters 5 and 6.

3. Indeed, it could be said that this joker discourse may be employed by Jacques's family to help diffuse moments of tension or discomfort that may arise in their community-based work as Jehovah's Witnesses. This is, of course, only speculation on my part.

4. See, for example: Aronowitz and DiFazio 1994; Cummins and Sayers 1995; Heath and Mangiola 1991; Howe and Strauss 1993; Gee, Hull, and Lankshear 1996; Reich 1992.

5. Reich identifies at least three categories of services that will be provided by workers by the year 2020: production services, in-person services, and symbolic-analytic services. He also claims that the bulk of the world's wealth will be owned by those who can provide symbolic-analytic services. Reich (1992, 177) estimates this will be five percent of the world's population.

6. Of course, work and business Discourses comprise only part of one dimension of Jacques's everyday life, both now and in the future. Nevertheless, they are an important part.

7. *Earn and Learn* (Vingerhoets 1993) is a commercially produced and complex role-play simulation of an adult community. It comprises a teacher's handbook and a set of photocopiable cheque books, wage sheets, drivers' licenses, and other bureaucratic paraphernalia. The *Earn and Learn* simulation sets in place only the institutional structures of a community (e.g., a bank, grocery store, real estate agent, car dealers, a casino). All else that transpires is constituted by the interactions of the students enacting their roles. This program is becoming increasingly

8. popular in upper primary grades in the Brisbane region, and suggests useful terrain for future research projects.

8. Technically, Jacques does not become a Jehovah's Witness until he publicly declares his commitment through baptism. However, because Jacques participates in activities as though he is a confirmed member, he will be referred to as such for the purposes of this discussion. This in turn raises interesting questions about official and unofficial memberships in Discourses, and the complexities attending decisions about the degree to which an unofficial member can participate in the Discourse.

9. For example, the overarching goal of the Queensland English syllabus is: "to develop students' ability to compose and comprehend spoken and written English fluently, appropriately, effectively and critically, for a wide range of social and personal purposes" (Department of Education, Queensland 1994, iii).

CHAPTER FIVE

Layla

Layla (12 years), like Nicholas, is tall for her age. She has dark brown, shoulder-length hair cut into a bob which she usually keeps off her face with a black headband. Layla can look quite serious at times; but when she smiles her face radiates warmth and good humor. She is keenly aware of "what's in" for teenage girls, buys *Girlfriend* magazine,[1] dresses in the latest fashions for teenagers, and identifies herself as a "shopaholic." Layla has lived in the same house all her life. Her parents, Beth and Ray, bought it over fourteen years ago when they were newly married. Their house is located in an older area of north Brisbane, now classified as inner city and becoming increasingly gentrified. Layla's family remodeled their Federation-style home (circa 1900–1910) during the 1970s, and it is now a large, comfortable two-story home. Ray is a partner in a tiling business and did much of this remodeling work himself. Beth trained as a nurse, and at present works during school hours as a medical secretary in a private hospital.

Layla's brother, Jonathon, is one year older than Layla and they share a relationship characterized by long periods of solidarity punctuated by moments of hostility. They regularly play Nintendo games together[2] (although Layla doesn't much care for the "fighting" ones) and talk to each other about their respective schools. Their favorite television show is *Ren and Stimpy*,[3] and one of Layla's most prized possessions is a brightly colored poster of Ren and Stimpy that has them outfitted in gas masks and standing in a room full of cheese. The caption for the poster reads: "Who cut the cheese?" Beth sighs and declares that the characters have "sick senses of humor" but seem popular with young people. Jonathon is in his first year of secondary school and is attending a Catholic boys' school. Layla currently attends a coeducational Catholic primary school, and is enrolled in a nearby Catholic girls' secondary school for next year. Jonathon has not yet decided what he would like to do when he finishes school, while Layla would like to "work with animals or travel."

Although Beth had promised herself that she would never send her children to Catholic schools or single-sex schools after her own experiences in both, she feels that in present times such schools offer the kinds of academic experiences she believes are important. These include, in relation to Layla: girls not being inhibited by boys, more opportunities for teacher attention than if boys were present, and higher success rates for girls. Beth emphasizes, however, that all she really wants from her children's education is that they become "good people" and hold "good values." Her mother's aspirations seem to have a strong influence on Layla's own actions and language uses. For example, when asked what she would wish for if she had three wishes, Layla nominated: "That everyone can be friends." Another time, she described instances of being caught in traffic jams on the Brisbane-Gold Coast highway ("the road to Dreamworld," a popular local theme park), and looking around at the people in the cars beside her only to have them give her "the finger." She tells how she ignores them as her mother advises her to do, but is dismayed by such reactions because she "isn't staring on purpose."

At home, Layla's family seems warm and close; they regularly take holidays or trips to theme parks together (e.g., Tasmania, Dreamworld), share humorous anecdotes about each other, and talk together as a family. Layla and Beth share a particularly close relationship and devote much time to talking with each other in the kitchen after school while Layla does her homework and Beth prepares dinner. They also watch television and movies together, as well as regularly go shopping together. Layla no longer participates in sporting activities due to a knee injury two years ago, and her present pursuits tend in the main to be physically restricted. In addition to spending time talking with her mother, Layla fills her spare time speaking on the telephone with girlfriends, watching television or video movies, playing Nintendo games with her brother, or sitting quietly in her bedroom writing letters to friends and penfriends in England and Japan. However, whenever Layla is swimming in her family's generously proportioned inground pool or mucking about with her group of friends, her energy seems limitless.

Layla has a close circle of female friends at the large Catholic co-educational primary school she attends. This group constitutes her main circle of friends both in school and out-of-school, and appears to be extremely important to Layla.[4] Unlike Jonathon, she has no one her age living close by with whom to spend time; consequently, she regularly has friends from her circle to stay the night on weekends, or she sleeps at their houses. Outside this group of close friends at school, Layla appears to associate cordially with most of her classmates and teachers. In Layla's class, there are no fixed seating arrangements. Groups of large tables fill most of the room. Pigeon holes under the banks of windows on opposite sides of the classroom hold students' school books and other belongings. Layla appears to share a warm and trusting relationship with her classroom teacher of two years—as do the majority of students in her year 6/7 composite class. Although Layla participates in most things in class (e.g., role-plays, collaborative writing, debates) and events associated with the school (e.g., the school musical, Mass), she appears to prefer operating in the background, rather than taking a prominent role. Her teacher, Mr. Wills, describes Layla as an "average" student.

Christian behavior codes and citizenship principles characterize Layla's schooling. Physical and spiritual "care for each other" are explicit ethics that infuse teachers', the principal's, and the priest's talk in the chapel, assembly hall, classroom, and playground. This is overwritten by public prayers and songs in which students participate.[5] Indeed, Layla repeatedly voices institutional expectations regarding fraternal relationships with others and being a "good person." Layla carefully explained to me, for example, why her friend Shona was trying to help repair relationships within another group of girls: "Our teachers said we have to help each other." Such emphasis on duty of care and (loving) relationships seems more pronounced at Layla's school and in her talk than in Nicholas's church-based school and his talk at school, and certainly more so than in Jacques's school.

At least two significant forms of life or social identities can be identified in this incomplete characterization of Layla's everyday life. These include: being a particular kind of female teenage friend, and being a particular kind of student. Accordingly, the following two snapshots and accompanying discussions attempt to hold in place for closer investigation the ways in which these imbricated forms of life and their motivations constitute everyday language and social practices for Layla.

SNAPSHOT 1: YOU NEVER KNOW WHAT YOU'RE GONNA GET.

(Tuesday 1 November 1994, 11:13 a.m. Day 7 of observations)
EVENT: MORNING TEA

It is a searing hot day. A group of girls from Layla's class and the other year 7 class sits in a circle on benches in the shade of a classroom block eating their morning snack. Seeming without any signal, they all begin singing in unison a song that is unfamiliar to me, but that is obviously popular with this group. They break off to poke fun at Layla's boiled egg that she has brought along to eat. She protests and shifts around on the bench, declaring that she *likes* boiled eggs. Sallie tells about a television advertisement where a man eats a raw egg whole. The girls groan "gross" or "yuck." Layla finishes her egg as attention turns to Shona, who is eating Nutella from a plastic and foil container. Sallie starts singing the Nutella advertising jingle and the others join in, which leads to singing the Caramello Bear jingle. This turns into talk about television shows, and everyone agrees that *Maxie's World* is "cool" and "so good." They discuss what happened on *Lois and Clark* last night, with different girls recounting the parts they liked best.

(11:18 a.m.) The girls finish eating and stand or sit in the shade, out of the glittering heat. A number of girls make different suggestions as to what they should do with the remainder of the break, and they decide to play Dare. Layla is chosen to carry out the first dare. The group send her off to ask a boy if he'd like to go out with one of them, but she returns without having carried out her task. There is much laughing and loud talking.

The girls stand around discussing who's going out with whom—the game of Dare apparently abandoned—and who is fighting with whom in Layla's class and the other year 7 class.

The school bell sounds deafeningly above us and Layla and Shona scream until it stops ringing. In the meantime, the others smile at each other and put their hands over their ears in a practiced manner. Layla announces to no one in particular: "My momma always said, life is like a box of chocolates—you never know what you're gonna get." The girls can be heard repeating this line from the movie *Forrest Gump* all the way up the stairs to their classroom.

This first snapshot holds in place patterns that were repeated countless times over the course of observing Layla in school and out-of-school contexts. It soon became obvious to me that Layla's language practices play a significant role in establishing the identity of this group, and in maintaining (and sometimes repairing) relationships at school and out-of-school. The following discussion focuses first on language practices that are—in Gee's term—coordinated by popular media, then shifts to a discussion of Layla's membership in a particular group of girls.

Life Is Like a Box of Chocolates

Time out of class for Layla's close circle of friends[6] is devoted to singing television and radio advertising jingles, recounting the latest episodes of and reciting lines from favorite television shows, sitcoms, and series, discussing movies and movie star exploits, talking about the latest in fashion trends (including comments on what teachers are wearing; cf. McRobbie 1991, 13), and dancing and singing their own covers of popular songs. It would be easy to discuss such language practices in superficial terms; claiming, for example, that Layla is simply moving through a "typical" female teenager phase and acting out the socializing influences of mass media and popular culture (cf. Beaumont 1995, 110). Matters are much more complex than this, however.

Although contributing important insights into popular media images and ideologies, many sociologists and cultural commentators tend to cast female teenagers as "agentless receptacles" (cf. Beaumont 1995; Kellner 1991, 1995). However, Layla and her close friends do not appear to be slavish consumers and imitators of mass media information and the scripted identities they proffer. Instead, this group actively reworks material pulled from popular culture sources (e.g., television, magazines, movies, radio) into pastiches that appear to serve a number of purposes. Perhaps most obvious are the ways in which they use these reworked pieces to amuse themselves and sometimes others outside their group (including their class teacher). For example:

> (Tuesday 25 October 1994, 11:12 a.m. Day 2 of observations)
> EVENT: MORNING TEA
> The girls have finished eating, and sit in a circle in the hot shade while discussing, among other things, what they'll be doing after lunch, the shoes a teacher is wearing, and love letters. Suddenly, Shona jumps up and begins singing Kylie Minogue's latest song in an exaggerated manner, complete with suggestive gestures and pout. The rest of the group laugh, applaud wildly, then discuss the merits and otherwise of the song, Kylie Minogue, Madonna, and their respective exploits.

Another purpose for these kinds of language practices appears to be implicated in an idiosyncratic and sporadic social commentary directed at immediate contexts or traditionally expected social roles (see below). At times, too, Layla and her close friends appear to use these language practices to resist certain teacher-supplied identity scriptings. This is particularly evident when they have a teacher other than Mr. Wills. For example, Layla's class was taught by Mrs. Moodie while Mr. Wills attended an in-service seminar. The students were familiar with Mrs. Moodie; however, her teaching style was much more regimental than Mr. Wills's and she did not seem to be popular with Layla and her circle of friends. In the particular event reported here, Mrs. Moodie had told the class that if they behaved she would "take them down to the oval and play a game." Layla and the others looked at each other excitedly, whispering alternately: "Basketball! T-Ball!" until Mrs. Moodie asked who had a tennis ball; the girls sighed and slumped low in their seats. Down on the oval, Layla's circle of friends launched into complex language games that lampooned the teacher's game and their participation in it.

> (Thursday 3 November 1994, 10:30 a.m. Day 9 of observations)
> EVENT: TEACHER'S GAME
> (10:33 a.m.) SUBEVENT 1: *Rules*
> Mrs. Moodie explains her rules for the game, then asks for teams of half girls and half boys.

Layla moves off calling: "Half girls over here!"

(10:38 a.m.) SUBEVENT 2: *Naming*

The teacher has organized the two teams with little cooperation from the students.

Layla's circle of friends has managed to remain intact. After discussing how "stupid" the teacher's game is, Sallie sets about renaming team members using the names of popular toys and TV characters. The rest of the circle of friends joins in, shouting "I'm Little Pony!" or "I'm Mr. Bucket!" or Layla's choice: "Crusher!"

Meanwhile, the game has begun.

The girls stand in a huddle on the field, repeatedly changing their "aliases" (their term) amid much laughter and singing. They occasionally direct other team members to fetch the ball. Layla is now "Yogi Bear" and will answer only to that.

(10:47 a.m.) SUBEVENT 3: *Subversion*

The teams have swapped fielding and throwing positions.

Layla tells me to sit and talk with them so that they don't have to participate. She announces her alias is now "Lamb Chops" and the group of friends break into singing the Kantong stir fry sauce advertising jingle. This is followed soon after by the *Lamb Chops* theme song from the television show.

It's Layla's turn to throw the ball, and the teacher calls her to the "home plate." After telling Mrs. Moodie to call her "Lamb Chops," Layla stands at the marker with the tennis ball in her hand. She looks around with an exaggeratedly helpless expression on her face saying: "I don't know how to throw. Do I just throw it?" The group shouts: "Just throw it!" etc., which she does. However, instead of running, Layla simply stands in her original position and there is no score. In the ensuing noise and confusion, Layla sticks out her bottom lip and protests: "That's not fair! They never told me to run!" and then sighs loudly, "Oh well. What a pity, I never ran."

She strolls away and discusses it loudly with Sallie and Melissa (who are now B1 and B2 from the *Bananas in Pyjamas* television show).

Mrs. Moodie did not visibly react to the actions and talk of Layla and her circle of friends. She appeared to patiently endure—or ignore—the girls' construction of the game. The circle of friends, on the other hand, seemed to revel in the opportunity to use particular language practices to mark out a social space for themselves within the constraints of the situation. From my perspective as an observer, there appeared to be localized (and temporary) shifts and overt tensions within the usual power relationships between this teacher and this group of students (cf. Walkerdine 1985, 220). Although Mrs. Moodie's institutional power remained relatively intact (i.e., the girls remained on the field and so forth), the group seemed to be challenging her personal power. These kinds of challenges to teacher authority, however, were never directed at Mr. Wills while I was observing. Indeed, Layla's usual classroom language uses and actions differ markedly from the event described above. This is the subject of the second snapshot to come.

In summary, it seems that Layla and her circle of friends are coordinated by and use information provided by popular media in their "enactment and exploration of possible identities" (Richards 1993, 25; also Carrington and Bennett 1996; Lumby 1996). This challenges claims that adolescents are (only) positioned by television and other popular culture media. This latter view can be interpreted as promoting adolescents as tabula rasa or as "victims" of consumerism (cf. Buckingham and Sefton-Green 1994; Rushkoff 1996b). Layla and her friends, although enculturated to some degree by popular culture, actively demonstrate flexible capacities to participate in aspects of it and—often seemingly simultaneously—demonstrate at least some metalevel understanding of the ways in which popular culture "works."[7]

Furthermore, this shared knowledge of popular culture and the circle of friends' patterns of interaction are used to establish contexts of resistance, although this kind of group action rarely occurs when their regular classroom teacher, Mr. Wills, is present. This suggests there are certain institutional or teacher-related boundaries to action and talk beyond which they hesitate to step, and possible boundaries are explored below. In addition, and as already signposted, these language and social practices establish a set of group membership norms, values, and expectations that define what it means to be a particular kind of friend, and thus, a member of Layla's circle of friends. These membership criteria also serve to distinguish insiders from outsiders and "wannabes" (my term).[8]

Friends, Barbie Doll Girls, and "The Fight"

Membership in Layla's circle of friends seems to be regulated by particular sets of criteria. From my own observations of interactions and the subject matter of these interactions, I propose that these sets of criteria are constituted in part by having access to popular culture, and by the degree of socialization that comes "free" via popular culture media (Arnett 1995; Luke 1993, 1997; Richards 1993). Thus, (shared) knowledge of the latest television shows, movies, music, and Hollywood star-related gossip is highly valued by this group. However, it is not this knowledge alone that guarantees a place in the group; for example, the ways in which this knowledge is shared or put to use are significant as well. Thus, public and often "showy" performances and actions also comprise part of this group's membership criteria (cf. Shona enacting Kylie Minogue). Nevertheless, membership in Layla's circle of friends involves much more than simply knowing about, or having access to and using appropriately, certain dimensions or components of current popular culture.

A second set of membership criteria is demarcated by members' explicit commitment to the group. For example, Layla is quite scathing about a group of year 7 females she calls the "Barbie Doll Girls," describing them as "boy crazy" and self-centered. Layla seems to regard what she sees as their dependency and focus on boys as a betrayal. She used to be close friends with some of these girls "but now they've turned right off us and gone over to the boys." It seems there are at least two values crucial to being a member of Layla's circle of friends: first, relationships with one's girlfriends are paramount, and second, girls should not act boy crazy and risk losing their identities by becoming "plastic ideals."

Indeed, much energy appears to be expended in keeping Layla's circle of friends tight-knit. From the range of possible interpretations available, Angela McRobbie's makes the most sense in the present case. McRobbie proposes that "[a] function of the social exclusiveness of such groupings is to gain private, inaccessible space" (1991, 14). This rings true in relation to Layla and her circle of friends; the language and social practices of this group of friends—consolidated during school breaks and in shared out-of-school activities—are usually elusive to (and thus exclude) outsiders and wannabes. This makes it difficult for outsiders and girls on the edges of the group to keep up with the play, or to interpret these practices in ways that are valued by the circle of friends. Indeed, I repeatedly found myself beset with difficulties in trying to interpret what was happening. For example, despite Layla's repeated claims that fighting is stupid, I observed a number of (potential) relational crises, such as on the fourth day of observations when Layla unexpectedly reported: "We're having a fight with Anna because she said we're ignoring her." Later, as Anna attempted to repair relations by sharing gossip with the others and loaning pens and paper—enacting what I would have interpreted as appropriate member practices—she is accused of "sucking up" to the others.[9] I was unable to establish whether or not Anna was being ignored, or whether she only thought she was being ignored, or why her actions were deemed unacceptable by the group. Thus, like Anna, I was nonplussed as to why she was being excluded.

It is easy to rely on an explanation that proposes Anna may not be a "full" member of this circle of friends, or that the Discourses that constitute Anna bring her unknowingly into conflict or tension with group members. However, given the complexity of the group's interactions, these explanations are too neat. Indeed, in McRobbie's eyes, the chimera-like qualities of membership criteria and the closeness of their group enable young adolescent females to "remain seemingly inscrutable to the outside world of parents, teachers, ... and boys as well" (1991, 14). Perhaps this inscrutability signals a limit to—but not necessarily a limitation of—the extent to which D/discourses can be mapped by outsiders. Such limits were signaled earlier in relation to Jacques and his joker discourse. This line of thought is taken up again later.

In addition, Layla's commitment to her circle of friends often included processes of self-surveillance. For example:

> (Tuesday 25 October 1994, 1:15 p.m. Day 2 of observations)
> EVENT: LUNCH TIME
> Layla and I go to sit and eat lunch by the assembly hall. Upon seeing the others sitting over by the canteen, Layla turns to me and says, "We'd better go and sit with them, otherwise they'll get angry."

Conversations with Layla, her close friends, her teacher and her mother, helped explain aspects of this pattern of self-regulation. This points towards a third set of membership criteria I see as constituted primarily by institutional norms and expectations. Layla's close circle of friends does not occur in a vacuum, and is situated within networks of relationships spanning Layla's year 6/7 class, other students, her family, and others. Layla, like Nicholas, differentiates between her close friends with whom she mucks around and spends time out-of-school, and those friends she talks to and sits next to at school but rarely—if ever—sees socially. These relationships are interwoven with larger networks coordinating and constituting the school, and other networks of relations that extend beyond this school.

Thus, Layla's interactions with others outside her immediate circle of friends also seem subject to a complex range of norms and codes of action. For example, a year 6 girl who appeared keen on becoming an insider (i.e., a wannabe) misinterpreted the "rules" for touching. In a high-spirited move during a raucous morning tea gathering she stuck her fingers down the collar of someone's dress and, to her great distress, was promptly accused of being a "Feeler." This is a derogative term with strong lesbian connotations that is perhaps aligned with certain institutional Discourses that do not regard homosexuality as socially acceptable (cf. Foucault 1967). Perhaps Layla's circle of friends is regulated by the values of these Discourses and simultaneously uses these values to regulate and/or judge others' actions. It seems that particular institutional norms and regulations do indeed bear directly on Layla's circle of friends, challenging in some ways McRobbie's claims that tight-knit groups of young adolescent girl friends are "inaccessible." I argue, in light of my findings, that groups such as Layla's circle of friends very often are already (and always) "accessed" by the strong and enculturating coordinations of school, home, church, and other institutions. Earlier in the year, for example, Layla's circle of friends had experienced rupture and fragmentation. Although Layla could not remember the exact cause of the fight, it was a recurring theme in her talk, and its significance in the life of the group was corroborated by her teacher, members of her group, and her mother. Unlike Nicholas and Stuart, whose falling out was over a rule in basketball (see chapter 3), Layla and her friends appeared to have clashed over a relational issue; that is, who liked whom best. Although the friends tried to deal with the situation, they found they were unable to resolve the conflict on their own and asked an "authority"—Mr. Wills—to intervene:

> (Tuesday 25 October 1994, 12:05 p.m. Day 2 of observations)
> EVENT: INTERVIEW 2
> SUBEVENT: *Talking about "The Fight"*
> Layla   Well we had to make a decision, like whether we should tell Mr. Wills or sort it out ourselves, and we ended up telling Mr. Wills 'cause it was getting like out of hand, and like—we didn't want—we're not allowed to get our parents involved, so it was better to tell Mr. Wills than let it go on, and we ended up sorting things out, and then we're just all friends again.
> And when asked to tell more about the fight:
> Layla   Oh well, it was Shona and I and... I think it was over the musical or something last year, but it was like when we came back to school and everything, and then I—and then Melissa and them went off and I wasn't friends with them, 'cause like.. Melissa and Shona are really good friends and I wanted to be friends with Melissa but not Shona at the time, so we ended up all.. apologising to each other 'cause it was really stupid.

Despite my efforts to inquire about the fight from a number of different angles, Layla's recount remained confusing. I repeatedly encountered difficulties in endeavoring to interpret whose norms and values were at work in this relationship crisis. To begin with, my initial interpretive problems were not ameliorated—as I had hoped—by trying to interpret recounted events in terms of Discourses; indeed, such analyses served to locate my reading of Layla's recount of the fight at an even more complex intersection of group, school, church, and family norms and expectations than I had initially assumed. Although this proved initially frustrating in relation to interpreting the rupture and reassembly of Layla's circle of friends, this "finding" supports my claim that any research employing Gee's theory of D/discourse requires multiple sources of information (e.g., observations, conversations with everyone involved) and is enhanced by mapping or coding data from a variety of interpretive angles (i.e., multiple coding of data within different discursive framings). In this way, revisiting and cross-examining data over and over enabled me to see the rich interpretive possibilities these complexities held for understanding more fully Layla's constant negotiations among the Discourses coordinating her everyday life. For example, a range of specific normative forces (or Discourse coordinations) operating on Layla's relationships at school are suggested in phrases like "we're not allowed to get our parents involved." When asked to explain what she meant by this, Layla murmured "Cause... ((exhalation)) then the parents get.. angry at each other I think.. so it's better for them to keep out of it." When asked who decided not to involve parents, Layla replied, "Uhm someone told us not to get the parents involved." The identity of this "someone" was left unrevealed, but I have a strong suspicion based on interviews and wide-ranging conversations that it might have been Mr. Wills.

In all honesty, it is impossible to identify with unquestionable assurance which Discourses are operating in the fight and in Layla's account of it. Nevertheless, it is possible to propose tentative and provisional coordinations. These include, among others: patriarchal Discourses that provide social scripts for females that cast them as emotional rather than as rational; nice girl Discourses that value caring relationships over stormy ruptures; Catholic Discourses that value confessing, recourse to a mediator, and forgiveness; and a primary Discourse that contributes particular sets of values, beliefs, practices, expectations for self and others, respect for parents, particular ways of solving problems, and the like. However, these kinds of interpretations are ever only provisional. In order to interpret in more detail the Discourses coordinating and constituting this fight—and its seemingly far-reaching effects—it would have been necessary for me to have observed Layla's group before, during, and after the fight in order to trace any changes in language use and actions that perhaps could be attributed to the coordinating effects of certain D/discourses. Once again, this emphasizes the need for ethnographic approaches to D/discourse research, and not just discourse analysis alone.

Institutional renderings of the friends and their fight seem to be captured in Layla's repeated claims that fighting is "stupid." Layla appears to use the term "stupid" as a coverall for describing something that is deeply felt, but that may be quite differentiated from one occasion to the next (e.g., "This is stupid" used to refer to a teacher-set task that she does not see as valuable, or that fighting is "stupid," meaning that it is unacceptable). Therefore, it is difficult to ascertain with any confidence to what extent her claims about fighting being stupid simply reiterate what someone (who is influential) has told her, and thus to what extent she genuinely believes it to be so. This difficulty is captured in her recount of Mr. Wills's comments on the situation: "He said it's just pretty ridiculous that you guys are fighting 'cause you've all been friends for a long time and... you're going to be friends for an even longer time." In contrast to the dynamic and, to me, seemingly telepathic interactions of the circle of friends, Layla explains that in the course of their meetings with Mr. Wills they "came to a decision where we should all just be friends." Indeed, I see an institutional influence on this decision in Layla's following comment about restoring order and re-establishing the circle of friends: "Oh well, it took a bit of time at first to get.. used to the idea ((laughs)). We ended up getting friends though." Nevertheless, despite "getting used to the idea" and as indicated above, relations are still not always smooth sailing for members of this circle of friends.[10]

The way in which Mr. Wills appears to have dealt with this relational rupture in his role as a representative of school and church values and practices sits in marked contrast with the way Nicholas's and Stuart's fight was dealt with (see chapter 3). In Nicholas's and Stuart's case, the vice-principal overtly exercised her authority in response to the disruption—of a physical sort—caused by Nicholas's and Stuart's altercation, and they were ordered to write a letter of apology to their teacher. Layla and her circle of friends' troubles were discussed over a period of time until consensus appeared to have been reached one way or another. Their relational problems were less physically disruptive to the classroom than Nicholas's and Stuart's, although these troubles did interfere with the values of friendship and care promoted by Mr. Wills and others at Layla's school. It is also interesting that the circle of friends invited Mr. Wills to intervene in their relationship troubles, and take on the role of mediator (rather than act as an overt judge). There appear to be interesting implications here regarding how school-based practices shape and how students enact gendered identities and practices, which resonates with a growing body of research produced at this particular junction.[11]

In addition, the influence of Layla's family on her attitude towards relationships is undeniably significant. Layla's parents value family relationships, and make this explicit to both children. For example, Ray is already at work by the time Layla and Jonathon wake each morning and Beth describes dinner time each night as "especially important. That's when we spend time together as a family." In addition, and after a long history of name calling, if Layla and Jonathon now call each other names (e.g., fatty, toothpick, idiot) they can expect to be punished. "So we don't call each other names any more," Layla laughingly declares.

Thus, the seeming "inaccessibility" of young female adolescent friendship groups as described by McRobbie (1991, 14; see also p. 135 above) is not the complete story. The group, no matter how close-knit or inscrutable, is also coordinated by institutional norms, values, and expectations. Therefore, while popular culture and mass media promote one form of enculturation, they are by no means the only influences at work in Layla's everyday life.

Teen Gals and Nice Girls

Being a member of Layla's circle of friends comprises much more than having access to and sharing aspects of popular culture, wearing particular kinds of clothes, and being variously a foil for or performer of humorous routines and improvisations. Although such things are important to the group, they do not necessarily ensure membership. As with Nicholas and Jacques and their social groups at school, certain phenomena and identities take on particular meanings in the shifting discursive threads and spaces of Layla's circle of friends. However, Layla and her close friends appear to draw their inspiration more explicitly from popular television, movies, and magazines than do Nicholas, Jacques, and their friends. For example, among hundreds of other possible examples, at various times their wristwatches become secret-agent mobile phones, lines from movies are used like passwords for group members, and intertextual aliases are preferred to real names; at other times these items are not accorded such status or roles. Indeed, it seems that members of this circle of friends must be alert to changed and changing relational nuances and exchanges, otherwise they will feel or find themselves to be on the outer edge of the circle. As indicated earlier, conceptions of Discourses are useful here in terms of claiming a complex array of influences, subject matter, and coordinations that constitute much of Layla's ways of speaking and acting as a member of this particular group of young adolescent females. For example, Layla and her circle of friends can be said to belong to a sub-Discourse of a larger set of practices that could be called—for want of a better term—a "teen gal" Discourse after the manner of the magazines they like to read.

Once again, I use the term *sub-Discourse* in a very particular sense in order to differentiate Layla's circle of friends' language and social practices from those of other groups in their schools and everyday lives, and from other configurations of similar teenage groups outside their school. Thus for me, Gee's term *sub-Discourse* can be used to describe the ways in which Layla's circle of friends' practices, values, beliefs, and so forth can be recognized as belonging to a larger and most likely more enduring (for now) teen gal Discourse while at the same time constituting a particular version of (and dynamic contribution to) this larger Discourse. Furthermore, members of this circle of friends enact certain social identities and subject positions that are constituted and coordinated by their relationships with each other and with others outside their immediate group. Gee uses the concept of *social networks* to help explain the identities that speakers signal in their language (e.g., 1991a, 5, 1996a, 131). However, after analyzing the data collected while observing and talking with Layla, Nicholas, Jacques, and Hannah, I find "interactive webs of relationships" a more dynamic and apposite concept than "social network" for describing possible social roles, identities, and subject positions (McRobbie 1994, 187; see also Lemke 1995a, 16). Layla repeatedly describes herself in terms of her relations within this circle of friends, as well as the relations to which she lays claim—or that lay claim to her—in her everyday life (e.g., within her family, with her Japanese and English friends). In addition, this interactive web of relations is threaded through with institutional expectations and responsibilities that extend beyond this circle of friends to other groups and individuals, and that exert considerable influence (recognized and unnoticed) on the ways in which this circle of friends acts as a composite of individual members.

From my perspective, much of this seemingly widespread web of relations appears to be coordinated by the intersection, or cross-seepage, of at least two Discourses. One of these coordinations I have previously labeled a Catholic Discourse. The ethos of the school overtly promotes a strong sense of belonging to a family and a sense of responsibility for others. This is achieved by a number of means, including: documented codes of conduct displayed on walls, the student council, teacher attitudes and modeled practices, and shared activities and rituals including school assembly and Mass where students repeat declarations of love for each other and sing of being members of the family of God (cf. Lesko 1988, 111–112). Students are clearly expected to look after each other physically and emotionally, and to behave in particular ways towards their teachers and others.

Another possible Discourse coordinating Layla's relationships with others appears to be characterized by social expectations of what counts as being a "nice girl" (cf. Steedman 1981; Walkerdine 1981, 1996a). For example, nice girls care for the emotional and physical well-being of others, often above and beyond their own well-being; nice girls are well behaved and sexually aloof outside long-term relationships with a male partner (Lesko 1988, 93–95; Gilbert and Taylor 1991, 15–16). This is a particularly pervasive Discourse in Australia and elsewhere, and drawing on regularly observed patterns of discourse and action, I propose that Layla's practices and relationships with others may be coordinated simultaneously by Catholic and nice girl Discourses (among others); and that substantial aspects of these Discourses are likely to be an organic part of her primary Discourse. These overlaps and seepages emphasize the complexity and overlap of Discourse memberships and coordinations in Layla's everyday life. These complex interrelationships bear directly on Layla's ways of acting and speaking in a range of contexts, and at times—as previously mentioned—are manifested in overtly self-regulating language and social practices. For example:

> (Tuesday 25 October 1994, 12:10 p.m. Day 2 of observations)
> EVENT: INTERVIEW 2
> SUBEVENT: *Discussing dealing with anger (utterances 209-211)*
> Layla   Well, I just try and keep it in myself that I have to settle down if I get angry or something. I try and settle myself down. Calm myself down and don't get really angry.
> Michele   Why's that?
> Layla   'Cause people just think you're stupid if you get angry at them. Like if you yell and things.

To sum up this section, it seems that in Layla's everyday life interactive and shifting webs of relations are woven from personally immediate, as well as from more enduring social and textual forms of life. As already discussed, many of her ways of speaking and acting outside the classroom are recognizable as aspects of larger cultural and social constructions or scriptings of being a certain kind of female adolescent.[12] Many of the possible ways of speaking and acting available to her are intertextual, comprising—in the case of her particular circle of friends—idiosyncratic configurations of lines and performances taken from television soap operas, cartoons, advertisements, and sitcoms; teen magazines; movies; comics; and from the Sunday papers, to list only a few.[13]

For me, using a more explicitly relational concept such as "interactive webs of relationships" to describe certain patterns of interactions expands Gee's original definition of Discourses to include the significance of interpersonal relationships in interpreting forms of life and social identities (cf. Brown and Gilligan 1992; Gilligan 1990). This also moves directly towards addressing Lemke's (1995a, 16) criticisms of Gee's focus on the "speaking individual." A more explicit relational plane of analysis can help contextualize interpretations of an individual's ways of speaking and acting within at least some of the webs of relations—and their coordinating Discourses—that appear to be implicated in her social identities. Moreover, I strongly suspect that Layla's complex uses of language and popular culture subject matter are aspects of a generation that is more able than previous generations to navigate a vast sea of diverse symbolic and social resources and their attendant social processes and practices (Buckingham and Sefton-Green 1994; Howe and Strauss 1993). Douglas Rushkoff, in his commentary on what he calls "screenagers," captures my point when he claims, "We [may be] afraid of the universal wash of our media ocean because, unlike our children, we can't recognize the bigger picture in its overall structure" (1996b, 194).

Likewise, Chris Richards suggests the "socialization" of young people is not so much the "incorporation of children into an (unchanging) society," but rather the "succession of generations" (1993, 47). Maybe, in relation to Layla's circle of friends and perhaps others like it, we are witnessing performances that are new enough to alter what counts as being a member of a teen gal Discourse, and which in turn, are altering the Discourse itself. This is only an informed guess, and some may argue that young adolescents have

Everyday Literacies 143

for a long time parodied radio and television language, images, and meanings. However, previous generations have not grown up with television and electronic technologies as an organic part of their everyday lives as has Layla and her generation (cf. Rushkoff 1996a, 1996b). Possible forms of life accruing for Layla's generation certainly warrant further discussion and study.

The second snapshot shifts interpretive attention from Layla as a friend and teen gal to Layla as a student. This snapshot contrasts noticeably with Layla's usually flamboyant actions and unapologetically dramatic use of language within her circle of friends.

SNAPSHOT 2: ROLE PLAYING (OR, "I'M NOT DOING IT!")

(Wednesday 26 October 1994, 12:10 to 1:15 p.m. Day 3 of observations.)
EVENT: LANGUAGE LESSON
SUBEVENT 1: *Orientation*
Mr. Wills and students are reconstructing and reconfiguring transactional conversations from a recent *Earn and Learn* session. Mr. Wills has pre-arranged for two students—one the owner of the Casino (Ivan), and the other the Federal treasurer (Victoria)—to re-enact the closing of the casino following revelations of a scam involving rigged "scratch-it" ticket sales.

He sets each table team[14] the task of changing one or more elements of the re-enacted conversation (e.g., contexts, sites, who is involved, who speaks first, language used, tone) to be presented to the rest of the class.

> Layla whispers "Oh God" then turns to Anna sitting beside her and says, "I don't get it."

Mr. Wills talks through an example for the class, demonstrating how the conversation would change if Ivan began speaking first, or if the conversation occurred in Victoria's office instead.
SUBEVENT 2: *Team task*
Layla's table team discusses possible changes that could be made to the original interaction, but does not appear to arrive at any sort of decision.
Mr. Wills informs the class, "Right, your time's almost up."

> Layla asks Melissa "Why are we doing this? I don't know—what are we gonna do?" and then, "Do we have to act this out? Are we acting it out?" Her team continues to discuss possibilities.

> **SUBEVENT 3:** *Class role plays and discussion*
> Layla's table team decides that they will change the scene by including an "advance party" that warns Ivan about the impending casino closure. Mr. Wills circulates around the room as teams continue working on their "conversations." When he comes to Layla's team, Sallie explains to him "We came up with like, Victoria told Melissa at the bank, and one of the tellers overheard and went over and told Ivan." Mr. Wills comments encouragingly, and moves off.
> Layla's team decide that she, in her role as a bank teller in *Earn and Learn*, will be the one to tell Ivan. Layla's eyes widen and she asks, "Why do I have to go over there?" The others explain that she is the only one who can do it. Layla suggests Shona instead, who is also a bank teller, but the others insist that Layla is the one to tell Ivan. Layla protests, saying anyone can do it, but no one appears to be listening.
>> Layla asks repeatedly: "What's happening?," "How am I going to do it?," "Am I going over?," and complains: "I don't get it" as the others continue to construct the proposed role play.
>
> Finally she declares, "I'm not doing it." In the end, another team member, Daniel, acts as the advance party to forewarn Ivan of the closure.

The lesson from which this second snapshot was lifted aimed at making explicit to students the ways in which the outcomes of a conversation are contingent on "purposes, context, subject matter, roles, relationships, mode, and medium" (Mr. Wills's lesson plan). Accordingly, students were given time within the lesson to experiment with interactions by means of changing one or more contextual, linguistic, or relational features. In the course of this language lesson—and others—Mr. Wills draws on a presumably shared language for talking about language with his students. This includes terms and phrases like: "unpack, reconstruct the conversation, context, tone, live analysis, visual change, role, the power position (in an interaction), reproduce the context," and so forth. However, as displayed below, Layla does not appear to understand the link between certain terms and the processes they denote.

In addition, and despite Layla's demonstrated competence in using language creatively, and her ability to poke fun at a range of popular culture and everyday practices, very little of this seemed to find its way into her language work in class during the time I spent observing her. Indeed, Layla—like Jacques—often seemed at a loss as to what was required of her, and relied on her teammates to fill her in. For example:

(Wednesday 26 October 1994, 12:10 to 1:15 p.m. Day 3 of observations) EVENT: LANGUAGE LESSON SUBEVENT 3: *Analyzing and modifying the original conversation*	
Teacher-led talk	Classroom underlife[15]
529 Mr. W: Okay, stop for a minute. I just want to find out where groups are at ((class falls silent)). So we'll just find out where groups are up to.	
531 Mr. W: We have four tasks: reconstruct, analyze, suggest a change, re-enact.	530 Layla: ((Very quietly)) Where are we up to?
	532 Layla: ((Whispers)) What are we doing?
533 Mr. W: All right? Now, who's—who has yet to do the first one? The reconstruction of the conversation. So everyone's had a go at that one? They've spoken through what they've said, they've stood in the right place and all that sort of—	534 Melissa: ((Soft voice)) Don't worry about it.
	535 Layla: What's "reconstruction?"
	536 Anna: We're analyzing it.
	537 Melissa: You know the—
	538 Anna: We're analyzing it.
539 Ss: Yeah.	
540 Mr. W: Right. So which groups are currently in the analysis stage of their task? Unpacking it, finding out how did you feel about it. All right, which groups are in the third stage of suggesting a change, or in the process of coming up with a change?....	541 Layla: What's the analysis?
	542 Anna: That's ((inaudible))
	((They continue to conference in whispers))

During interviews, Mr. Wills emphasized the importance of developing and using a shared metalanguage with students: "I see it as part of my role to give them a language to think about their language. Otherwise, how can they possibly improve it?" Within the language lessons I observed, Mr. Wills attempted to develop metalevel understandings of the way language works, and how it can be changed in order to make oneself more effective in conversations. Indeed, "improvement" and "becoming more effective" are recurring themes in Mr. Wills's classroom talk and school-related conversations. Layla seemed attuned to this; hence her efforts at improving herself through a self-directed reading program (i.e., "Mr. Wills says reading a lot improves your knowledge of words"), and her self-corrections in conversations with me (for example: "Uhm, well I thought that if there was something wrong I could get worse—sicker—more sick"). In addition to developing a metalanguage, Mr. Wills repeatedly tries to draw students' attention to links between their out-of-school lives and what they are learning about language in the classroom. For example:

(Wednesday 26 October 1994, 12:10 to 1:15 p.m. Day 3 of observations)
EVENT: LANGUAGE LESSON (utterance 636)

Mr. Wills   If we were compiling a list of "Dos and Don'ts" to be effective in conversation, say we're going to put out a little booklet so we're going to list each one in point form. Like this: If you want to be effective in your conversation in business, do this." What would we put on the "Do" side?

It seems that being a member of Mr. Wills's class includes, among other things, being able to use language to talk about language, demonstrate a metalevel understanding of the functions of language, and make links between classroom language practices and everyday life beyond school. It appears that Mr. Wills aims at apprenticing his students to (particular kinds of) "real world" language practices that will help them negotiate their way in an adult world. Indeed, when asked about her school-based language learning experiences, Layla identifies them as usefully relevant to possible workplaces, and comments on the importance of having a "real" purpose for writing:

> (Wednesday 2 November 1994, 4:30 p.m. Day 7 of observations)
> EVENT: INTERVIEW 2
> SUBEVENT: *Talking about school and language learning (utterance 495)*
>
> Michele   Do you think school is teaching you the kind of language that you're going to need?
>
> Layla   I think so because... if you went out to like, the real world and went and got a job and everything, you'd have to know how to use proper language and, use it properly... instead of just... If you were in like an office, you'd have to make lots of phone calls and know how to speak and things. And in conferences, you'd have to know how to... how to get up and say what you think
>
> Michele   Mr. Wills talks about the purpose of writing and things like that. Do you think it helps if you know why you are writing something, and who you are writing it for?
>
> Layla   Yes, because if you don't know who your audience is, like who you're writing it to, and you're just writing a letter for the sake of it, you really wouldn't get much out of it because you're just not giving it to anyone. Well, you could give it to someone, but you don't know who you're writing it to. Like, at our school camp we were asked to write a letter to a person and Mrs. Champion would post them all, but like, we never heard anything from them, because we didn't know who we were writing to or anything. So, it made the letter, harder to write—more difficult.

It seems that having a meaningful purpose for writing is paramount for Layla. For example, when asked about the lesson on conversations (see snapshot 2 above), Layla responded vaguely that it was about "analysis or something." In addition, she seemed to reinterpret Mr. Wills's focus on a business discourse in the lesson in her summary of this lesson's learning outcome, which she identified as: "Conversations with best friends are different from conversations with worst friends." Letter writing looms large in Layla's talk about purposeful language uses, and in her own social practices out-of-school. However, when Layla is presented with an opportunity at school to use her interest and competence in letter writing in ways that would enable her to access increasingly powerful ways of interacting in the real world (i.e., emailing) the opportunity is cast in terms of a detective game. This is not to deny her the recreational aspects of email; nevertheless, if this is the only kind of email experience to which she has access, then possibilities for engaging in real world uses of email are seriously curtailed.

(Monday 31 October 1994, 8:50 a.m. Day 5 of observations.)
EVENT: KEYLINK[16]
SUBEVENT 1: *Introduction to email*
Layla, two female and two male students are grouped around a computer located in the year 7 class adjoining theirs. This computer has an external modem and Mr. Wills demonstrates how to set it up and dial into Keylink "headquarters" using the computer keyboard and an email software package. He logs off, then points to a list of handwritten instructions that he had compiled that morning before school and tacked to the wall above the computer terminal. Layla keys in various passwords and commands as Mr. Wills talks the group through the logging on process. At times she looks quizzical and hesitates until helped out by a classmate or by Mr. Wills; she laughs and continues. As they work through the list of instructions, Mr. Wills explains passwords, user names, sending and receiving mail, organizing mailboxes, session menus, creating files, scroll bars, the mouse, printing in economy mode, and closing down connections. Mr. Wills also explains that their task is to "agree to pretend"[17] they are detectives tracking down a criminal by means of a trail of clues provided by other participating schools. He reminds them of the *Get Smart* television show and movie. He talks about using nonsexist language, thinking divergently, and about organizing the information they collect.

SUBEVENT 2: *Agreeing to pretend*
The group opens their electronic mailbox and finds their first clue: "Criminal was overheard talking about traveling north to gamble." The group moves to nearby tables and begins leafing through short descriptions of participating schools that each had submitted to Keylink prior to the start of this project. Some of the students consult atlases to check the location of a suspected school. All of them make notes and discuss possibilities before reaching consensus that the message refers to a school in Townsville.

> *(Keylink continued)*
> They use pen and paper to collaboratively draft a suitably cryptic email message—or "letter" as Mr. Wills describes it—to this school.
> SUBEVENT 3: *Sending a message*
> Mr. Wills sits at the computer and talks the group through the process of sending a message, drawing their attention to the relevant instructions on the wall.

The group spent the next four weeks before and after school and in lunch breaks logging on, checking their mailbox, decoding and encoding clues, and sending messages to other schools around Australia. When asked about participating in the project, Layla commented on how she had enjoyed it, although she didn't really understand why they were doing it, or how it all worked.

Now You See Her, Now You Won't

At one level, Layla does not seem to fit with the kind of student Discourse Mr. Wills promotes. In class, Layla appears to resist drawing attention to herself, and devotes much of her time to avoiding public attention and potentially embarrassing displays of knowing or not knowing. For example, Mr. Wills encourages students to have confidence in themselves and their own knowledge (e.g., said publicly to Layla: "Why do you doubt yourself?," or "Have a go"). However, Layla repeatedly expresses minimal confidence in her own abilities (e.g., "What a fluke. I just guessed"). I was struck by the ways in which she seemed to construct herself as an "invisible" student in Mr. Wills's class. This included: evading eye contact with Mr. Wills whenever possible, answering only when she knew she had a good chance of being right (e.g., had asked a classmate the answer first), preferring to answer in a chorus (and then usually having a bet both ways; such as, if the teacher asks about sending a friend or foe, Layla answers: "Friend, foe, friend"), or by retreating into silence when the attention of her teacher or the class is focused on her alone.

There are available any number of interpretations of Layla's behavior in class; for example, her reticence may be motivated by a fear of failure, boredom, not wanting to draw attention to herself, or by a conviction that girls are not to demonstrate that they are knowledgeable (cf. Davies 1993; Gilbert and Taylor 1991). Any or all of these could serve as reasonably adequate explanations. Perhaps, instead, she is motivated by a strong need to belong (and to be seen to belong) to a group rather than to subscribe to the "rampant individualism" that is so often promoted in schools in countries like Australia (cf. Lesko 1988, 8–10). Although this latter interpretation lies again in the realm of speculation, it nevertheless usefully explains some of the striking contrasts between Layla's academic invisibility and restrained language uses in class and her theatrical performances and lavish language repertoire when in the company of her circle of friends. I suspect that Layla is demonstrating how well she has been enculturated by the interactive web of social relationships and secondary Discourses that currently help shape and constitute her various social identities and language practices, particularly in terms of being a nice girl and a good friend (more so than being a good student). For example, it seems that Layla is being apprenticed most thoroughly to Discourses that value relationships; indeed, her teacher is quite explicit about at least one aspect of this:

> (Tuesday 1 November 1994, 12:00 p.m. Day 7 of observations)
> EVENT: INTERVIEW 2 (utterance 091)
> Mr. Wills I keep trying to tie in values all the time; that if underlying your language is not having respect for other people, then we're just wasting our time. If we're not learning to relate and show some kind of respect for other people, and concentrate instead just on what each "I" wants to happen, then it's kind of pointless. And... this is one of the problems I have with school text genres. They don't involve relationships with people. They are just cold, dry, and clinic.

This position also resonates with Layla's mother's hopes that her children will grow up to be "good people" with "good values" (i.e., one aspect of the family's primary Discourse). This kind of citizenship apprenticeship is not in itself a negative thing; indeed, many theorists and commentators have long advocated the inclusion of this dimension in social analyses and projects.[18] However, if this is the only kind of apprenticeship that Layla believes to be valued by those in authority, then there may be a risk that Layla will regard herself as incapable of the kind of analytic work of which Reich (1992) speaks, despite the burgeoning analytic skills demonstrated in her exuberant, creative, and parodic uses of language, and their increasing cachet in certain workplaces (see Howe and Strauss 1993; Aronowitz and DiFazio 1994).

These concerns are neatly captured by the Keylink project in which Layla participated. Email is fast becoming an indispensable technology in myriad workplaces, and rapidly assuming a front row seat in new configurations of powerful Discourses (Kurland 1996; Rheingold 1994; Taylor and Saarinen 1994). Email is used, for example, to collect and disseminate information, communicate with others about issues or to "add value" to an idea or product, and/or to build and maintain communities of users with common interests or purposes. Unfortunately, the Keylink project did not apprentice Layla to any of these real life uses and practices of email—or believable simulations of them—and their coordinating Discourses.

A PROVISIONAL CONCLUSION (AND SOME MODIFICATIONS TO THE THEORY)

There is of course much more that can be said about Layla and her everyday language and social practices. My interpretations of Layla as a teenager, a friend, and a student, however, are necessarily tentative. During the initial stages of the analysis process, I found it difficult to tease apart patterns of specific influences, props, actions, ways of speaking, values, and coordinations. In Layla's case (as with Hannah; see chapter 6), I initially found these multiple and intersecting coordinations and sets of practices indissolubly interrelated to such a degree that my efforts at interpretation were for a long time paralyzed. Indeed, simply having a theory of D/discourses proved insufficient. I found I needed to also know about the Discourses I was claiming for Layla almost as much as an insider would—or at least know enough about them—in order to be able to identify them with any confidence. Thus, it seems that identifying Discourses with any authority requires a great deal of knowledge about various "worlds" and possible forms of life.

Paradoxically, I also found that interpreting Discourses requires at least some degree of professional distance between one's own Discourses and the Discourses of those being studied. Hence, I attribute some of the initial difficulties in interpreting Layla's Discourse coordinations in part to my own close familiarity with the Discourses that constitute and coordinate Layla. Indeed, I found myself constantly comparing and contrasting my own adolescence with Layla's experiences. I was also reminded repeatedly of tensions I experienced as a young teenager in trying to make a space for myself while at the same time trying to please everyone else. I managed to create some professional distance from Layla by setting aside, for quite some time, the information I had collected about her. This seemed to produce a degree of detachment from the data. In the meantime, reading additional feminist critiques of education along with studies of and commentaries on adolescent girls in school and out-of-school contexts also helped with final analyses. In addition, I endeavored to address the potentially confounding effects of my own Discourses on my interpretation of Layla's language and social practices by reflecting as far as I was able on my own experiences as a year 7 student and so on, and then carefully crossexamining these data using what I considered to be trustworthy evidence in support of my interpretations, all the while keeping my self-reflections in mind. I also verified my interpretations by means of member checks and "outsider audits" by colleagues.

Gee's notion of coordinations coupled with McRobbie's conception of interactive webs of relations proved especially helpful in describing the complex ebb and flow of constraints, influences, social relations, and social and language practices constituting Layla's membership in a range of Discourses (without having to identify each of these Discourses beyond provisional labels). This also helped me to see how Discourses can extend beyond social groups, and how members and nonmembers interact and thus define a particular group, a practice, and so forth. In response to Bennett's (1993, 574) call for evaluating the importance of a Discourse for a particular person, I am only able to speculate in Layla's case. Layla was often inscrutable, even in interviews where I had the opportunity to probe for more detailed responses. However, given the high status of popular culture in Layla's group, I would say that this Discourse is important to the identity of the group as a whole. Beyond that, it is difficult to separate Discourses Layla values and Discourses she believes she *should* value. Indeed, those Discourses of which she is most fully a member may be the least apparent to her, and most likely would not enter into the (consciously) "valuing" stakes. Thus, regardless of whether or not Layla values the Discourses in her everyday life, they nevertheless coordinate and constitute her identities, and her everyday social and language practices. Seen from this angle, Bennett's criticisms seem to miss the mark.

Endnotes

1. *Girlfriend* is aimed specifically at the young "teen girl" market. For example, the contents page of the November 1994 issue includes:
FASHION	**43 Water Babies**	The coolest cossies to look hot in
CELEBS	**62 Just Chillin'**	Celebs spill how they chill out
FEATURES	**40 Flirt Alert**	How to know when he's hitting on you!

2. Jonathon has a full-sized television in his room that he uses almost exclusively for playing Nintendo.

3. *Ren and Stimpy* is an animated television cartoon. Ren is a neurotic chihuahua, and Stimpy is a large, dim-witted cat.

4. Unfortunately, there does not seem to a "female" equivalent for the concepts of "mate" and "mateship." Despite the cohesiveness and loyalty that the term "mate" connotes, its cultural associations make it unsuitable for describing Layla's group. Accordingly, the label "circle of friends"—although still inadequate—is used to describe Layla's close girlfriends and their interrelationships. The term "circle" was chosen deliberately because most of the group's interactions were conducted while sitting or standing in a circle. This was not the case with Nicholas and his mates, nor with Jacques, who usually talked with others while engaging in some sort of physical activity, such as playing basketball or roaming the playground.

5. This includes songs such as: *Come Together* with the repeated lines: "We are part of one family...," *A Life of Love* with the repeated lines: "Love one another," and so forth. Prayers include lines such as: "...walk in the newness of life as your adopted children," and "Lord Jesus you have made us your brothers and sisters in Baptism."

6. In the sense that this is the group to which Layla sees herself belonging, rather than denoting any sort of ownership of the group by Layla. Indeed, the group appeared to be organized around general consensus, with no permanent leader observable.

7. This is not to deny the historical effects of Layla's family and other institutions on her social identities. These other coordinating forces are foregrounded in discussions that follow.

8. *Wannabe* is a popular derogative term used to describe a person who is perceived by others as desperately and hopelessly wanting a particular social identity or to be a member or a particular group (e.g., I wannabe like Madonna).

9. Contrary to my predictions, however, this rupture appeared to have been resolved completely by the following day, and was never mentioned again during the observation period.

10. This is confirmed by a number of small ruptures in friendships I observed during the time I spent with Layla and her circle of friends. However, unlike the large fight, these were quickly repaired and smoothed over.

11. See, for example, among others: Davies 1989, 1993; Gilbert and Taylor 1991; Giroux 1991; Gowen 1991; Graddol and Swann 1989; Jones 1986, 1993; Lesko 1988; McLaren 1991b; McRobbie 1994; Roman 1992; Smith 1995; Swann 1993; Tannen 1994.

12. This is exemplified, among myriad other occurrences, by Layla and her circle of friends' liberal use of words such as: "like," "cool," "totally," and "not" (the latter used to negate claims and denote resistance or sarcasm) which are generally spoken with a North American accent. These expressions and intonations appear in a range of media designed specifically for teenage markets, and I overheard these words and intonations being used in all four classrooms I observed for this study. For further discussions of this aspect of teenage cultures, see, for example: Gilbert and Taylor 1991, 57–58; McRobbie 1994, 180.

13. North American produced movies and television shows appear to be a significant influence in the life of Layla's group. Following this thread of investigation in detail unfortunately lies outside the scope of the present thesis, but signposts interesting terrain for future research (cf. Giroux 1996; Luke 1997; Rushkoff 1996a).

14. *Table team* is a term shared by members of the class to describe groups of students working collaboratively on a project or teacher-set task. These table teams are fluid and are defined principally by where one happens to be sitting for that lesson.

15. In the manner of Kris Gutierrez and her colleagues' focus on the richness of classroom underlife (e.g., Gutierrez, Rymes, and Larson 1995).

16. Keylink is a national government funded initiative designed to introduce primary school students to electronic mail. Each Keylink project runs for approximately four weeks.

17. This is a shared term the class uses to distinguish between being in role and being a regular student.

18. See, for example: Lankshear and Knobel 1997; Mills 1959; Rheingold 1994; Searle 1993; Gilligan 1982.

CHAPTER SIX

Hannah

Hannah (12 years) is small for her age. Her slight build and brown, shoulder length hair, worn mostly in two neat plaits, tend to make her look younger than she is. Hannah has an open face, with bright, blue eyes framed by gold glasses. She has an impish smile and a quirky sense of humor. Hannah is well known for speaking extremely quickly and animatedly when talking about things she enjoys, or in which she is interested. Her favorite outfit comprises her "denim shorts and blue top," because in Hannah's words, "they're fashionable." After school she wears light sundresses or comfortable shorts and tops. She appears to spend her time after school watching television, reading, playing with her younger sister, working on craft projects, or listening to her mother talk about growing up in rural northern New South Wales. Hannah particularly enjoys hearing her mother and aunts retelling childhood events while sitting around the kitchen table.

Hannah's family is one of the few in the area who own the home in which they live. Most of the houses around them are either Housing Commission homes, or rented. Hannah's home is well kept, with a neatly trimmed lawn and a number of tidy garden plots. This is in stark contrast with many of the houses in the same area. The satellite city in which Hannah lives is officially designated "disadvantaged" by the Department of Education and other government bodies, and is generally recognized as having high unemployment and crime rates. This area is also extremely diverse culturally and linguistically, and spending time in the local shopping mall reveals a broad mix of cultures, languages, apparent socioeconomic situations, and probable lifestyles.

Hannah lives at home with her mother and father, her older brother, Craig (15 years), and younger sister, Laura (7 years). Her father, Peter, trained and worked as a chef, but now drives delivery trucks for a large carrier firm. He is currently contracted to Coca-Cola and organizes the delivery loads for the thirty or so trucks that operate out of the depot where he works. On weekends, Peter also runs a business that cleans small trucks and industrial buildings, and both Hannah and Craig regularly work for him. Peter was on late afternoon and night shifts during the observation period, and I rarely saw him. Hannah's mother, Julia, trained and worked as a nurse before marrying Peter and insists that she she is content to be "just a housewife," and does not want full-time wage-earning work. She is a tireless volunteer worker at Hannah's school, and takes an active interest in her children's schooling. Julia, however, expresses strong feelings of alienation towards the area in which they live, saying, for example:

> (Thursday, 1 December, 4:47 p.m. Day 9 of observations)
> EVENT: INTERVIEW 4 (with Hannah and Julia)
> SUB-EVENT: *Talking about a recipe book Julia had just bought because it reminded her of her mother's recipe book (utterances 529–531)*
>
> Julia   I don't belong here.
> Michele   You don't?
> Julia   No... No, I don't fit into this area, sort of thing. I don't really fit the type ((soft laugh)).

Hannah's family seems a close and loving one, although at the time of observations Craig appeared to be testing various outer limits of social practices acceptable to his parents. Hannah shares a room with Laura and they appear to get on with each other very well. Her family regularly spends time together, usually camping and water-skiing with Peter and Julia's brothers and sisters and their families. Everyone has bought different bits and pieces of equipment, and the families pool their boats and gear for skiing sessions. They mainly waterski on a large lake in New South Wales, near where Julia and her siblings grew up. In addition, Hannah's family regularly holiday together; when I first phoned them about my intended research, for example, they had just returned from two weeks in the Blue Mountains near Sydney.

In school, Hannah is one of the few students who wears the school uniform, and hers is always pressed and spotless. The school has a large student population, from predominantly working class and underclass families. The school is culturally, ethnically, and linguistically diverse, with up to 40 different groups represented, and "acceptance of others" is promoted actively throughout the school by the teaching staff. Hannah is in a double class of 54 students, with two teachers, Mrs. Evans (called "Mrs. E." by the students) and Mr. Brunner. Compared with other year 7 classes I have spent time with, this class seems by no means an easy one to teach. The class is culturally and linguistically diverse, and has a high rate of transience, a number of explosive personalities, and students who in the main seem far more worldly wise and street-smart than students in the three other classes I observed. In startling contrast with most of her classmates, however, Hannah is a "model" student. She rarely talks during lessons and works at her tasks without seeming to be distracted by other events occurring in the classroom. Her teachers, too, comment on Hannah's ability to apply herself to her schoolwork. For example:

> (Thursday 1 December, 3:43 p.m. Day 9 of observations)
> EVENT: INTERVIEW WITH MR. BRUNNER
> SUB-EVENT: *Discussing local high schools (utterance 343)*
> Mr. Brunner   I don't believe Hannah will have a problem wherever she goes. She's got that type of attitude and she doesn't let things around her bother her.

Hannah's teachers rate her as "above average" in language and literacy competence. Hannah identifies reading in class and at home as one of her most favorite pastimes. Her preferred authors at the moment are Enid Blyton and R. L. Stine.[1]

Hannah is well liked by her teachers and classmates and appears to enjoy school very much; for example, when asked what she would wish for were she to have three wishes, her immediate reply was:

> (Tuesday 22 November, 4:30 p.m. Day 2 of observations)
> EVENT: INTERVIEW 2 (utterance 119)
> Hannah   I'd wish that all the people in my class and friends and stuff,

> and my school, was like out in the country—that we lived out in the country. So we're like based out in the country, and I still have all my friends and teachers.

Hannah has a very small group of close friends at school, which includes her best friend since year 1, Virginia. This group is completed by another two girls, Jing and Yee, from Cambodia and Vietnam respectively. Virginia, however, appears to be the only friend with whom Hannah socializes regularly outside school (aside from Hannah's cousins). All four girls are well behaved in class, and are generally quiet and unassuming. During lunch hours, however, these friends create and practice elaborate and often raucous skits and dance routines which they are allowed to perform occasionally for their class. Hannah and Virginia are also involved in the school Drama Group and are currently rehearsing for an end-of-year concert.

From this brief and incomplete characterization of Hannah, it is possible to identify at least three overlapping social identities that appear to play a prominent role in her everyday life. These include: being a "model" student, being a performer, and being the member of a particular family (which, in Hannah's case, manifests itself in her interest in the "olden days" and life in the country). The following three snapshots attempt to freeze some of the complexities constituting these various identities for the purposes of investigating and interpreting possible Discourse memberships and the ways in which they might coordinate her everyday life. As with Layla, however, this initially proved to be no easy task.

The following discussion of Hannah's language and social practices concludes with reflections on a number of interpretive difficulties I ran up against at various times within this case.

SNAPSHOT 1: GETTING DOWN TO THE TASK AT HAND

> (Monday 28 November, 11:10 a.m. Day 6 of observations)
> EVENT: LANGUAGE LESSON
> SUBEVENT 1: *Silent reading (after morning tea)*

The students move into the classroom and find their seats, or mill about talking to each other. Hannah sits at her desk without speaking to anyone and takes out her book, *The Door in the Wall* (Ashton Scholastic). Mrs. E. and Mr. Brunner wait for everyone to be seated, then set about identifying which students are yet to hand in their Novel assignment. Hannah seems engrossed in her book while this is happening.

Jethro,[2] who sits beside Hannah, leans over and takes a pair of scissors from Hannah's desk. She appears to ignore him. Jethro sits and trims the green fuzz from a tennis ball with the scissors, then gently jabs Hannah in the arm with them before putting the scissors back on her desk. Hannah reads on.

(11:15 a.m.) Mrs. E. informs the class that they have five minutes of silent reading left before moving into their reading groups. Students around Hannah are variously engaged in reading novels, magazines, novelty books, chatting, or simply sitting with their heads on their desks. Jethro shifts around in his seat, bounces the tennis ball on his desk a few times, and yawns loudly. Two students from another class come to the door and ask who would like to play softball for Friday sport. Hannah looks up briefly, then returns to her reading.

SUBEVENT 2: *Introducing the next section of the lesson*
(11:22 a.m.) Mr. Brunner tells his student group to come and sit in the large space in the center of the room. Hannah puts her book away and sits on the floor, somewhat on her own. Virginia sits with another girl. Mr. Brunner explains that the task he is about to give them is part of their final assessment for their current unit on Greek mythology. Hannah appears to listen carefully, regularly raises her hand in response to Mr. Brunner's questions, and is called on to provide answers. The students are sent back to their desks with a worksheet each, and Hannah begins working immediately.

(11:31 a.m.) After some time, Hannah raises her hand, but Mr. Brunner is engaged in redirecting a student who is in the wrong group. Hannah lowers her hand, then fetches a dictionary from the bookshelves and appears to look up a word. A group of students discuss with Mr. Brunner where the Achilles tendon is located. One student loudly suggests that it's "in my bum." Hannah continues working.

Classroom events and practices like the ones above were repeated over and over again during the two weeks I spent in this classroom. Indeed, I found that the bulk of my fieldnotes were more about other students than about Hannah. Once I had described the task she was involved in, there was often very little else to write about her for long periods of time. Hannah was never reprimanded by her teachers, but neither did she seem to be teased by her classmates for behaving in ways that some may have regarded in others as being a "goody-goody" or "teacher's pet" (and therefore generally unacceptable).[3]

The kind of student sub-Discourse constructed by Mrs. E. and Mr. Brunner was markedly different from the other three classrooms I had observed. Both teachers repeatedly reinforced, among other things, respect for others and their property, the ability to make reasoned decisions, and the ability to take responsibility for one's own actions. For example, one lesson I observed focused on decision-making (and built on a previous lesson that addressed concepts and issues associated with freedom and responsibility). The class discussed situations where they had been forced to make important personal decisions, and then talked about factors that had influenced a range of such decisions. Mrs. E. used personal anecdotes to support or explain points she was making. Following this discussion, Mrs. E. listed a set of steps on the chalkboard that could be used to guide decision-making: (1) State the problem, (2) Gather information, (3) Examine choices, (4) Consider the consequences, and (5) Decide and evaluate. Next, the class watched a video of a scenario that involved peer pressure to shoplift. The students then worked through the decision-making steps listed on the chalkboard in deciding what they would do in such a situation.

Another example was highly visible and played an ongoing role in classroom life. A large, permanently displayed chart at the front of the room listed actions that disadvantage others. These actions included: spitting, answering back, comments, doing little work, deliberate disobedience, bad language, and lying. From the way it was written, this chart appeared to be the result of a brainstorming session, and additional actions looked as if they had been added at later dates. This chart was referred to a number of times while I was observing this class, particularly when a student was being reminded of what counted as acceptable and responsible behavior in the classroom. Students were also encouraged to take responsibility for their school work. For example, work contracts were employed for major assignments (e.g., the novel-based assignment mentioned in snapshot 1) and students signed an agreement that they would complete a specified amount of work by a given date. This document also established the content and the quality of the final product expected by both teachers.

From speaking with Mrs. E. and Mr. Brunner and listening to what they said in class, it was apparent that they were also interested in equipping their students with—at the very least—"survival" language abilities and social skills. For example:

> (Thursday 15 December, 3:15 p.m. Day 11 of observations)
> EVENT: INTERVIEW 3 (utterances 180–184)
> Michele   So what would you see then, as their language needs?
> Mrs. E.   Very functional. With the genres that we've done, we've purposely concentrated on functional genre because we felt that for these students to end up in the world and survive, they really need to be able to fill out forms, to know how to deliver or take a message, all those sorts of things... And hopefully, at the same time, we'll be teaching them some basic social skills. Just procedures and things, you know.
> Mr. Brunner If they can get those things out of it, maybe when they're older they can go on and do something.
> Mrs. E.   That's right.
> Mr. Brunner If they've got a grasp, a good understanding of those things, they might decide, "All right. If I want to get somewhere, I've got to start learning how to do these things."

In summary, Mrs. E. and Mr. Brunner worked to establish students as independent, self-motivated learners who would be able to "survive" in terms of language abilities and social skills outside school. Most students within this class, apart from Hannah, did not seem to enact or aim for these values and goals. Hannah, however, certainly appeared to embody her teachers' aspirations for their students.

A (Model) Student

To begin with, I found myself somewhat at a loss in trying to interpret the Discourses that may have been constituting Hannah as a model student. It would have been easy to claim that Hannah was fully and unquestioningly complying with the student sub-Discourse championed by her teachers. Or, as with Layla, it would be possible to say that Hannah is coordinated by Discourses that require young girls to act in respectful and dutiful ways. Indeed, these interpretations are confirmed by Hannah herself. During the familiarization visit, for example, Hannah described how in class she sits next to Jethro, who, despite his reputation with her teachers, she finds very funny. In her words, "I try not to talk to him, but sometimes *I just have to risk it*" (my emphasis). Numerous times, too, I overheard Hannah telling someone not to talk to her during class work times. In addition, Hannah had explained to a classmate (who subsequently told me) that one of the reasons she doesn't hang around with Ramona and the in-crowd of girls is that they get into too much trouble. Thus, it seems that examples such as these signal Hannah's membership in and coordination by a particular student sub-Discourse and/or nice girl Discourse.

I am convinced, however, that these Discourses are not the only ones coordinating Hannah's identity and subjectivity as a particular kind of student. To begin with, Hannah demonstrates a remarkable self-sufficiency both at school and at home. For example, Hannah and Virginia did not usually sit or work together during class, even when given opportunities to do so. I initially interpreted this as a falling out with each other; however, when I asked Hannah about it, she explained that they both like to sit with and talk to other people as well as each other. This contrasted markedly with Layla and her circle of friends, who were very tight-knit and interdependent (see chapter 5). In addition, Hannah works independently in class, and often solves any difficulties she encounters in her schoolwork on her own (see, for example, snapshot 1 above). This is confirmed in her semester school reports. For example, her school report for semester 1, 1994, describes Hannah as "a friendly, courteous class member who works quietly on tasks with minimal supervision."

Hannah's self-sufficiency also appears to be coupled with self-confidence and self-assurance. She is willing to try new things, even though she knows she might not be highly successful at them (e.g., deciding to play softball even though she is not athletic). Indeed, she was encouraged to do so by her parents. For example:

> Excerpt from Parent/Guardian Survey conducted by Hannah's teachers in September 1994 and responded to by Julia:
> 2. *What in your opinion does your child do well? (strengths)*
> Hannah appears to do well in most things. Scholastically she's the strongest but she tries most things with varied results. We both encourage her to have a go at everything that comes along.

This "have-a-go" attitude of Hannah's was different from, and often contrasted with, the self-improvement discourse that characterized many of Layla's comments. One reason for this difference could be that Hannah feels comfortable with who she is and is confident of her ability to master (or at least enjoy) new practices. However, despite my strong impression that this is indeed the case, this interpretation is difficult to support with concrete evidence.

At home, Hannah also appears to be encouraged to be self-sufficient by her parents, and particularly by her mother. For example, during the afternoon of the second day of school-based observations, Hannah asked whether I would mind not sitting with her group of friends at lunchtime anymore because her friends "can't be themselves when you're around." [4] Later, Julia explained to me that this had been a dilemma for Hannah, and that Hannah had wanted Julia to approach me about lunchtime observations. Hannah, however, was told that it was her responsibility to ask me. Another time, Hannah telephoned after my official fieldwork had finished to invite me to come and watch her and her three friends perform a number of skits for their class. After hanging up, the telephone rang again, and Hannah was phoning back to invite me to her graduation ceremony the following day. Hannah explained at the end of this second conversation that she had felt awkward for some reason about phoning back to invite me, but that her mum had asked her, "What have you got to lose?"

At the risk of over-interpreting these and other similar observations, I propose that the self-sufficiency enacted by Hannah is not reconciled easily with nice girl Discourses alone, which in the main tend to emphasize dependency and acquiescence (cf. Gilbert and Taylor 1991; Lumby 1996). Conversely, the student sub-Discourse promoted in Hannah's class values independence, both in terms of learning and personal decision-making.

However, and as indicated above, I propose that Hannah is also being coordinated by values, beliefs, and practices that characterize her primary Discourse and, in particular, her relationship with her mother. Julia often includes the word "cope" in her talk about her everyday life and, for a number of reasons—including months of ill health after the birth of Laura—has had to find ways of dealing with the everyday demands of raising a family successfully in an area in which she feels she doesn't belong. Indeed, whenever I spoke with Julia, I sensed a strong determination to provide her children with a warm, stable home environment and positive experiences of schooling. Julia often remarked, for example, that there were "so many children in the area who are not given a chance at a decent life." Neither did she feel comfortable with many of the parenting practices she saw enacted in her local community. For Julia, these practices included: women not feeding their children balanced, wholesome meals; parents and children speaking disrespectfully to each other; parents telling their young teenage children to leave home; no fixed bedtime hours for young children; children often left at home on their own, and the like.

In addition, Julia described her own time at school in which she was constantly compared (usually unfavorably) with older and younger siblings by her teachers and how she ended up hating school because of it. Julia deliberately planned her children's births some distance apart so that they would not suffer the same fate, and avoids praising one child over another in relation to their school performances. However, Julia also observed with an unmistakable inclining of her head in Hannah's direction, that it also means that one child may be "under praised." Despite her obvious competence in a range of areas, Julia appears to have little confidence in her own abilities. At times, too, I had the distinct impression that Hannah was trying to protect or help her mother by, among other things, behaving impeccably at home and at school (unlike her brother, Craig). Once again, this is only a tentative supposition and cannot be substantiated with material evidence from fieldnotes or interviews. Nevertheless, I am convinced that Julia's values, beliefs, actions, practices, and so forth, directly coordinate much of Hannah's primary Discourse, and hence, the ways in which

Hannah acts out certain identities in class and at home. This claim is revisited and discussed in the context of snapshots to come.

As previously signposted, and in stark contrast with her in-class identity, Hannah usually spent her lunch hours devising elaborate and humorous skits and dance routines with the help of her three friends. These skits were mostly spoofs on popular culture (e.g., supermodels, designer clothes), and often included messages about class differences (e.g., differences in actions and reactions of a "snob" and a "poor person" seated near each other in a restaurant). These skits were developed largely by Hannah and Virginia, and spoke to their vivid imaginations and keen senses of humor. This love of performing constitutes the subject matter of the second snapshot.

SNAPSHOT 2: ACTING UP

> (Thursday, 1 December, 1:00 p.m. Day 9 of observations)
> EVENT: HANNAH AND HER FRIENDS PERFORMING SKITS
> SUBEVENT: *The second skit*
> The entire class is seated in one half of their large classroom, with the dividing curtains pulled across to form the wings of a makeshift stage. Hannah primes the audience as to what lies ahead, explaining that Virginia is a model who is trying to draw attention to herself. Virginia's hair is tied into myriad small pigtails, held in place with strips of brightly colored cloth. Each girl has a long strip of cloth and uses it in ways similar to how models and cabaret singers use feather boas.
>
> They strut down the "catwalk," swinging their hips, pouting, shimmying their shoulders, and singing "We're models, on the catwalk. I wave my tush on the catwalk" in a direct and hilarious parody of the popular song, *I'm Too Sexy*. Hannah and Virginia make a second run down the catwalk and when they reach a certain point Virginia breaks into a frenzy, pushing Hannah out of the way, and singing at the top of her voice, "I'm too sexy for my socks, too sexy for my undies," and so forth.
>
> Their classmates and teachers are shrieking with laughter by now. Hannah grabs Virginia, gives her a good shake and asks her what she's doing. Virginia explains that she does indeed want more attention than Hannah.

> *(Snapshot 2 continued)*
> Hannah stamps her foot, and says that they'll have to do it all over again. They try two more times, threading their way out into the audience, seductively dragging and draping their strips of cloth over everybody as they sing. Twice more, Virginia reaches a certain point and explodes into unrestrained singing about how sexy she is. Eventually, Virginia agrees to behave, and they finally manage to complete their song about models on the catwalk. Just as they are about to leave the "stage," however, Virginia runs close to the audience and sings her own version of the song at double-speed, before being chased off by Hannah. Their classmates and teachers cheer and clap.

There was a startling incongruity between these girls' identities and practices during class, and the practices and identities explored during lunch hours and occasionally performed for their peers and teachers. In addition to these skits, Hannah explained that the four friends also practiced dance steps they had learned during Drama Group, or that had been shown to them by classmates who attended dance lessons (e.g., Ramona). As mentioned earlier, both Hannah and Virginia belong to the school's Drama Group, which meets during class time. Student involvement in this Drama Group is voluntary, and at the time of observations, this group was preparing for an end-of-year concert. This includes regularly practicing professionally choreographed dance routines to a number of songs that were popular at that time,[5] and rehearsing two or three short plays and excerpts from popular musicals.[6] The Drama Group is organized and run by a drama teacher, the school's music teacher, and a professional dancer from the community.

It's Easier Without the Script

For Hannah, it seems that devising and practicing dance routines and humorous skits is an important part of her life. When asked about the skits in particular, Hannah explained that last year she, Virginia, Roger (a classmate from last year), and Virginia's older brother used to devise skits at school and occasionally perform them for their year 6/7 composite class. It was difficult, however, to pinpoint the origins of this play-making; Hannah's teachers suggested that concert nights at school camps had been a trigger, while Hannah attributed it primarily to the fact that Virginia and her family often created and performed short plays at home. When asked how they went about devising each skit, Hannah explained "We just do, it's too hard to explain." I also asked whether they wrote scripts or plot descriptions for each skit, and Hannah explained, "No, we just remember the words. It's easier without the scripts." Another time, Hannah explained that the main aim of each play was to make other people laugh, therefore the principal criterion for initially judging the quality of a skit was whether or not it made them all laugh while they were devising it. Hannah later declared that if people did not laugh at their plays, then she felt silly. Perhaps, too, this may help explain why she presents a synopsis of each skit to her audience just prior to it being performed.

Unlike Layla and her circle of friends' impromptu performances, Hannah and her friends' skits and short plays are carefully rehearsed. In fact, I know of one play they had been rehearsing and fine-tuning for over a year, waiting for a chance to perform it. Hannah described how the group of four girls (with occasional "extras" drawn from the class) are forced to devise and practice their skits during their lunch breaks because "we don't visit each other at home much." The skits produced by these girls appear to send up aspects of popular culture such as sport, supermodels, television advertisements, and soap operas, or poke fun at upper middle to upper class people (or "posh" people in their terms). For example,[7] one skit involved Virginia and Yee going shopping for new clothes. They entered a store and began "ooohing" and "aaaahing" over the various items of clothing as they put them on, while speaking with toffy English accents. When they had finished dressing, they turned to the audience and leapt into the air singing, "Oh what a feeling.... St. Vinnie's!"[8] This was a send-up of a frequently appearing television advertisement for Toyota vehicles, advertisements that endeavor to sell "image" along with particular clothing labels, and people who fall for such image-mongering. Spoofing certain images or identities was underscored in the closing segment of this skit when Virginia and Yee strolled over to Jing, who had just emerged from an expensive hotel, and they declared in loud voices—to Jing's enacted shock—that *she* absolutely loved what *they* were wearing. Another, more elaborate skit opened with Virginia lying languorously on a "couch" of desks, deciding to "holiday in the country." Of course, all manner of unpleasant things befall this "rich city lady" during her visit to a farm.

All of the skits I saw performed by this group were unrestrained in nature, and often sexually or socially daring, engaging Hannah and her three friends in a range of usually extroverted roles. Again, this was in stark contrast with their subdued and restrained actions and discourses in class. Interestingly, these skits also contrasted sharply with the activities of the Drama Group. For example, Hannah was Little Red Riding Hood in a short play of the same name destined for presentation at the end-of-year school concert. Hannah had obviously put much time into learning her part and was able to speak her lines unaided, while other students still needed scripts to prompt them. During this particular practice session, Hannah's body movements and gestures were less extravagant than those I had seen in her skits with Virginia and the others; nonetheless, she was "in character" and skipped about the stage. To begin with, she spoke her lines in a high-pitched, simpering voice; however, one of the two teachers present interrupted Hannah's performance to tell her to "speak in your normal, clear voice," and the other teacher told Hannah she was speaking too quickly. For a fleeting moment Hannah looked crestfallen, then she took a deep breath and began again. This time, she more or less talked the part through, and her gestures and movements were much more restrained, even wooden.

The dance routines performed by the Drama Group were tightly choreographed. Repeated formations of dancers included lines, serried rows, and synchronized movements. Hannah rarely smiled during dance practices, even though she declared emphatically in conversations with me that she loves dancing and wishes she could take lessons. In addition, she could be seen carefully counting the beats of the music to herself, and although she danced in perfect time with the music, her movements seemed restricted and self-conscious. This was also the case during the final, public performance; none of the dancers smiled on stage, and Hannah could be seen counting the beats to herself. Her mother, Julia, commented after the concert that Hannah had taken jazz ballet lessons for a number of years and had always been very precise in the way she approached dancing. Julia joked, "Everyone else can be out of time together, but Hannah will always stick to the count."

At least two D/discourses appear to be constituting and coordinating Hannah's membership in the Drama Group. The teacher most responsible for the functioning of the group explained to me that the objectives underpinning each public performance fall into two categories: skills and outcomes. Skills objectives aim at developing: listening skills, concentration, team skills, cooperation, the ability to follow directions, and self-control. Outcomes-based objectives include: developing standards of public performance, critical reflection in order to evaluate personal and group performance, and meeting "professional standards" in public performances. In this particular drama group, students appeared to be apprenticed to a "professional performance" Discourse, whereby the values and work ethics of professional arts-related groups are employed in devising and polishing the group's concert production. The drama teacher is very explicit about this, and is himself heavily involved in amateur and professional theater troupes out-of-school. The Drama Group's work with the professional dancer underscores this sense of apprenticeship.

In addition, a Discourse that values self-discipline and bodily control appears to be constituting this drama group in interesting ways.[9] One version of this Discourse found in most schools is indissolubly linked to the normative and regulatory role of schooling (cf. Luke 1992a, 1992b; McLaren 1991b). For example, Allan Luke draws on the work of Bourdieu and Foucault in his critique of schooling, and discusses the "technologies of regulation" and "disciplinary inscription of the subjectivity of the student" that work to produce certain types of students (1992a, 115). Likewise, Peter McLaren proposes the term *enfleshment* to describe "the dialectical relationship between the material organization of interiority and the cultural forms and modes of material production we inhabit subjectively" (1991b, 154). Without doubt, schools are sites of enfleshment which becomes intextuated[10] into the student body in much the same way that power relations are inscribed in the "body politic of the society-at-large" (155). Hannah's drama teacher had very specific ideas about how each dance and play should be performed, and there was little—if any—student consultation or negotiation involved in selecting and devising each dance routine or play staging. In a very real sense, this teacher is also insisting that these student performers be amenable to being regulated, as well as able to manage and maintain their own self-regulation.

Both of these attributes are valued widely in schools and by mainstream social groups in Australia and elsewhere. Generally, the students in the Drama Group complied with this regulation.

However, this is not to argue for an "education as reproduction" position. Indeed, such interpretations have been problematized and shown to be more complex than traditionally conceived. That is, students are not necessarily passive recipients of the identities scripted for them by the school and other social institutions.[11] Indeed, Hannah and her friends' skits and self-devised dances constitute contexts for exploring and experimenting with a range of identities and subject positions other than those offered by their schooling, or by their primary Discourses. Although this group draws on television, magazines, and personal experiences in devising skits, this does not appear to be a simple matter of "writing themselves as girls" and perpetuating a patriarchal Discourse that very often scripts particular social identities and subject positions for girls at school (Gilbert 1989, 263).

Even though the skits performed by this group of young female adolescents featured symbols, artifacts, and practices often associated with "being (a particular kind of) female" (e.g., cloth strips as feather boas, an interest in clothes and eating, being beautiful, being jealous), these things were not always presented in terms of enacting "positions that rely upon a hierarchical construction of male/female relationships" (Gilbert 1992, 3). Pam Gilbert identifies such reliance as common practice for adolescent females; however, the theme recurring most in Hannah's short plays is class difference rather than male/female relationships or nice girl identities. Accordingly, these plays were performed in ways that showed "poor" (or working class) people to be resourceful and strong, and "posh" (or middle upper to upper class) people as ineffectual and weak. This does not necessarily reflect the socioeconomic status of Hannah and her friends' families, but it certainly captures themes familiar within this school and its encompassing community.

In addition, wherever the girls did seem to conform to cultural images of "being female" in their plays, such as in the supermodel skit, they very often exaggerated their roles and flaunted their sexuality in ways that simultaneously parodied and explored these identities. It certainly seemed as though the girls, and Hannah and Virginia in particular, were "trying on" a range of adult women roles in ways made safe through humor and acting.

Thus, in one sense, Hannah and her friends were practicing and experimenting with identities already claimed and enacted by many of the girls in their class (albeit in perhaps less safe ways). These other girls usually dressed in clothes and jewelry better suited to older women, read teen gal and young women's magazines such as *Dolly, Cleo*, and *Cosmopolitan*, demonstrated more obvious interest in boys, and generally seemed more worldly than Hannah and her three friends.

To pick up a point made earlier, Hannah's claim that her friends "couldn't be themselves" while I was watching them during their lunchtime rehearsals was intriguing to say the least. It left me wondering which "self" they were being during their lunch hour; obviously it was not the usual "self" of the classroom. Perhaps Hannah was suggesting that the personas they enacted in their plays were closer to their inner lives than the schooled bodies they presented during class, or perhaps these personas were in some way how they perceived/would like to perceive themselves, or have others see them. Alternatively, these girls may have been constructing ways, no matter how seemingly inconsequential, of resisting identities and subjectivities that have been mapped for them by others, according to the community in which they find themselves; for example, being mothers, having husbands, being powerless, and the like.[12] Once again, this complex of events, conversations, and observations is not easily interpreted in terms of specific Discourses. Nevertheless, a set of patterns of values, beliefs, practices, and so forth can be discerned in these performances.

This interwoven array of Discourse coordinations may mark a period of "coming of age," or a transition in Hannah's life, whereby her primary Discourse is becoming increasingly noticeable to her as she engages more and more with secondary Discourses of adulthood and womanhood. At home, for example, Hannah appears to be negotiating her way—not always smoothly—between being a child and being a teenager. She remarked to me one day while we were discussing how she learns dance moves from Ramona at school that, "Up until just a while ago I was mostly interested in silly things, but now I'm starting to become more interested in dancing and [popular] music." Nonetheless, and despite this claimed burgeoning interest, Hannah still holds fast to many things associated with her childhood, such as her Cabbage Patch dolls, a letter from Santa Claus, various collections of Garfield and Lion King wares, and stories of possible fairy visits to her backyard. In addition, Hannah's mother is not keen on Hannah growing up too quickly. For example, during a conversation about Hannah's clothes, Julia described how Hannah often wants to buy clothes that she sees her 19-year-old cousin wearing (e.g., platform sandals), and how Julia won't let her, saying "There's plenty of time for being an adult later."

Hannah's identification of Enid Blyton and R. L. Stine as her two favorite authors neatly captures some of the curious juxtapositions and possible tensions in Hannah's everyday life. For me, these seemingly strange bedfellows, one writing about fairies or groups of young people who solve "devilishly tricky" mysteries and the other writing about gruesome events and the dark side of the supernatural, signaled some of the complexities with which Hannah was dealing in her everyday life. On the other hand, however, Hannah's liking for both authors is logical given that both follow a predictable storyline formula and the young protagonists always triumph over paranormal forces or unlawful adults.

In summary, the skits performed by Hannah and her friends appeared to be coordinated and constituted by a number of Discourses. Likewise, Drama Group performances seemed to be similarly complex, but coordinated by a number of possibly different Discourses. Yet it is difficult to neatly label particular Discourses to which Hannah and her friends may be consciously or unconsciously subscribing in both kinds of performance practices and events. That being said, however, whether or not Discourses can be reliably and exhaustively labeled is of small concern to me. What *is* important is that a conception of Discourses enables fruitful insights into the complexities which coordinate and constitute Hannah's everyday life. This is borne out in the analysis of the third snapshot below.

Narratives about Julia's childhood appear to be an important part of Hannah's interactions with her mother. As mentioned earlier, Hannah liked nothing more than to hear her mother and aunts swapping tales about growing up in northern New South Wales. Indeed, Hannah encouraged her mother to include me in these patterns of talk by telling Julia to recount to me particular events that Hannah obviously knew by heart, but which still entertained her. For example, Hannah begged Julia to tell me the story "about the thistles and the cart and the electric fence" while we

SNAPSHOT 3: THE OLDEN DAYS

(Tuesday 29 November, 6:05 p.m. Day 7 of observations)
EVENT: INTERVIEW 3
SUBEVENT: *Discussing the relative value of money*
(utterances 102–107)

Julia	Mum always said they'd never leave the farm. Her father was a soldier-settler, on a farm outside Casino, and then uhm, they were there for X number of years and then moved into town, and they were up here in West End for a short while with a corner convenience store. She tells the story of parents giving these kiddies a penny and they could buy all these lollies ((small laugh)). It was very frustrating for her because a penny would buy so many lollies. This must've been back in the thirties, the late thirties sort of thing.
Michel	They'd get a penny's worth and there'd be a whole bag full?
Julia	Yeah, it used to drive her parents insane!
Michele	Yeah, I bet. ((To Julia)) Well you'd remember going into a lolly shop and they'd have all these jars, and you'd say "Oh, I'll have five cents worth please," and y'know, you'd get five for a cent, and things like that.
Hannah	Yeah, I read about it in books, like *February Dragon* [Thiele, 1965], and they go into this shop—February Dragon was the big Ash Wednesday thing, and Miss Barratt had it—and there's this shop called "Barnacle Bill's" and they go in and they had a penny and they got a whole lot of aniseed for a penny, a penny worth of aniseed. And each one wanted aniseed ((small laugh)), and the shopkeeper kept on putting the jar up, and then uhm, the little boy goes "But," and the shopkeeper goes "What do you want?" and he goes "But," and the shopkeeper said "You better not want anything," he goes "But, but" then the shopkeeper puts the jar up, and he goes "Can I please have *half* a penny worth of aniseed?" and the shopkeeper goes "What? Get out of here!" ((laughter)).

were sitting having a cup of tea at the kitchen table. Julia told the tale, with elaborations and asides from Hannah.

As snapshot 3 suggests, Hannah also enjoys telling stories herself, and appears to model them on the narrative patterns established by her mother. Whenever Hannah did not have personal experiences on which to draw in telling a story, she recounted events she had read in books as though she had been there herself. Moreover, in her conversations with me, Hannah very often associated her mother's childhood and the setting for these narratives with talk about "the olden days" and wanting to live in the country when she was older.

The Olden Days and Living in the Country

I noticed that many of the books Hannah said were among her favorite—aside from R. L. Stine's *Goosebumps* series—were often set, and usually written, three or more decades ago.[13] Hannah herself commented explicitly on this penchant: "I like books that are like, the olden days and stuff." In addition to nominating that she would live with her teachers and class out in the country when asked what she would wish for if she was given three wishes, Hannah also chose:

(Tuesday 22 November, 4:30 p.m. Day 2 of observations)	
EVENT: INTERVIEW 2 (utterances 119–120)	
Hannah	That all the violence goes away, that there was no pollution and that it would never happen again, and that we did stuff like in the olden days.
Michele	Oh, what do you mean by that?
Hannah	Horse and cart, so we wouldn't cause pollution and, like, did stuff so it wouldn't cause pollution, or we used stuff that didn't cause pollution.

Hannah seemed to prefer country-style furniture and accoutrements, too: "I like the old country stuff. I don't like the new stuff that's come out. Some of the new chairs, they've got like green seats and black backs and go like this ((indicating the shape of the chair back with her hands)). They're awful."

Her desire to live in the country was expressed repeatedly to me in conversations:

> (Thursday 1 December, 4:28 p.m. Day 9 of observations)
> EVENT: INTERVIEW 4 (utterance 164)
> Hannah   I just really love the country and the farming life. I mean like, I've got a cousin and I asked her where would she rather live, in the country, a suburb, or in the city, and she said "the suburbs," and I asked Mum what it was like living in the country, and she said it was kind of lonely and stuff. But, I just really like the country and like, farms and stuff. And, I'd like—I'd *love* to live on a farm. Well, at the moment I would, I don't know if I'd actually live there. I might have animals and paddocks and stuff. It might come out of reading Enid Blyton books and stuff like that.

Julia, too, seemed interested in times past. For example, Julia told Hannah and me about the recipe book she had bought recently because it reminded her of the recipe book her own mother had put together from pages cut from magazines. Julia explained: "My mother had made her own recipe book. She used to cut recipes out of *New Idea* and the *Women's Weekly*, and this book actually had some of those pictures in it, so buying it was a nostalgia thing ((laughs))." Hannah's interest in the country and the olden days seems, to me, to be indissolubly linked with a strong sense of family relationships and history, often strengthened and supported by written texts in particular and family traditions in general.

During my visits with this family, Julia repeatedly stated her belief that family and family gatherings are important for children. For example, both Hannah and Julia spoke fondly of past and present Christmas traditions and rituals belonging to their immediate and extended family (e.g., late, long lunches where everyone brings along their favorite food, handmade bon bons). Many of these rituals, even though some are no longer practiced, are preserved, it seems, in Julia's narratives. For example:

> (Thursday, 1 December 1994, 5:15 p.m. Day 9 of observations)
> EVENT: INTERVIEW 4
> SUB-EVENT: *Discussing family Christmas traditions (utterances 467–471)*
>
> Julia   I used to.. make bon bons. I used to make my own bon bons. For years... about five years.
> [I made bon bons for—
>
> Hannah   [Yeah, she made it for all the family, and put in little gifts.
>
> Julia   Yeah, everyone at the Christmas table, and then I'd go and find a little tiny gift to put inside... I'd sort of try to stick to a price limit and I'd try and find a gift, for each person that they actually liked, or they would be interested in. It was a challenge to see what you could find actually. I used to sort of look for little Christmas stickers. One year I had little silver angels that I put on, and I printed their name in the angels sort of thing. It was really good. And it was very interesting actually. It sort of got a bit out of hand at the end though, so I stopped it. It just got to the point where you were putting... It started off with just bits of trivia, and then I sort of built up and built up... Then it got to the point where people weren't very happy with what was in it, and it was too hard keeping up with it all.
>
> Michele   Seriously? They complained about what was in their bon bon?
>
> Julia   No, just really didn't want it sort of thing. And it was... you sort of felt you had to find bigger and better things, and it was just easier to stop it. I did it for about five years. It was a real challenge.

Hannah regularly elaborated on aspects of her mother's narratives which indicated a close familiarity with each recount, and suggested that many of these stories were perhaps themselves "ritual" aspects of Hannah's interactions with her mother and intrinsic to being to a female member of this particular family. Thus, it seems to me that Hannah is being apprenticed in her primary Discourse to oral narrative telling by means of her access to a group of experts in the form of her mother and aunts in particular. Hannah's peers in this apprenticeship are her siblings—especially Laura—and her female cousins. Hannah's mother also provides Hannah with opportunities for guided participation which Hannah takes up whenever she elaborates on or shares in the telling of her mother's stories. Hannah is also provided with opportunities for participatory appropriation as demonstrated by Julia's encouragement of Hannah's own narratives and Julia's willingness to listen to them.

In addition, Hannah appears to transport many of the literary qualities of her mother's stories coupled with Hannah's own extensive reading into narratives she produces at school. Her school report for creative writing in semester 1, 1994, reads: "Hannah produces interesting, lively and creative stories. She uses a rich vocabulary to enhance her work." However, the skits in which she excelled at scripting and producing were not accorded any explicit academic status by her teachers in relation to conventional "school success," although she did seem to accrue social status in the class by means of these skits. Even though Hannah employs her imagination, creativity, and storytelling abilities with some recognized success in class—either in terms of written narrative ability or kudos accruing from her performances—it is difficult to predict the degree to which these narrative capabilities will be recognized and enhanced by school authorities in secondary school, where literacy emphases shift to reasoning and objectivity, and report and argument writing (cf. Gilbert 1989, 1991, 1992; Goodson 1995).[14]

DISPLAYING SELF AND IDENTITY

Unlike the girls studied by Angela McRobbie (1991, 1994), Leslie Roman (1992, 1996), and others with similar research agendas, Hannah did not openly resist schooling or authority (except perhaps to some degree in her skits and self-choreographed dances), was not openly interested in boys, did not place her relationships with her friends before everything else, and neither did she seem interested in popular youth culture in quite the same ways as, for example, Layla or many of the other girls in Hannah's class. Instead, Hannah seemed to be most interested in her own immediate family and network of relations; adding to her various collections of dolls, teddy bears, fairies, and *Garfield* and *The Lion King* figurines; working on self-initiated craft-projects; and reading. In addition, her particular interest in her mother's childhood, her mother's narratives about family events and practices, the "olden days," and "living in the country" says much, I believe, about some of the values, beliefs, and practices constituting and coordinating Hannah's primary Discourse.

One possible way of interpreting the role of narratives and the motifs of "the olden days" and "country life" in Hannah's everyday life is offered by Deborah Schiffrin, who claims, "[t]he ability of narrative to verbalize and situate experience as text (both locally and globally) provides a resource for the display of self and identity" (1996, 167). I prefer to expand Schiffrin's conception of the relationship between narrative and identity, however, and claim that narrative plays a significant role in *constituting* identity and self, rather than merely displaying such things (cf. Vilko 1994, 273). Before discussing Hannah's social identities in more detail, however, it is useful to begin with a brief and necessarily circumspect discussion of her mother, Julia.

Julia, as mentioned above, feels alienated from the community in which she has lived for over 16 years. She feels duped by the real estate agent who showed them homes only in this area because, she believes, their down payment was funded under a government housing scheme initiative for first-home buyers below a certain income threshold. Julia does not define herself in relation to the people she encounters in her neighborhood or at Hannah's school, except in terms of contrast: "they're just a different class, you see. No other way to say it." Thus, it could be that her narratives about her childhood and her family then and now, are indeed displays of self and identity, or perhaps are reassurances that she is not like the people she sees outside her home in terms of class and, therefore, in terms of the family's primary Discourse. Indeed, it is interesting to speculate on possible relationships between the recurring theme of Hannah's skits and her mother's expressed sense of alienation from the general community in which they live.

Perhaps Julia's sentiments, attitudes, and narratives also serve to constitute and coordinate aspects of Hannah's social identities so that Hannah, too, defines herself primarily in terms of her family relationships and her mother's childhood. In addition, Hannah may see the world of her mother's childhood—conveyed by Julia's narratives—as a time when and place where everyday life was much more simple than their lives at present. Indeed, many of Hannah's comments about life in the country seemed idealized and somewhat naive. Julia's comments on farm animals and

Hannah's perceptions of them certainly lends credence to this interpretation: "On the farm, which is something Hannah doesn't realize, is that we had *work* animals, not pets! ((laughter))." Similarly, Hannah's interest in the "olden days" is perhaps a hankering after more innocent, perhaps more safe and seemingly uncomplicated, times. Again, her mother's alienation from their local area may have much to do with Hannah's attitude towards the country and times past in the sense that their present community is not necessarily one of Julia's choosing.

NEGOTIATING DISCOURSE MEMBERSHIPS

The preceding discussion of Hannah is, of course, far from complete, but nevertheless demonstrates my point that notions of D/discourse enable engaging insights into some of the complexities characterizing Hannah's everyday life at a given moment in time and space. I have found in the course of this study that interpreting Discourses requires both *knowledge of* and *professional distance from* (a range of) Discourses. In Layla's case (see chapter 5), I repeatedly found it difficult to maintain what I felt to be sufficient critical distance from the data in order to be able to interpret it in ways that were communicatively valid and trustworthy. However, in the case of Hannah, further difficulties were encountered with respect to identifying—and knowing about—possible Discourses constituting and coordinating her social identities. Thus at first, Hannah appeared to be a "limit case" to Gee's conception of D/discourses as a theoretical framing for ethnographic case study research.

Somewhat ironically, her model behavior in class initially made interpretations virtually impossible by dint of difficulties in collecting observations about someone who was always on-task, quiet, and well behaved. Hence, any number of claims could have been made about possible Discourse memberships, although such claims could be grounded only in suppositions. As indicated, it seemed too easy to simply assert that Hannah thoroughly complied with nice girl and good student Discourses. Indeed, it was impossible for me to tell from my observations whether or not she was a full and unquestioning member of these Discourse, or only *appeared* to be so. This dilemma captures an inevitable limitation of taking an ethnographic approach to D/discourse research which does not in the main incorporate methods for obtaining insights into sociocognitive processes. An example makes my point.

Hannah's self-sufficiency, exemplary behavior, concern for others, and so forth in class certainly matched the social and educational identities promoted by her teachers. Nevertheless, after observing Hannah for a few days, I developed a strong suspicion that matters were far more complex than my initial interpretation suggested. This intuition was strengthened when Hannah asked me not to sit with them at lunch-times, as well as when she told me about the skits they had performed for their class, and the new skits they were currently practicing. These hunches remained unsupported, however, until I revisited the data I had collected about Hannah after analyzing the three other cases involved in this study. Thus, it was only after I had carefully event mapped my fieldnotes and scrutinized transcripts by means of interaction and message unit analyses, that I was able to interpret a number of patterns of values, beliefs, practices, discourses, actions, and so forth in the data collected about Hannah.

This mapping work enabled me to see how certain tentative claims about Hannah's everyday practices could be supported by cross-referenced evidence. In many cases, patterns or divergent instances of social and language practices, comments, and observations that I had not connected or compared during data collection were found to be significant in terms of my interpretations (e.g., Julia's comments about her alienation from the community in which they lived juxtaposed with her childhood narratives and Hannah's skits set in the country). In Hannah's case particularly, event mapping and interpretations grounded in conceptions of D/discourses helped unravel at least some of the complexities constituting Hannah's everyday life, and confirms the potential usefulness of this approach to language research.

Hannah's Discourse memberships appear to be complex indeed. Her identity as a "model" student in class contrasted sharply with the images she projected and the identities she enacted in performing the skits she scripted with Virginia and the others. These performances also contrasted with those produced by the Drama Group, which required a particular "schooling" of her self and body that was different again from the schooling of her self and body in class. I may also have been party to a period in Hannah's life when she was shifting from being a full member of Discourses that valued childhood innocence and pursuits (e.g., Cabbage Patch Dolls, fairies, letters from Santa, Enid Blyton books)—coordinated by her primary Discourse—towards Discourses that value, among other things, modern music, contemporary dancing, authors such as R. L. Stine, and fashionable clothes (e.g., particular teen gal Discourses, professional theater Discourses). This is not to suggest that her primary Discourse will be abandoned, but that it may become more open to questions and negotiations by means of having access to other Discourses. In this way, her primary Discourse is opened to critique and may be even changed in some way. Obversely, Hannah's primary Discourse may also provide her with ground from which to critique other Discourses.

Unlike Layla, Hannah did not mention having a self-improvement agenda; rather, she talked about becoming "more interested" in certain things (e.g., music and dancing), than she had been in others (now identified as "silly things"). Perhaps, too, her skits—such as the supermodel one—were ways of negotiating some of the tensions accruing between her primary Discourse and her coordination by other Discourses that are conceivably more adult-seeming to her. Indeed, Gee's distinction between primary and secondary Discourses proved invaluable in interpreting Hannah's possible Discourse memberships, coordinations, and social identities. Moreover, and as with the previous three case studies, this distinction provided useful inroads into interpreting what at first seemed to be contradictory practices; in Hannah's case, for example, apparent anomalies among her often childlike practices at home, her model student behavior in class, and her exuberant and worldly skits. In addition, Hannah did not seem to value friends in the same way that Layla or Nicholas did. Her interactive webs of relations, for example, appeared to be grounded first and foremost in family interrelationships, and extended variously to include her three school friends, her teachers and her other classmates. Indeed, Hannah's relationships with her three friends and her class, as well as her perceptions of herself as a student in this class, are certainly complex and difficult to pin down for analysis. For example, when asked to respond in writing to a question I asked: "At the moment, the people I like to be with the most are...," Hannah first wrote "friends," then crossed it out and wrote "my class, because we muck around and have lots of fun." Hannah's actual enactment of "mucking around" certainly differs from that of, say, Nicholas's and his mates, and although her classmates certainly did muck around, Hannah was never observed doing likewise. Once again, this example signals some of Hannah's complex to-ing and fro-ing among a range of (possible, or wished for) social identities and subject positions in her everyday life.

In closing, the interpretations of Hannah's social and language practices offered here are by no means the only ones available, nor are they posed as complete. However, Hannah's case clearly illustrates some of the complexities involved in negotiating memberships in Discourses that are not necessarily compatible. Without doubt, Green and her associates' data mapping techniques and Gee's theory of D/discourses proved invaluable in coming to understand more fully what at first seemed to be a fairly straightforward case.

Endnotes

1. R. L. Stine is the author of a popular horror story series for young adolescents. Each story features young middle class American adolescents either rescuing each other or rescuing themselves and a number of adults from certain doom. Enid Blyton wrote serial tales of adventurous, independent, and thoroughly English middle class young female and male adolescents who solve mysteries that have eluded or frustrated the police and other law-abiding adults (e.g., The Famous Five and The Secret Seven series). She has also written a series of fantasy tales (e.g., *The Magic Faraway Tree*) and anthropomorphized toy narratives (i.e., the *Noddy* books). Hannah's liking for Blyton and Stine is a striking, yet also logical, juxtaposition; and one that is discussed later.

2. Jethro is 12 years old, but is approximately 175cm (5' 9") tall and weighs about 70kg (154lbs). He has a volatile temper and few students deliberately cross him. Remarkably, however, he seems to get on well with Hannah.

3. I found this absence of teasing strangely surprising; particularly when I observed other, quite cruel treatment of some class members by their peers. Perhaps a statement by one of her male classmates sums up the general feeling towards Hannah: "Hannah's good. If someone's down, she tries to help them."

4. This was intriguing because Nicholas, Jacques, and Layla had each looked out for me at lunchtimes and the like. Hannah's request is difficult to interpret, but I have a strong sense that these four girls used lunchtimes to explore a range of ways of speaking and acting and so forth that were in marked contrast to their usual identities and actions in class, and perhaps out-of-school. Hannah's claim that her friends "couldn't be themselves" is fascinating, and is taken up again in relation to the second snapshot.

5. These songs included: *Go West* by the Village People, *Prince Ali* sung by Elton John for the *Aladdin* movie by Disney, and *The Never Ending Story* from the movie of the same name.

6. For example: *Little Red Riding Hood*, a section from the movie musical *Aladdin*, and a short skit about baking a cake.

7. Descriptions of the group's skits will be written as the events were intended to be "seen" by the audience. That is, an actor will "walk through a door" rather than be described in terms of "pretending to open a door and walk through it." This narrative strategy is used deliberately to help capture some of the imaginative qualities of these dramatized events.
8. "St. Vinnie's" is a commonly used nickname for the St. Vincent de Paul Society Store, a chain of cheap secondhand clothing and home-goods stores run by the St. Vincent de Paul Society and stocked by means of community donations.
9. See discussions of bodily regulation and surveillance in, for example: de Certeau 1984; Bourdieu 1977; Foucault 1977.
10. From de Certeau's (1984) notion of "intextuation," meaning the "transformation of bodies into signifiers of state power and law" (McLaren 1991b, 155; also de Certeau 1984, 131–153).
11. See, for example: Davies 1993; Gutierrez, Rymes, and Larson 1995; Macedo 1993; Steedman 1981; Walkerdine 1981, 1996a.
12. See also, for example, among others: McLaren's notion of "modes of resistant subjectivity" (1991b); Steedman's discussion of four eight-year-old girls resisting "normalized" female roles in their writing (1981); Gotfrit's exploration of dance as a site of resistance for woman (1991); Walkerdine's use of film narratives as a medium for telling "new stories about subjectivity" (1996b).
13. For example, Hannah listed: *Ash Road* by Ivan Southall published in 1966, *Seven Little Australians* by Ethel Turner published in 1894, *Little Women* by Louisa May Alcott published as a serial in 1868 and 1869.
14. Four years later, Hannah has now appeared in the chorus of two school musicals, *Joseph and his Technicolour Dream Coat* and *Jesus Christ Superstar*. Both musicals were practiced outside school time, and required hours of dedication and practice. Hannah told me she loved every minute. In one letter to me, Hannah also described how she and her friends had "so much fun" performing a Can Can dance during a "multicultural night" organized by her French class to raise money for a trip to New Caledonia.

CHAPTER SEVEN

Doing school

The four young people who participated in this study collectively enacted diverse arrays of language practices in their everyday lives. These practices encompassed a broad range of contexts, identities, subjectivities, and purposes; from impromptu drama or singing performances to teacher-controlled drama performances, cryptic on-court language during lunchtime basketball, letters to pen-pals and relations, technical terms associated with learning to play the piano, ways of speaking and reading in church, through to ways of speaking, viewing, and writing while engaging with various electronic technologies. As this abbreviated list suggests, the range for each participant was far from seamless, and the complexity of observed social and language practices indicated that all four participants laid claim to—or were claimed by—a multitude of D/discourses and D/discourse coordinations. This chapter focuses on the teaching practices observed in all four classrooms. This sets the scene for discussing themes and issues pertaining to language and literacy standards-setting and students' access to mature and valued secondary D/discourses that were raised in the previous four case study chapters. Thus, the approach taken is similar to cross-case analysis, but not with the intent to generalize "findings" to all year 7 teachers and their students everywhere.

Teachers and Adolescents' Everyday Lives

The five teachers observed in this study professed a general knowledge of primary school students' out-of-school lives; however, they were inevitably more vague about specific social practices and co-constitutive language uses in the lives of Nicholas, Layla, Jacques, and Hannah. For example, Mr. Lasseter[1] explains:

> (Thursday 20 October 1994, 12:45 p.m. Day 10 of observations)
> EVENT: TEACHER INTERVIEW 2 (utterance 074)
> SUB-EVENT: *Discussing Nicholas's language uses*
> Mr. Lasseter I'm not aware of any outside activity really. He might've said something, but I can't recall. I know he delivers the newspaper, I know he plays basketball. He loves going out with his mates. I know he says he goes to the movies sometimes.

Although Mr. Lasseter is able to identify a number of Nicholas's out-of-school activities, none of them appears to inform language and literacy tasks encountered in his classroom, and school purposes for completing teacher-set language tasks seem to prevail. Of course, it is impossible for any teacher to address every student's out-of-school interests or pursuits, and my aim is not to privilege only student-selected texts and practices in classrooms. To suggest a neo-Summerhill curriculum would be naive and irresponsible.

I am convinced, however, that effective approaches to language and literacy teaching begin with experiences and practices familiar to students before they are introduced to more abstract concepts pertaining to language practices. Of course, making explicit links between lesson content and students' everyday lives does not necessarily ensure that meaningful learning will take place; indeed, many teachers who try to make such links often oversimplify or exaggerate connections and risk shifting the focus of lessons away from processes and skills and focus on students' already-in-place cultural knowledge. For example, a lesson with phonemic awareness objectives quickly becomes a lesson on the dietary habits of kangaroos, at least in the minds of the students, when the teacher stops halfway through reading a big book on Australian mammals to the class for a prolonged discussion of what kangaroos eat (cf. Baker and Freebody 1989; Freebody et al. 1996). Nonetheless, it still proves useful to discuss some of the possible implications a lack of teacher awareness of students' out-of-school lives might have for classroom practices and language learning opportunities (cf. Heath and Mangiola 1991; Moll 1992; Walkerdine 1990).

Analyses of observed classroom language lessons and interviews with the five teachers directly involved in my study suggest that at least four of them focus primarily on written texts and attempt to extrapolate textual features or generic structures to social practices. If you recall, Ms. Bryant, Jacques's teacher, had her class analyze the similarities and differences between two cultures using a proforma photocopied from a textbook (see chapter 4, snapshot 1). Although some students may have understood the role of the activity in learning certain "higher order" thinking skills and strategies for writing effective information reports, this did not appear to be the case for Jacques. Instead, he seemed unable—or unwilling—to extrapolate these compare and contrast strategies from one lesson to the next. Thus, for Jacques, the compare and contrast lesson appeared to hold little meaning. However, out-of-school, he was able to construct effective oral texts in meaningful contexts and for particular "real world" purposes using compare and contrast strategies.

Perhaps this disjunction between Jacques's school and out-of-school literacy practices is a result of his teacher grounding the lesson in school and textual purposes, rather than in—for Jacques—more meaningful reasons and goals that can be found in "real world" contexts outside school. This is not to make his teacher solely responsible for this disjunction; indeed, teachers in Queensland primary schools—as with teachers anywhere—are also constituted by institutional Discourses pertaining to education, their social roles as educators, and the ways of "being a student" they are expected to promote. In addition, and as signaled in chapter 1, a new English syllabus for years 1 to 10 has been recently introduced in Queensland schools. This syllabus is grounded explicitly in genre theory and "language in use" approaches to planning, teaching, and assessment.[2] The goal of this syllabus is to develop students' knowledge of, and competence with, a range of written, visual, and spoken genres, their social functions, and their linguistic features (Department of Education, Queensland 1994). However, a general, often-voiced, lack of provision for professional development and reflective practice exacerbates the demands placed on teachers during the course of each school day. This has far-reaching implications in terms of teachers coming to grips with the rather sophisticated theoretical underpinnings of this syllabus and subsequent opportunities for maximizing classroom language and literacy learning experiences (cf. Carr 1996; Freebody 1993).

Unfortunately, limited funding or release time from class is made available for such activities and time-pressed teachers are often forced to take shortcuts in the language and literacy learning process, like the one described earlier. Perhaps a more telling example is provided by the teacher who used a different proforma to teach her students how to write an argumentative essay. This proforma provided students with a step-by-step structure for writing their essays, which included: stating their position, describing three reasons for this position, then concluding by restating their thesis. This teacher talked students through an example she had written on an overhead transparency, then set them to work to produce their own individual essays on a topic she had chosen. The proforma itself had come from a book borrowed from another teacher, and this book was regarded by this teacher as a "godsend." She knew students needed to be able to write argumentative essays for secondary school, but she wasn't sure—in this, her first year of teaching year 7—how best to go about it and this proforma seemed a quick, straightforward approach.

This "quick fix" approach—repeated in many other classrooms I have observed recently—does not augur well for the implementation of literacy standards and methods used to ascertain students' "levels" of competence, unless they are accompanied by careful and exhaustive explanations and demonstrations of procedures and, more importantly, ways of incorporating standards assessment into effective classroom teaching practices. Otherwise, these standards and benchmarks will usurp language and literacy syllabus guidelines and the teacher's own ideas about effective language and literacy content, and, in a worst case scenario, these standards and benchmarks will become licences for transmission or banking approaches to education.

Ample evidence of this effect can already be found in the recent introduction of the Year 2 Diagnostic Net, mandated for Queensland primary schools by the state government. This diagnostic and intervention program is designed to "catch" students with literacy (and numeracy) problems in the early years of schooling, and channel them into intensive prepackaged remedial programs (e.g., Reading Recovery; see, for example, Clay 1992) or specially designed "independent education programs" within the classroom. Each year 2 student in Queensland is tested by means of a kit of diagnostic tools that focus on the student's ability to accurately read a text aloud, identify individual letters of the alphabet, spell accurately and identify text structure, recognize and write single words, and the like. This diagnostic process, therefore, is strangely at odds with the conception of literacy and literacy learning promoted in the Queensland English syllabus. In addition, anecdotal evidence suggests that troublesome practices are emerging in response to pressures for teachers to minimize the number of students caught in the Net tests who then require remediation at considerable expense to the school. For example, student-teachers are returning from practicum sessions and reporting to me how they spent their time in year 1 and year 2 "helping" students *study* for the Year 2 Net tests (c.f. Lankshear and Knobel 1998).

Indeed, for many students at present, language learning opportunities at school are often only code-breaking or "doing school" tasks (cf. Freebody 1992; Luke and Freebody 1997). Nicholas, for example, seems to think that in Mr. Lasseter's class all he has to do is crack the task code (whether it be genre or content related, etc.) and he is virtually guaranteed success. This is demonstrated in Nicholas's attempt to use only the resource book from which Mr. Lasseter drew the assessment criteria for the project set as a class assignment (see chapter 3). Likewise for Hannah, a model student, the purpose of language lessons seems to be interpreted generally in terms of "doing school" rather than in connection with social practices. For example, the reason she gave for completing a worksheet that required her to punctuate a passage was: "It was part of [my teacher's] assessment." Even in classrooms rich in "lifelike" language and literacy experiences, such as Layla's, not all students appeared to make connections between class work and language practices outside school settings. When Layla was asked about possible out-of-school uses for the wide range of genres to which she was introduced and given ample opportunity to practice in class, she identified only letter writing as being useful outside school.

Of course, it is easy to criticize teachers, especially when only partial glimpses are provided of the complex contexts in which they operate. Thus, comments made about these five teachers who gave so generously of their time are intended only as additional "telling cases" that must be read within the context of the current—often tumultuous—state of play in education in Queensland at present. In fact, I was forced to rethink my own role as a teacher—and as a teacher educator—in the process of observing classroom practices from a researcher's perspective, rather than from a teacher's perspective (to which I am most accustomed). I was able to see first-hand how the normative role of schooling, the boundaries established by the institution, and how students' own social agendas impinge on learning opportunities. When I was a classroom teacher, deeply involved in classroom life as a member rather than primarily as an observer, these things had been much less visible. During the time spent in the four classrooms visited for this study, I observed how timetabled interruptions for specialist lessons (e.g., choir, physical education, foreign language learning, library), incidental interruptions (e.g., school photographs, rehearsals, intercom messages), other demands on teachers' time (e.g., assessing and reporting student progress, speaking with guidance officers, participating in school curriculum development), and student engagement in various activities seemingly unrelated to the task at hand (e.g., note passing, throwing bits of rubber, daydreaming) siphoned off the bulk of actual learning time.

The teachers themselves spoke of difficulties in finding time to plan and implement the kinds of lessons they would have preferred to teach. In some cases they saw their approach to teaching inhibited by a class of students they felt required more structured lessons and content or information-based teaching than they would otherwise like to teach. Nevertheless, and although there are myriad constraints presently operating on primary classroom teachers in Queensland and elsewhere, the ongoing work of researchers and educators such as Anderson and Irvine (1993), Buckingham and Sefton-Green (1994), Green and Yeager (1995), Heath (1983, 1992; and Mangiola 1991; and McLaughlin 1994), Irvine and Elsasser (1988), Moll (1992), Searle (1993), Thomas and Maybin (1997), Torres (1997), and Wallace (1992), to name only a few, offer effective—and heartening—approaches to classroom-based language and literacy education that are not unmanageably complex affairs requiring large investments of time and costly collections of resources.

Indeed, the strategies employed by educators like those listed above are often elegantly simple, and emphasize purposeful and meaningful language and literacy experiences for students. These strategies include: having students pose a question about language or about a social practice that then becomes the focus of investigation (e.g., how to clean up a local beach or park; how to promote a sense of community in their local area; how to teach parents to be responsible drivers in the school car park); devising prereading (or writing, or viewing, etc.), while-reading, and postreading activities that encourage peers to reflect on their language and social practices and develop a language for talking about language; and providing students with opportunities for developing their own strategies for analyzing contexts and language practices (e.g., producing a class handbook that explains shared terms and meanings, practices, and expectations pertaining to this particular class). I am convinced that these kinds of approaches to language and literacy pedagogy have rich potential for meeting the stated requirements and benchmarks of mandated literacy standards, with ample flexibility for going beyond these basic requirements to enact a more fully "social" literacy in the classroom. However, there does remain a risk that explicitly sociocultural classroom practices like those mentioned above will become just another way of "doing school," particularly if teachers themselves are not equipped with sound, working theories of language as a social practice. This has significant implications for teacher education, and these are discussed in the final chapter of this book.

Literacy for what?

The purposes for teaching particular texts and textual features identified by the five teachers directly involved in this study encapsulate the four broad categories of language curriculum theories or approaches that Peter Freebody (1993) identifies as seminal influences in Australian language and literacy education. These theoretical and pedagogical trends are not confined to Australia, but tend to circulate and reverberate among English-speaking countries and their colonies, and include skills, growth/developmental, cultural heritage, and social-critical approaches to language education (indeed, the writers of the Queensland English syllabus explicitly locate this syllabus at an intersection of all these bodies of theory) .

In relation to the present study, three participating teachers seemed to rely almost exclusively on skills-based models of pedagogy for teaching different text types, and students were regularly provided with grammar worksheets and genre proforma which they completed in the course of a lesson. In addition, these skills-based approaches were often linked with a limited means-ends rationalization for the content of various language lessons. For example:

> Some things I teach because I know they're going to get it in high school. And I think sometimes I do it because I know that they have to get it *there*, and then from *there* they go on to university, or to wherever. I know some things that I teach here, you know, they may not need at all when they're out working.

In one sense, this also gestures towards a developmental or growth model of learning, but one that is constrained by school contexts. One participating teacher, for example, was challenged by a student about the reason for learning how to write argumentative essays (Student: "Why do we need to do this, and what do we need it for?"), and subsequently explained it in terms of high school assessment and writing-based occupations. No matter how well-meaning these explanations are, such responses from teachers suggest a limited understanding of language as a socially constituted and constituting practice. Indeed, the overall effect of using high school as a rationale for language lesson content promotes a notion of school-produced texts as ends in themselves, rather than as connected to social practices outside school.

Another teacher, Mr. Brunner, explained to me that learning about myths was an important part of learning how to write in a different genre and of understanding how the Greeks used myths to explain the world. This teacher's comments invoke cultural heritage motifs operating in Australian education (and education institutions elsewhere). He explicitly aligned himself with genre and whole language approaches to language teaching, but structured lessons around a commercial kit of resources on Greek myths. This was in a school regarded as disadvantaged in terms of the school community's general working class and underclass socioeconomic status and transient population. Although learning about myths and mastering the genre will prove helpful for many of these students in certain high school classes, there appeared to be few opportunities for students to move beyond the structured tasks provided in the kit or by the teacher (e.g., find-a-word puzzles, punctuation exercises, writing their own Greek myth). It is difficult to reconcile such tasks with, for example, the teacher's goal that each student develops an appreciation of ancient Greek culture and its impact on modern societies. Despite wanting to equip his students with "survival" English capabilities, there seemed little in this unit of work that would enable these students to compete effectively in a fast-shrinking employment market when they leave school.

From my perspective, at least one teacher did seem to promote social approaches to language and literacy in his classroom. This teacher also claimed to purposefully avoid an overtly academic imbalance in the language learning experiences he orchestrated for his students. He reasoned that not all students in this class would be going on to higher education and it was his duty to equip them with a range of understandings about how language works in life outside school (although this did not necessarily include analyses of power structures and relations, etc.). He repeatedly drew attention to the role of context and purpose in constructing effective oral, written, and visual texts, and encouraged students to experiment with a range of genres. I am convinced that this teacher has an extensive metalevel understanding of language and social practices, and is able to bring this to bear on classroom language and literacy experiences. If this conviction is well founded—and I believe it is—this, too, has significant implications for teacher education (see chapter 8).

Turning again to Nicholas, Jacques, Layla, and Hannah, it seems that on the whole they usually associated language and literacy learning in their classrooms with instrumental goals or teacher purposes. For example, Nicholas offered a critique of skill-based grammar education that demonstrated metalevel understanding of the seeming ends-means rationalization of some of the language learning experiences in his classroom. Jacques, as another example, claimed that school prevented people from becoming "duds," which can be interpreted in both an academic and a social sense. Perhaps Jacques recognizes aspects of the normative role schools play in producing particular kinds of people, which, for him—and doubtless many others—has very little to do with his own purposes and everything to do with school (and other institutional) goals.

Layla appreciated developing letter-writing skills at school which she put to good use in maintaining relationships with her various pen-friends (including me, long after data collection had finished), but regarded most other language practices in class as relating only to school purposes. For Hannah, language and literacy activity at school was often an end in itself.

For example, when asked about a writing conference she had with one of her teachers, Hannah observed, "I like getting my stuff checked, because then your good copy has no mistakes."

Despite school-enclosed justifications given to students as reasons for completing tasks, or rafts of grammar worksheets to keep them floating above the literacy failure line, and so on, all five teachers involved in this study agreed independently that students' language uses have changed over the past decade or so. Each teacher was quick to point out what they saw as the cryptic and often aggressive language young people used when playing electronic games. In addition, two teachers commented specifically and at length on students' familiar way of speaking to teachers and other adults. This contrasted with these teachers' own experiences of growing up when, for example, speaking as an equal to a nun or a teacher was either never contemplated or brought severe and memorable punishment. Others described how most of their students hardly ever read novels at home, and seemed more interested in magazines, comics, and television. Indeed, some of these teachers even described themselves as having to compete with the pace and garishness of television and the seductiveness of computers in catching and maintaining students' interest. For example:

Teacher	So I think [the classroom] can be far more interesting. But perhaps it has to be like that to keep up with all the other stimuli that they have.
Michele	With all the other...?
Teacher	Like, you know TV. And like, their lives are fast. These kids lead fast lives, so teachers have to make everything... more exciting and interesting.

These five teachers generally viewed current language and social changes as detrimental and worked at getting their students to speak politely to adults and to each other, to write neatly, to speak slang only outside the classroom, and so on. There appeared to be little room in these classrooms—apart from one classroom perhaps—for new, emerging, or blurred genres that may be valued in society already, or are likely to be valued in the future (cf. Freebody 1993; Lemke 1993, 1995b).

In addition, all five teachers agreed with the principles of genre theory espoused in the English syllabus and emphasized explicit modeling of generic structures and direct teaching of text features in their classrooms. However, their energies appeared to be directed in the main towards students mastering academic genres (i.e., conventional narrative forms, information reports, expositions, argumentative essays, etc.). Yet despite these teachers' efforts to equip their students with processes for constructing academic texts, many of the observed lessons appeared to focus on the *content* of the task—at least from the four students' points of view—rather than on the language processes being developed and the interrelationship of these processes with social practices. For example, Jacques claimed that the aim of the compare and contrast lesson described above was to learn more about Balinese and Australian customs, and not about developing a strategy for engaging in analytic work. One lesson in another classroom involved students in using a proforma for extrapolating the main ideas from an information text. This exercise was completed collaboratively by the entire class and then again—using another text—on an individual basis. When asked, many of these students identified "completing the sheet" as the purpose of the lesson, rather than learning about how to identify key words and topic sentences as the teacher had intended.

Time constraints and pressures on primary school teachers to produce students who are able to write, read, and spell at an "appropriate level" by the time they reach secondary school (cf. Clinton 1997; Curriculum Corporation 1997b; Kemp 1997) encourages transmission models of teaching that focus on content knowledge or promote quick fix approaches to learning. Paradoxically, however, knowledge is no longer the main preserve of schools and universities, and increasingly, what "counts" as knowledge—and who selects it, and the criteria used—is decided increasingly outside of them (cf. Aronowitz and DiFazio 1994; Giroux 1997a; Popkewitz 1991). Robert Reich's (1992) predictions concerning the role of symbolic analysts in workplaces in the next millennium suggest that current students need to be taught much more than merely school-selected content and how to write or construct arguments by simply "filling in the blanks." Even allowing for Reich's stark economic agenda, this re-emphasizes problems inherent in reducing language and literacy to a list of demonstrable skills and insulating classroom language and literacy learning from "real world" or mature practices.

Thus, when teachers focus intentionally or unintentionally on school purposes and practices in language lessons and other language-related experiences they may ultimately disadvantage students. Although Hannah's mastery of spoken and written narrative genres stands her in good stead at primary school, it remains to be seen whether she is able to master writing nonnarrative texts in ways that equal or surpass, say, Nicholas's understanding and production of such texts (e.g., report, explanation, argument). It is well recognized that it is the latter kind of text types that are usually most valued in secondary and higher education (cf. Martin 1985, 1993; Poynton 1985). Nicholas has both acquired and learned how to write successful expositions and arguments, and has had a longer period of time to practice writing them than has Hannah. Although only speculating, I believe these differences often go unnoticed in primary classrooms to the disadvantage of those with less opportunity for practicing language and literacy skills and processes, and for developing metalevel understanding of language and social practices and their interrelationship[3] (cf. Gee 1992b; Freebody, Ludwig, and Gunn 1996).

Language and literacy competency standards grounded in skills or lockstepped processes, and which are often constrained by developmental models of learning, are only a thin representation of what it means to be "literate" (cf. Gee 1996a; Lankshear 1997a). Thus, promoting national literacy standards and benchmarks as a means of ensuring that all students are able to read, write, and spell by certain ages, and, as a direct corollary, who therefore will be able to participate fully in society as citizens and workers, is a cultural illusion. Access to social goods and participation in social services requires much more than simply meeting a list of language and literacy performance criteria. Thus, along with Gee, Lankshear, and others, I argue that it also involves much more than being able to read, write, and spell.

Complex and dynamic relationships exist among social groups, social institutions, and D/discourses, and issues arising at the intersection of language, options, and power are never as straightforward as some educators and policy makers would like. For example, Nicholas can be said to use language "powerfully" when interacting with the boys in his class; he is able to noticeably regulate or shape their actions and language uses. Both Nicholas and his friend, Stuart, are involved directly—whether consciously or unconsciously—in deciding what counts as being an insider in a particular group of lads. This kind of "personal power," however, does not necessarily extend beyond their membership in a mateship Discourse as evinced, for example, by the "power" of some female classmates to control Nicholas's actions in class by refusing to help him with his math until he speaks nicely to them. As another example, Nicholas is well on his way to mastering aspects of technological D/discourses that are regarded as (potentially) "powerful" at present in Australia and elsewhere. However, employing this burgeoning D/discourse expertise in class is curtailed by his teacher and is made "unpowerful" in this particular classroom.

Even though the findings of the present study are limited to only four cases, they challenge claims like those championed in the recently introduced National Plan for Improving Literacy and Numeracy Skills of Young Australians (Curriculum Corporation 1997a). These claims make recourse to "research" to support such arguments as: "young people's participation in education, workforce and society is influenced significantly by their level of ability in literacy and numeracy" (1997a, n. p.). This echoes claims made in the previous Australian language and literacy policy, which declared among other things that "[t]here is a strong and well-documented link between low levels of literacy or English language competence and high levels of unemployment and other forms of social disadvantage" (Dawkins 1991, 1). The cases of Nicholas, Jacques, Layla, and Hannah strongly suggest that the relationship between education, employment, and citizenship is not so simple or linear.[4] In response to these findings, I suggest that teachers who do not have at least *some* understanding of language as a complex social practice can not claim to be providing language and literacy competencies and understandings that are likely to contribute to the future economic and social well-being of their students. Indeed, the benefits accruing for, say, Jacques now and in the future might derive primarily from working with his father, more so than from his learning experiences at school. Jacques's entrepreneurial skills and understandings were acquired through access to expert performances in a business Discourse and could never have been acquired at his primary school as it is configured at present. However, it is highly unlikely that Jacques's current literacy failure at school will correlate directly with his experiences as a citizen and worker, or that he will experience "high levels of unemployment and other forms of social disadvantage."

Nicholas, on the other hand, might be disadvantaged by *not* having access to language and literacy learning opportunities at school that extend or enhance his existing capabilities. In his case, however, his parents have the wherewithal to compensate for gaps between schooling and everyday life. Not all children, of course, have such effective backing and may accrue fewer options at school for life beyond compulsory schooling. Indeed,

> classrooms that do not properly balance acquisition and learning, and realize which is which, and which student has acquired what, simply privilege those students who have begun the acquisition process at home, engaging these students in a teaching/learning process, while others simply "fail" (Gee 1992b, 115).

This position provides defensible ground for arguing that schools which do not incorporate at least some aspects of mainstream Discourses into their curricula—rather than only some of the texts coordinated by these Discourses—risk denying students opportunities to practice or critique significant aspects of these Discourses that ultimately prove powerful beyond school (but that are not necessarily tied to what constitutes "school success"; cf. Jacques). Numerous theorists currently working at the intersection of language and education research are recognizing that many potentially useful understandings of language and how it works are gained increasingly beyond traditionally configured schools and classrooms.[5]

There are, however, a number of snags in this line of argument; "powerful Discourses" cannot be packaged and taught holus-bolus to students, and apprenticeships (in Rogoff's sense) to such Discourses are logistically difficult in most primary schools as presently configured and resourced. This is not to say that the outlook is devoid of hope, but it *is* a reminder that developing professional development packages and programs that are designed to show teachers how to "teach" students to identify and analyze D/discourses is to miss the point. Perhaps one way of beginning to address this problem involves teaching students methods for investigating and critiquing aspects of powerful Discourses in ways that are meaningful and purposeful to them.

For example, Mark Taylor and Esa Saarinen (1994, Interstanding 10)[6] claim schools need to teach dynamic and interactive ways of *understanding* a range of social phenomena, rather than doling out chunks of knowledge to be ingested across 10 to 12 years of schooling.[7] This resonates with Reich's prediction regarding the seminal role symbolic analysts will play in the world of work in the next millennium. Other educators interested in challenging mainstream social practices and language pedagogy involve young people in projects that require them to explore their own immediate community and everyday practices, reflect on and promote a range of social identities by means of constructing internet pages (e.g., *Virtual Valley, Digitarts, Black Voices*),[8] design and publish an array of alternative hard-copy and internet-based guides to inner Brisbane, and produce and perform dramatic, narrative works, among other activities that explore issues and practices identified by the young people involved as being important to them (cf. Knobel and Lankshear 1997; Stevenson 1994). These projects simultaneously develop metalevel understandings of social and language practices and enhance these young people's language and literacy capabilities.

Policy writers and teachers in the language education arena cannot afford to turn a blind or only partial eye towards the significant social, institutional, and economic changes already accumulating in a decade characterized by electronic technologies, information proliferation, and wide-ranging communication and service networks. Of course, technology is not the only arena of significant social and economic change in present times. Its impact, however, is becoming increasingly obvious and inescapable and, as such, warrants close attention. Nicholas's parents are well aware of changing times and language uses, and are equipping their children with hardware, software, and "wetware" that are valued already in the present,[9] and will be even more so in the future. A letter from Debra, Nicholas's mother, in response to reading draft sections of this study, underscores my point. Debra describes in her letter how the family now has an internet connection. She writes, "This has been invaluable socially and educationally. We use it all the time to research information for school and university assignments, to email friends and fellow work mates, to talk on internet relay chat (Joshua, Nicholas, and Jacinta all have friends overseas, especially the USA) and just to have fun. This makes me painfully aware of how far behind most of our schools are with computer literacy and technology. Even at the school where I teach, where we have one internet connection, and 25 well-equipped computers, I fear the methods I use are painfully outdated, compared to what the technology could provide" (17 August, 1996).

Perhaps one answer lies in developing teaching and learning strategies that blur the boundaries between school and life outside school.[10] Following Taylor and Saarinen's lead, language and literacy teaching approaches also need to be developed to equip students with strategies for distinguishing between contextually useful and useless—or even dangerous—information, and with the ability to turn knowing into understanding (see also Burbules 1997; Burbules and Callister 1996). Such strategies may even require, at different times, a reconfiguring of student-teacher roles. For example, students' understanding and mastery of technology is outstripping that of many of their teachers. This offers purposeful opportunities for students to use their technological expertise to enact genuine teaching roles and for teachers to become genuine learners (cf. Papert 1993; Lankshear and Knobel 1995). Once again, however, I am not suggesting that these kinds of teaching approaches and relationships will prove to be easily implemented magic cure-alls, or that students will necessarily *want* to engage in these kinds of learning opportunities. Nevertheless, I believe that investigating successful learning and teaching collaborations in relation to technology and language education is an area worth further research and collaborative work among language education researchers, classroom teachers, and students.

Conclusion

In summary, all four adolescents (and most of their friends) involved in this study demonstrated a wide and diverse range of everyday language and social practices. Concomitantly, each young person's language and social practices covered a broad spectrum of situations and goals-in-the-making;[11] for example, convincing parents that buying rollerskates was a useful and necessary thing to do, challenging a teacher's authority in classroom contexts without jeopardizing academic success, signaling simultaneous memberships in sometimes conflicting social groups, entertaining peers and teachers to deflect attention from academic troubles, experimenting with different social identities, and so on. In addition, I repeatedly observed sharp differences between each participant's exuberant, intertextual, and often witty language use outside formal classroom spaces and his or her (official) in-class language and literacy production, which was often minimal and usually bordered on the pedestrian. All four adolescents obviously enjoyed playing with and experimenting with language, and it was clear that playful uses of language were important aspects of their everyday social and language practices and interactive social networks. In addition, wider reading strongly indicates that these kinds of language uses and their associated cognitive strategies and Discourses are likely to become increasingly significant in these students' not-so-distant worlds of work and (most likely global) citizenship.[12]

On the other hand, when "academic" language and literacy strategies, understandings, and practices were taught in the four observed classrooms, they were often delivered prescriptively, or the lesson was unclear in terms of the teacher's objectives. I propose that such experiences in classrooms further serve to alienate school-based language and literacy learning from everyday social and language practices. These experiences also interfere with students' abilities to make their own connections among what they have learned about language use, and other subject areas, assignment work, and their possible future lives. Not all four study participants might pursue additional study or overtly academic text practices beyond schooling. Nevertheless, they may be able to benefit from effective language and literacy understandings and strategies obtained in school if they were able to employ these understandings and strategies in critiquing mainstream practices and in meeting a range of "real-life" purposes that are genuinely meaningful to them. Drawing on enacted exemplars, these might include: critiquing media images through creating and publishing alternative images; lobbying for environmental or social changes using email and other electronic media; writing letters, songs, or raps of complaint broadcast to corporations or government bodies asking for environmental change or responding to draft policies; calling for social action through public poetry readings; researching information pertaining to an illness, legal issue, or investment; designing and constructing effective and creative internet pages that have been commissioned by local businesses or groups; and so on.

The sweep of everyday language and social practices enacted by these young adolescents was broached unevenly within the four observed classrooms. In many respects this is hardly surprising as the Queensland English syllabus, even when used only heuristically, offers little guidance in relation to these kinds of language and literacy practices and their associated social practices. Indeed, the heavily emphasized genre approach to language education operating within this syllabus appears to me to be based on a narrow range of literacy practices that prevailed twenty or thirty years ago. In addition, at least four of the teachers observed during this study generally employed instrumental approaches to teaching language and literacy, and language lessons were interpreted repeatedly by the four participating students more in terms of "doing school" than as interactive apprenticeships to valuable and worthwhile language and literacy understandings and practices (and their coordinating Discourses). This suggests that existing conditions and pedagogies need to be scrutinized before implementing sets of language and literacy benchmarks or standards, and teachers need to be provided with ample opportunity to examine these benchmarks in relation to their own theories of literacy and learning in order to minimize instrumental approaches to meeting these standards. This is discussed in more detail in the next, and final, chapter.

Endnotes

1. Throughout this chapter, teachers' names are generally left unstated, except for instances where they can be readily identified from the context or content described and the use of his or her name facilitates the point I am making, or where there is a risk that a classroom practice may be wrongly attributed to a particular teacher.

2. In Australia, systemic functional linguistics (e.g., Halliday 1978, 1985) has been appropriated by educators who perceive a need to address schooling "disadvantage" and subsequent limited life chances through language and literacy education. To this end, they assert that some social groups—and their characteristic genres—enjoy more "power" than other groups (and their genres) under existing conditions in Australia. These "genre theorists" explicitly link genre mastery with teaching and learning. They claim that genres and their social purposes can—and should—be identified and taught explicitly to students, and particularly to students from marginalized and/or non-English speaking backgrounds (cf. Christie 1987, 1989, ed. 1990; Christie and Rothery 1989; Cope and Kalantzis eds. 1993; Cranny-Francis 1992; Hasan and Perrett 1994; Knapp 1989; Martin 1992, 1993; Martin and Rothery 1993; Williams 1993). Oftentimes, however, such claims appear to posit causal relationships among explicit teaching, linguistic and genre choices, and social transformation. In short, many of the genre theorists' claims appear to suggest that if the language (and text-types) are changed, then we can change the relationship between power structures and biography. Extended critiques of these claims are found in: Gee 1994c; Kamler 1994; Knobel 1997; Luke 1993; O'Sullivan et al. 1983; Reid ed. 1987; Richardson 1992.

3. See also Wayne O'Neill's (1970) illuminating and far from outdated discussions on the promotion of "improper literacy" in schools.

4. See also detailed critiques in: Brown, Leavold, Tate, and Wright 1994; Carnoy 1993; Freebody 1994; Freebody and Welch eds. 1993; Gee, Hull, and Lankshear 1996; Gowen 1991; Hull 1993; Lankshear 1993; O'Connor ed. 1994a and 1994b.

5. See, among many others: Cummins and Sayers 1995; Green and Yeager 1995; Heath and Mangiola 1991; Heath and McLaughlin 1994; Lankshear 1993, 1997a; Moll 1992; Rheingold 1994; Rushkoff 1996b; Taylor and Saarinen 1994.

6. Taylor and Saarinen's book *Imagologies* (1994) is not numbered conventionally from the first page to the last. Instead, their book is divided into numerous sections (e.g., Telewriting, Interstanding, Netropolis, etc.), and each section begins with page 1.

7. Taylor and Saarinen actually use the term *interstanding* to emphasize this dynamism and the interrelationship among understanding and interactions with others and the world.

8. *Virtual Valley*
   <http://www.ps.odyssey.com.au/GRUV/vvalley/welcome.htm>

   Digitarts
   <http://digitarts.va.com.au>

   Black Voices
   <http://www.ps.odyssey.com.au/GRUV/black/blkhome.htm>

9. *Wetware* refers to the cognitive strategies and social practices for effectively using technology and associated technological literacies for achieving a range of purposes (cf. Der Derian 1997; Yukawa 1993).

10. See, for example, strategies outlined in: Anderson and Irvine 1993; Buckingham and Sefton-Green 1994; Cummins and Sayers 1995; Heath and Mangiola 1991; Janks and Ivanič 1992; Searle 1993; Shuman 1993; Wallace 1992.

11. "Goals" in this sense are identified *post facto*, and may or may not be the intended product of each person's original intentions or aims (cf. Lemke 1995a).

12. See, for example: Cummins and Sayers 1995; del Rio and Alvarez 1995; Poster 1995; Reich 1992; Rheingold 1994; Rushkoff 1996a and 1996b; Taylor and Saarinen 1994; Stone 1996.

CHAPTER EIGHT

D/discourse research and literacy education

This chapter shifts discussion to wider terrain, and particularly to considerations of language and literacy research and education. Prior to this, however, the efficacy of event mapping and D/discourse theory as analytic constructs in case study research is discussed and evaluated.

D/DISCOURSES AND EVENT MAPPING: AN EVALUATION

In retrospect, a conception of D/discourses coupled with event mapping strategies proved to be a useful analytic and interpretive device. Without doubt, it enabled the teasing apart of *some* of the complexities constituting four young people's everyday lives. In terms of research, combining event mapping and D/discourse theory has gone some way towards developing an effective research methodology that enables dialogical analyses between the individual and the social.

Mapping Data

Data were collected from a range of contexts by means of a variety of tools and techniques, then mapped in multiple ways (e.g., event mapping through to message unit mapping). This enabled the weaving together of threads of evidence from multiple sources in support or disconfirmation of D/discourse claims and interpretations made about relationships among the individual and the social in the present study.[1] This also facilitated the examination of participants' language and social practices on a moment-by-moment basis, as well as over time and across contexts.

Mapping strategies, derived originally from Judith Green's research work (e.g., 1977) and the subsequent research work of Green and her associates, gave added dimension to data analysis and reporting as they required each reported event, utterance, or message unit to be contextualized by means of identifying location, time, date, place in the sequence of observations, the participants involved, and so forth. Even though this book concentrates more on narrating findings than on demonstrating analyses, these mapping strategies proved invaluable within this project in terms of identifying patterns of—or divergences in—practices across time and contexts. These patterns were read as signals for Discourse memberships and/or coordinations. Although this approach to analyzing and interpreting data was not the only one available, it certainly proved useful and provided complex and invaluable insights into four students' everyday lives. Consequently, these four "telling cases" can be used to interrogate claims made about young people's language and literacy fluencies and disfluencies, about language and literacy standards setting, and about English language policy and syllabus assumptions.

D/discourse Theory and Research

While boundaries among Discourses will always be provisional in any study, using Gee's D/discourse theory as an interpretive frame certainly helped to explain some of the seeming contradictions and tensions, multiple identities, subject positions, and language and social practices coordinating and enacted in the lives of Nicholas, Jacques, Layla, and Hannah. Arriving at satisfying interpretations of Discourses, however, called for a great deal of experiential and/or vicarious but verifiable knowledge about multiple forms of life and what it seemed to mean to be a member of each. I soon discovered that insufficient knowledge renders a Discourse more-or-less invisible to a researcher, even when repeated patterns of interactions, utterances, and actions suggest that some sort of coordination by a Discourse is being enacted by and upon a person. Paradoxically, I also found that identifying and interpreting Discourses requires degrees of analytic distance from participants and their forms of life. That is, too much (perhaps unconscious) familiarity with a Discourse (or an intersection of Discourse coordinations) may also make a Discourse invisible to the researcher.

For example, I found it easier to interpret Nicholas's and Jacques's Discourse memberships, than I did Layla's and Hannah's. One possible explanation is that both male participants' ways of speaking, acting, relating to others, dressing, and so forth, were sufficiently alien from my own experiences and memories of being in year 7 for me to identify how these various Discourses, actions, and processes coalesced in repeated sets of social practices. Conversely, the fine-grained details I recorded while observing Layla (and nodding in recognition) often obfuscated analysis and at times threatened to paralyze interpretations. While observing Layla, I well recalled the constant negotiations, ducking, and weaving that characterized my own early adolescence whereby I tried to please everyone, especially my friends, family, and those in authority. This often resulted in the kinds of tensions I observed operating in Layla's school life.

Perhaps much of my interpretive problem lay in trying to avoid projecting my own experiences onto my observations and interpretations of Layla. With this possibility in mind, I was scrupulous about reporting only those things for which I had multiple sources of corroborating evidence, and in obtaining member checks from Layla and her family. This is not to suggest that I have (over)simplified interpretations in cases where I have less immediate grasp of their complexity. I certainly did not want to settle for answers that were too simple or too clearly circumscribed. At times, this required conscious immersion in writing lives by means of fieldnotes, audiotapes, books and magazines they read, television shows and movies they watched, notes they passed in class, and myriad other physical and verbal traces, in order to see the complexity of a case. At other times, a different tactic was required when I needed to step back from the data in order to build an overall picture of patterns and particularities constituting the case. This was a difficult balancing act at times.

Another explanation for the difficulties encountered might be that "male" patterns of language and social practice lend themselves more readily to interpretation in terms of Discourses, whereas "female" patterns of action and interaction may be less readily identified and interpreted by means of Discourse categories. Quite distinct gender differences among patterns of language and social practices were enacted or described by the male and female participants in this study. These differences resonate with a large body of literature found at the intersection of language, education and gender studies in particular.[2] Without question, both Jacques and Nicholas were noticeably more physically and verbally active in most school and out-of-school contexts than Hannah and Layla. This, too, made it easier to identify shifts between events, patterns of language and social practices, and even the caliber of their relationships with various people. With regard to Layla and Hannah, however, I recorded large stretches of time where they appeared outwardly to be simply sitting still, or—in Hannah's case particularly—to be working industriously on school tasks. There was little left to record after describing the scene and context. However, to simply describe Hannah, for example, as complying fully with the student Discourse operating in her classroom and/ or a nice girl Discourse seemed an insufficient interpretation in light of her elaborate and extroverted performances in other contexts. Then again, it may be that the methodology I am aiming to develop is skewed towards privileging observable action over other sorts of activity. This will certainly be monitored in subsequent projects.

Another difficulty I repeatedly ran up against in investigating Discourses was how to verify interpretations of phenomena that were not exactly visible to me as a researcher, but which nevertheless seemed to be operating in significant ways in participants' everyday lives. For example, Layla's actions and language uses in class can be interpreted in a number of equally valid, but difficult to verify, ways. For example, one possible reading of Layla's silence in class is that she finds it difficult to follow the thread of lessons and often becomes confused about what she should be contributing to the lesson. Another interpretation could be that she is afraid of making a public mistake and chooses instead to remain silent and therefore less open to ridicule. Yet another possibility is that she has been thoroughly apprenticed to a nice girl Discourse, whereby she believes that a well-behaved female student is one who is silent in class. Perhaps she prefers to rely on her friends rather than her teacher for learning opportunities, or she is simply enduring each lesson, or she may be just lazy, or, indeed, any one or more of these could be the motive on different occasions. Admittedly, some of these interpretations are less probable than others, and any interpretation claiming validity would need to be more complex than those I have offered above. Nevertheless, the point I am making is that there seem to be aspects of students' everyday lives that are not overtly available for ethnographic scrutiny. These aspects usually prove difficult to track in terms of patterns of social practice, cognition, and Discourse coordinations. Gee explicitly accommodates social cognition in his theory of D/discourses and promotes an integrated view of mind, body, and society in his discussions of apprenticeship, acquisition, and learning (e.g., 1992b, 1996a). However, in practice, these dimensions of everyday life are difficult to investigate ethnographically. Perhaps, as Gee himself indicates (e.g., 1992b, 1996a, 1996b), recent research in the area of social cognition holds fruitful possibilities here for enhancing approaches to D/discourse research.[3]

Another interpretive hurdle occurred in Hannah's case. I found I had little knowledge on which to draw in constructing interpretations of her everyday social and language practices, apart from what I obtained from reported studies (e.g., Freebody, Ludwig, and Gunn 1996; Heath 1983; Walkerdine 1988). This was also confounded by the fact that Hannah's family did not "fit the mold" of many other families and family situations in the area. Upon reflection, the problem may be that I have not spent enough time in communities like Hannah's, or with families like Hannah's, and have only a limited "fund of knowledge" to use in interpreting her Discourse memberships (cf. Moll 1992). This dilemma is by no means unique to my own research, nor to the particular theoretical framing I am employing (cf. Delamont 1992; Roman 1992). Neither are there any simple solutions to this dilemma of simultaneously requiring funds of knowledge and professional distance in data interpretations. Nevertheless, in the present study I have taken steps along this interpretive tightrope that may perhaps contribute to additional insights and methodological work in the future.

In addition, and still focusing on methodology for now, using Gee's theory of D/discourses may have predisposed me to "find" Discourses in the collected data. This is not an insurmountable problem provided adequate strategies are employed throughout the study to enhance the validity and trustworthiness of proposed interpretations. In the present study, I liberally employed member checks, outsider audits, data cross-examination, cross-references, and the like to strengthen my claims (cf. Carspecken 1996; Fetterman 1989). Although the reader is the ultimate judge of the interpretations and analyses presented in this book, and notwithstanding the difficulties discussed above, I am convinced that Gee's theory—with some modifications—has enabled me to examine some of the complex interrelationships among language uses, sets of values and beliefs, social practices, social groups, and social institutions that co-constitute and coordinate the everyday lives of Nicholas, Jacques, Layla, and Hannah.

A D/discourse Anatomy

This next section presents evaluations of key concepts in Gee's theory of D/discourses and their usefulness as research devices. These concepts include: membership, sub-Discourses, primary and secondary Discourses, apprenticeship, and social networks.

Membership. The notion of membership in a Discourse establishes useful criteria for identifying social identities and possible differences among Discourses and their coordinations. However, in the course of my research I was forced to rethink the conception of Discourse "membership" used in this study. This had focused originally on defining a member in terms of values, beliefs, perspectives, ways of speaking and acting, and so forth that were shared with other members. It soon became obvious that I also needed to examine possible explanations of *how* members came to be members and perhaps nonmembers of different Discourses at different times.

Discourse memberships are complex. Some memberships appear to accrue by default, particularly those connected with institutionalized Discourses. For example, most children in Queensland are recruited as students by the state and are apprenticed to various ways of "being a student." Concomitantly, however, this also makes available a range of (often conflicting) ways of "being a student." Thus, some Discourse memberships may be deliberate choices, diligently practiced and defended from outsiders, or they may have elements of deliberate choice in terms of sub-Discourse membership. Differentiating between different *types* of Discourse memberships helps explain some of the observed contradictions or tensions (or both) among social identities, subject positions, and sets of language and social practices in at least these four young people's everyday practices. Nicholas's complex negotiations between the expectations of his mates and his teacher is a case in point. Moreover, I found that distinguishing among different types of memberships was facilitated by Gee's conception of "sub-Discourses."

Sub-Discourses. The "sub-Discourse" construct proved invaluable in distinguishing between what I saw as more easily recognized institutionalized Discourses and those that are much less bound by traditions of social convention, norms, and expectations. For example, I was able to use distinctions between Discourses and sub-Discourses to interpret possible social identities such as "being a student" in more complex terms than is often the case in reported classroom-based sociolinguistic research (e.g., the construction of "student" in Morine-Dershimer 1985). This provided additional insights into the ways teachers and students constructed various versions of "being a student" in their classroom, and how these constructions served to coordinate a range of practices. In turn, this generated multilayered and complex contexts for interrogating assumptions and claims made about teachers, students, and language and literacy standards (discussed later in this chapter). Similar insights were obtained in relation to memberships in sub-Discourses that bore allegiance to teen gal, nice girl, or mateship Discourses, and so on.

Primary and secondary Discourses. Distinguishing between primary and secondary Discourses also proved a useful interpretive strategy. I found, however, that the value of the distinction did not lie in allocating various sets of beliefs, values, practices, and so forth to one or the other. Such labeling and tidiness is impossible and unnecessary. Thus, the value of the distinction lay not so much in trying to identify the *kind* of primary Discourse enacted by each participant, but in identifying the possible *range* of secondary Discourses which each participant may have access to, courtesy of their primary Discourse. Thus, a person may be predisposed (or not be predisposed) to becoming a full or partial member of a Discourse due to a particular range of secondary Discourses that have seeped into her primary Discourses. Or, membership in a secondary Discourse may occur almost by default due to specific beliefs, values, knowledges, practices, and so on that also constitute aspects of a person's primary Discourse. These concepts were particularly apt for proposing possible interpretations of noticeable dissonances between home and school language and social practices.

Admittedly, interpretations of boundaries and overlaps among participants' primary and secondary Discourses are largely speculative and always provisional. Nevertheless, these accounts intersect with, and are supported by, a large body of reported studies available at the intersection of education, everyday life, discourse, and ethnographic or case study research (or both).[4] In addition, differentiating among primary and secondary Discourses helped construct a rich conception of *apprenticeship* that adds to Gee's explanation of how we come to be "full" or "mature" members of a Discourse.

Apprenticeship. Gee's concept of apprenticeship which applies equally to primary and secondary Discourses can be put to useful interpretive work in terms of explaining students' access to secondary Discourses and/or competence in certain practices. For example, Jacques's extensive understanding of "being a worker" and of business Discourses was neither innate nor inexplicable. Such understanding was both acquired and learned from watching and working with his father and other workers and is usefully explained in terms of apprenticeship to particular knowledges and sets of practices.

As analysis progressed, however, Gee's dyadic conception of apprenticeship was found to be somewhat limiting when it came to describing *processes* of acquisition and learning in the lives of the four young people studied. Instead, Rogoff's definition of apprenticeship as an indissoluble mix of sociocultural activity, learning, and acquisition proved more useful. The mutually constituting components of her theory of apprenticeship to a community of practitioners, guided participation, and participatory appropriation enabled more full-bodied interpretations of Nicholas's, Jacques's, Layla's, and Hannah's everyday lives. In turn, Rogoff's (e.g., 1995) sociocultural conception of apprenticeship challenges the "developmental" and technicist assumptions underpinning most standards-setting or benchmarking activities in education. If we consider literacy standards in terms of student access to secondary Discourses, then benchmarking agendas become far more complex—if not sinister—than many policy makers would have us believe. Aside from issues pertaining to school "success," Rogoff's conception of apprenticeship highlights the significance of social networks, or interactive webs of relations, in these four adolescents' Discourse memberships and coordinations.

Social networks. Complex theories become even more so in practice, it seems. For me, one area of Gee's conception of Discourses requiring further theoretical attention concerns the role of social networks in defining membership and Discourse parameters. Gee defines a social network as "people who associate with each other around a common set of interests, goals, and activities" (1992b, 107). However, in the course of analyzing data, I found I needed to attend to the ways in which these social networks coordinated members *and* nonmembers, as well as degrees and types of full or partial membership. Accordingly, McRobbie's (1994) conception of "interactive webs of relations" seemed to more fully capture the complexity of the Discourse and social group coordinations constituting and sustaining these four case study participants respectively. These webs of relations extended across Discourses (including opposing Discourses) and sub-Discourses, and were variously fleeting or more abiding (cf. Hinkson 1991). For example, Nicholas's concern for and association with outsiders contrasted with the observed mores of his group of mates.[5] For Layla, even more than for Nicholas, relationships within and across Discourses were of paramount importance, and appeared to be key factors in shaping her social identities. A dynamic and interactive conception of relationships also helps to explain how it is that any one person can lay claim to or be claimed by more than one Discourse membership at any time, and how these various memberships are negotiated and enacted.

One additional point: Bennett's challenge. My aim of developing an effective methodology for investigating the usefulness or otherwise of Gee's D/discourse theory in research conducted at the nexus of language and education was sparked by Adrian Bennett's criticisms of Gee's approach to D/discourse analysis (see chapter 2). To reiterate, Bennett posed two methodological problems pertaining to Gee's approach to D/discourse analysis:

(i) how to evaluate specific interpretations of meaning; and
(ii) how to evaluate the role or significance of the discourse under analysis in the lives of people who produce it.

In the present study I have gone some way towards addressing Bennett's first methodological problem by building communicative validity and trustworthiness procedures into my research design. And, as said before, I am convinced it is the reader who ultimately evaluates a researcher's data interpretations and the soundness of the argument presented; it is the researcher's responsibility to provide enough evidence to facilitate this evaluation.

Bennett's call for Gee and other researchers to evaluate the role or significance of a Discourse in the lives of the people who produce it is much more complex than he appears to assume. To begin with, Discourses can be evaluated differently from a range of perspectives serving different interests. For example, Nicholas's mother judges technological Discourses as having a significant role to play in Nicholas's life, whereas his teacher, Mr. Lasseter, appears to judge otherwise. In addition, a nice girl Discourse seemingly plays a significant role in both Layla's and Hannah's everyday lives, but to ask whether or not they value this Discourse is to miss the point of Gee's Discourse theory, which is interested in—among other things—how people are coordinated (consciously, unconsciously, etc.) by Discourses and how this affects their opportunities for accessing social goods and services. Bennett's call for researchers to evaluate the significance of Discourses for members therefore misses its mark when there is little choice over whether or not one is coordinated and engaged co-constitutively by one or more D/discourses.

Finally, despite some of the initial interpretive difficulties I encountered, analyzing data in terms of D/discourses afforded useful and rich insights into the everyday lives of these adolescents that were not made available by simply reading through the data. I am convinced that Gee's D/discourse theory—with some modifications—obtains invaluable insights into complex phenomena. Concomitantly, this provided me with the kinds of data required to interrogate claims and assumptions currently being made by governments, policy makers, and the business sector about primary school students' present and future language and literacy "needs." In closing this section I am not suggesting that research into the usefulness of this theory is complete; rather, the present study sets an agenda for further investigations into D/discourse theory at the intersection of research into language, education, and social practice.

WAYS FORWARD

Possible Directions for Future Research

Theorists working with sociolinguistic approaches to language research have long called for "antireductionist" interpretations of interrelationships among the individual, discourse practices, and the social. Any such interpretations would need to avoid positing the oversimplified cause-and-effect relationships between language and social practice that plague many current sociolinguistic methodologies. In the present study, I have attempted to translate Gee's theory of D/discourses into research practice in ways that maintain the complexity of his theory and that capitalize on the possibilities it provides for richly interpreting interrelationships among language use and social practice.

The results of this work, useful in themselves I believe, also signal a number of possible avenues for subsequent, more sophisticated work, particularly in the areas of social cognition and D/discourses. At the same time, the usefulness of Green and her colleagues' approach to data analysis has been explored by employing it beyond the instructional conversations which characterize much of this group's work. Nevertheless, there remains much more refined work to be done in bringing together D/discourse theory and data mapping practices in mutually enhancing ways, and this book is intended to be part of an ongoing conversation, rather than the final word. Aside from methodological concerns, the telling cases of Nicholas, Jacques, Layla, and Hannah can also be used to inform classroom practices in tentative yet possible ways.

Enhancing Classroom Language and Literacy Practices

Schools enact at least three overlapping roles in countries like Australia. As public institutions, they play a normative role in producing particular kinds of citizens and workers. Schools are also tied intimately to the societies that produce them. Thus, teachers are deemed responsible for providing students with a common base of content knowledge, values, and competencies from which to participate effectively in a diverse range of social institutions and practices. This includes providing learning opportunities that prepare students for adult life in a rapidly changing world. Moreover, schools are seen as responsible for developing the individual to the reach of her capacities in ways that are personally satisfying, as well as in ways that produce members of groups who will contribute to the overall well-being of society at large. National and state governments like our own capitalize on these themes and build them into national literacy plans and intervention programs (e.g., Clinton 1997; Curriculum Corporation 1997a, 1997b).

The cases of Nicholas, Layla, Jacques, and Hannah are indeed telling cases, and there is much in their everyday lives at school and out-of-school that will resonate with other young people's language and social practices. Within the scope of the present study, I found various dissonances among opportunities for acquiring, learning, and practicing language and literacy that these four young people are able to access out-of-school compared with opportunities made available in their classrooms, and those promoted by the Queensland English syllabus. Misalliances also seemed to occur between the language and social practices championed in three out of the four classrooms observed and those practices valued in the adult world of work and citizenship. If this is the case in relation to the four students studied, then the question must be asked as to what extent these dissonances are experienced by other students who do not have the same kinds of predominantly mainstream opportunities variously accessed by Nicholas, Layla, Jacques, and Hannah.

Accordingly, the remainder of this chapter sketches a number of possible responses for addressing what I believe to be widespread disfluencies among syllabus goals, classroom practices, and students' present and (possible) future language and social practices. The dangers of generalizing from a small body of work to wider arenas are fully recognized, and the following ideas are offered as tentative suggestions only. These ideas are themselves constituted and coordinated by a range of Discourses and need to be explored in more detail than provided here. Nevertheless, I have a strong feeling that much of what I have to say will resonate with many educators' experiences and their own ideas about directions for language education.

The following discussion focuses on what I see as a responsibility of teachers to identify and address in their classrooms different ways of "being literate," and to understand and act on as far as possible a broad range of literacy practices and their co-constituted social practices. This is particularly the case with electronic technologies, which many students now experience as organic aspects of their everyday lives. In addition, the need for teachers to critically reflect on the role schooling plays in producing particular kinds of citizens and their own role in such production is also emphasized. These ideas are not new at either primary, secondary, or tertiary levels of schooling. Nevertheless, they continue to hold fruitful possibilities for enhancing aspects of language and literacy education in primary school classrooms and, concomitantly, teacher education in the area of language and literacy.

Language, literacy, and schooling. The past few years have seen a surge in the number of prepackaged language and literacy in-servicing programs developed for Australian primary and secondary teachers (e.g., *Boys and*

Literacy 1996, *Literacy in the National Curriculum* 1995–6, *Pathways to Literacy* 1994, *Talking Our Way Into Literacy* 1996). Most of these packages have been funded directly by federal or state government departments. Briefly, *Boys and Literacy* (Alloway, Davies, Gilbert, Gilbert, and King 1996) was written by academics from James Cook University and developed in collaboration with classroom teachers. This project was supported by funding granted under the Strategic Initiatives Element of the National Professional Development Program, a program managed under the aegis of the Commonwealth Department of Employment, Education, Training and Youth Affairs. This in-servicing program was developed in response to research that suggested that boys were more likely than girls to participate in reading remediation classes and low-level streams of English classes. This research also suggested boys read less widely than girls and were less likely than girls to claim they enjoyed classroom literacy programs or endeavors. The program particularly concentrates on enhancing teachers' understanding of concepts such as "masculinity" and its social effects on literacy competence and practices (see also Davies 1997).

Literacy in the National Curriculum (Kempe, Anstey, Bull, and White-Davison 1995–6) is a National Professional Development Program orchestrated by academics at the University of Southern Queensland, education consultants, and classroom teachers in Toowoomba and elsewhere in Queensland. This initiative was funded by the then-named Commonwealth Department of Employment, Education and Training and additionally supported by the Darling Downs Council of the Australian Reading Association. The principal aim of this in-servicing program is to develop teachers' understanding of the National English Curriculum Statement and Profile. Other aims include addressing social justice issues (e.g., rurality, isolation, special needs learners, race, class, ethnicity, gender) and facilitating long-term change in language and literacy classroom practices.

Pathways to Literacy: A Professional Development Program for Senior Secondary and Technical Teachers (Searle 1994) was developed by the Department of Education, Queensland, in conjunction with Technical and Further Education, Queensland, and with additional support from the State Department of Employment, Vocational Education, Training, and Industrial Relations. The principal aim of this package is "to increase teachers' awareness of, and skill in dealing with, the language and literacy requirements of a range of subjects, including vocational education and training for all students" (4). This program encourages teachers to reflect on the literacy practices required in their subject area, and to develop methods for making these practices explicit to their students.

Talking Our Way Into Literacy (Department of Education, Queensland 1996) is a professional development package designed by Education Queensland[6] and based on the findings and data of local research into everyday literacy practices in low socioeconomic urban communities and schools (see Freebody, Ludwig, and Gunn 1996). The main aim of this program is "to provide clear and specific methods for educators in schools and the community to plan appropriately for more effective literacy practices in increasingly complex social and cultural contexts" (5). This in-service package requires teachers to research and reflect on their own literacy-related classroom talk, and to examine the ways in which "literacy" is subsequently defined for their students.

This listing of professional development packages is comprehensive, although not exhaustive, and some schools have developed their own programs to meet perceived language and literacy "needs" of specific school populations. Some programs have begun to address aspects of the issues and problems raised in this chapter and elsewhere in this book in relation to language and literacy education. Nevertheless, teacher access to such programs remains uneven and underfunded. The fallout from this situation may be that teachers attempt to teach "new" ways of using and thinking about language by "old" means without grappling with these "new" language and social practices in any way. Jim Cummins and Dennis Sayers (1995, 98) describe a similar situation in North American schools. They claim that very little has changed pedagogically in the past thirty years, despite the waxing and waning of "child centered" approaches, "whole language" approaches, and "discovery learning" (see also Cook-Gumperz 1993). Similarly, a comment I have heard repeatedly from a range of primary school teachers in response to the current Queensland English syllabus is: "But this is what I've always done, they've just given it new names." However, if students such as Nicholas, Layla, Jacques, and Hannah are anything to go by, and I believe they are, then teachers "doing what they've always done" must always be insufficient wherever there has been no engagement with current language and literacy theories or pedagogies on the teacher's part.

Allan Luke and Peter Freebody (1997; also Freebody and Luke 1990; Freebody 1992) outline a conception of reading that involves more than developing encoding and decoding skills in classrooms and suggests a possible multipronged approach to classroom language and literacy planning and teaching. Although Luke and Freebody focus primarily on reading, their insights apply equally to all other forms of text processing and practice. These education commentators directly link models of reading with models of social order, and emphasize that in current times "the means and practices of reading [have] changed significantly in important ways in relation to cultural, economic, and social developments" (1997, 191). Accordingly, their set of reading practices and resources embody historical and relatively new perspectives on reading pedagogy, and include: coding practices, text-meaning practices, pragmatic practices, and critical practices. These reader "resources" can be used as components or elements of "successful reading" (Freebody 1992, 49) and to embody in classrooms "a richer understanding of literacy that recognizes and builds on students' prior cultural resources, experiences, and knowledges in all instruction and programs" (Luke and Freebody 1997, 221).

Coding practices describe processes whereby decoding skills and habits are used to "unlock" alphabetic codes or scripts. The kinds of questions a reader asks while (de)coding include: "How do I crack this text? How does it work? What are its patterns and conventions? How do the sounds and the marks relate, singly and in combination?" (Luke and Freebody 1997, 214). Coding practices alone, however, are insufficient for reading meaningfully. Text-meaning practices inscribe the reader as a "participant": someone who is able to make meaning from a text by bringing to it additional cultural knowledge about texts, the subject matter, discourses, and the like. Thus, reading for meaning "entails the practice of drawing into play previous experiences with statements to recognize recurrence, similarity, and difference in the text" (Luke and Freebody 1997, 215). The kinds of questions a text participant might ask are: "How do the ideas represented in the text string together? What are the cultural meanings and possible readings that can be constructed from this text?" (215).

Pragmatic resources are brought into play in text-mediated social activities or events. The reader is able to match texts and contexts, and can tailor her reading accordingly. Luke and Freebody remind us here that a great deal of everyday reading practices for most people is "tied to everyday responsibilities of citizenship in the industrial workplace, family, and everyday life" (213). Freebody (1992, 53) suggests, however, that pragmatic resources are "transmitted and developed in our society largely in instructional contexts, some of which may bear comparatively little relevance to the ways in which texts need to be used in out-of-school contexts." His claim strongly resonates with many of the findings of the present study.

Drawing on critical reading resources engages the reader in analyzing probable worldviews and assumptions constituting a text. Thus, the reader as text analyst and critic is acutely aware that texts are also idea and value systems, and that readers often comply unquestioningly with these positions. Critical practices in reading require the reader to have metalevel understanding of how, why, and in whose interests texts work, and be able to employ complex sociocognitive processes in interrogating representations of "how things are" in texts. This is facilitated by questions such as: "What kind of person, with what interests and values, could both write and read this naively and unproblematically? What is this text trying to do to me? In whose interests? Which positions, voices, and interests are at play? Which are silent and absent?" (Luke and Freebody 1997, 214; also Wallace 1992; Kress 1985).

A successful reader is one who draws on all four sets of resources or roles in meeting their text processing needs. These roles are not meant to describe neat categories of activity; rather they are one way of trying to make explicit the complexities involved in teaching students to be effectively (or "properly") literate. Teaching language and literacy as though it is a fixed system of meaning that is cracked like a code will ultimately disadvantage students who do not have access to other ways of "being literate" (cf. O'Neill 1970). Instead, like Freebody, Luke, and others, I am convinced that students, even primary school students, will benefit most from an approach to language education that engages them in investigating how language is a social practice, and how meanings along with their own social identities and subjectivities are socially constituted (cf. Buckingham and Sefton-Green 1994).

There are indeed many literacies and ways of being literate, most of which involve much more than merely cracking the written code.[7] Jacques is a case in point. Despite his difficulties with language and literacy at school, I consider Jacques to be highly literate in at least two adult D/discourses. Both Discourses (i.e., business Discourse and Jehovah's Witnesses Discourse) require him to engage with a bevy of texts for specific "real world" purposes (e.g., reading dials on the dashboard of a truck, speaking cogently and persuasively while witnessing). These literacy practices involve much more than merely encoding and decoding (usually) written texts. Instead, these literacies are part-and-parcel of Jacques's everyday life and Discourse memberships which include sets of particular social practices, ways of speaking about things, certain values and assumptions, and ways of interacting with others.

Concomitantly, these literacies constitute significant aspects of his social identities. Thus, despite Jacques's literate competence in the adult world, many of the language and literacy practices expected of him at school seem to be alienating (cf. his parodic treatment of the Writer's Center in his classroom and his teacher's process approach to writing; see chapter 4). Much the same could be said for Nicholas, and doubtless many other students as well. Accordingly, in light of Jacques's case particularly, some teachers may need to rethink the kinds and range of literacy practices they are promoting in their class, and what they count as "being literate."

In addition, and keeping in mind the various time- and role-related constraints acting on teachers, some teachers may also need to examine the content they are using to teach language and literacy skills, knowledges, and processes. Layla, whose literacy practices include playing Nintendo, writing letters to friends, reading teen gal magazines, and talking for hours on the telephone, professes a deep lack of interest in writing a book report on *Ash Road* (Southall 1967) for their substitute teacher. On the other hand, although she does not necessarily "enjoy" them, she identifies the language and literacy practices her regular teacher engages her in as being more meaningful and engaging. These include, among many other examples: being taught how to research and write a library-based "research report," being taught various strategies for analyzing and organizing information to suit a range of (mostly school) purposes (e.g., "compare and contrast," "list and describe," "cause and effect," and "problem and solution" organizational strategies for texts she produces), and being given opportunities to present completed tasks in a variety of ways (e.g., by means of a debate, a poster, role plays). In addition, her teacher, Mr Wills, regularly draws students' attention to links between text types and methods of organization and their possible uses out of school.

Indeed, findings from the present study suggest that students—at least those who are like the four young people in this study—may engage more readily with language and literacy learning experiences when meaningful and purposeful links are established by their teachers between what is learned at school and students' everyday lives. Taylor and Saarinen (1994, Telewriting 2) support my claim when they chide people who bemoan the "fact" that young people no longer read "as we did at their age." They wryly suggest that the problem may not lie with these young people, but with the kinds of texts to which they are given access. To this I add that much of this perceived "literacy crisis" could also be due to what they are being made to read and write at school. Additional specific examples supporting this claim include Nicholas's subversion of a reading session based on a book taken from a commercial reading development scheme (i.e., a basal reader, as reported in chapter 3), Jacques's elaborate strategies for avoiding reading and writing, and Layla's anguished whisper to her tablemates, "God, get me out of here!..." as the substitute teacher read a long-winded story to the class from a basal reader.

I am convinced as well that teachers themselves need to be aware of and able to analyze at least some aspects of current and wide-reaching social changes and conditions if language and literacy learning in classrooms is to have currency beyond schooling (and I believe that as much of it as possible should). Or, at base-line, they need to be able to understand language as a complex social practice. I am not claiming that such understandings are easy to come by; nonetheless, I believe them to be important enough to explore—at the very least—in light of the present study. For example, students like Nicholas provide indices of the extent to which text processing has changed dramatically in the past decade. For him, drafting texts by hand is tedious and inexcusably labor intensive. Using a computer enables him to write more efficiently and more effectively, which he does at home. Indeed, at home he has long been apprenticed to a technological Discourse that is apportioned high status, and to employment opportunities in society in general. However, this expertise has virtually no currency in his classroom as an aspect of either technological or literacy practice as constructed by his teacher and indeed, by his school.

Although Nicholas's teacher is in one sense disadvantaged by not having a computer in his class all year round, this does not have to be an insurmountable problem. In addition to finding alternative ways of exploring technology as a social practice by means of magazines and newspapers, Mr. Lasseter could perhaps make the sites of text production in his class more flexible so that students use that computer as one "workstation" in a series for one or two afternoons a week, or initiate a tutoring system whereby the year 7 students are responsible for teaching year 1 students a range of technological skills and processes. Once again, however, this points to the need for teachers themselves to understand technology in terms of social practices rather than in terms of instrumental learning outcomes.[8]

Perhaps, to paraphrase Taylor and Saarinen (1994, Interstanding 10), the current "literacy crisis" that is said to be plaguing (yet again) Queensland primary education may not be an absence of or decrease in skills, but rather, that new forms of literacy and being literate arising in our communities are not being appreciated or sufficiently accommodated (cf. Rushkoff 1996b, 3–13). Indeed, Nicholas is far from an unusual case in primary schools.[9] Perhaps, as mentioned already, one way of capitalizing on students' technological expertise in a classroom where the teacher is unfamiliar or uncomfortable with all things technological may be to reconfigure at various moments teacher and student roles when working with computers in class. In this way, student expertise is recognized and capitalized on, and the teacher comes to understand more of the practices associated with working with computers. This has already proved successful in a range of classrooms (e.g., Cummins and Sayers 1995; Papert 1993). However, this kind of role exchange does not mean an abdication of pedagogical responsibilities for the teacher. Indeed, it seems to me that teachers have important roles to play in providing students with opportunities to theorize or at least come to some sort of metalevel understanding of their technological literacies in terms of a wide range of social practices.

The final point to be made here focuses on the exuberant and playful language practices in which Nicholas, Jacques, Layla, and Hannah participated outside their respective classes. Each used this kind of language in quite specific ways, and all four obviously derived much pleasure from experimenting and playing with what they said, and how they said it. For example, Hannah used language to explore a range of identities and subjectivities in her skits, such as singing in a husky voice, "I'm too sexy for my body, too sexy for my cat" as she flounced down an imaginary catwalk to shrieks of laughter from her classmates and teachers in an obvious parody of models, fashion show glamour, and television music videos. Layla often used lines or personas from movies she has seen to make her close friends laugh, or to use the assumed bravado of a screen star to challenge or turn the table on traditional roles, like the time a boy in her class was bothering her and she turned to him and said huskily, "Hello, gorgeous" and pouted Marilyn Monroe-style, reducing the boy to stammers and blushes and her friends to tears of laughter.

Nicholas and his mates also seemed to thoroughly enjoy commentating on their clowning around on the basketball court and using a particular style of language that seemed to be a distinctive mix of language used in North American soap operas and movies, as well as ways of speaking used by sports commentators. An example of the latter is found in the way Nicholas reported on the state of a player who was knocked over during a bid for the ball in a fast-paced basketball game. After checking to see if his mate was all right, Nicholas calls out to no one in particular, "It's all right folks, he'll be okay. And the game has re-*sumed*!" as he intercepts a pass and tries for a basket. Jacques, too, uses language exuberantly and distinctively, especially when messing around with his older brother. For example, during Friday night rehearsals at Drama School, Jacques and Gerard repeatedly innovated on the script and characters to create their own stories within stories. Jacques's character was supposed to be a reasonably seasoned gangster, and Jacques experimented with different ways of delivering his lines, such as using a high-pitched winsome voice, drawling them cowboy-style, saying his lines but without any sound then pretending to turn a volume knob and speaking more and more loudly, and on through a repertoire of gags and personas. Needless to say, his drama teacher soon became frustrated, but Jacques and his brother (who was experimenting in similar ways) found it hilarious.

These kinds of language practices are fascinating, and worth more sustained investigation. In addition, I believe that space should somehow be made for such language practices in classrooms. The often instrumental approach to genres and social purposes practiced in classrooms could perhaps, to some extent, be pushed beyond narrowly functional terms by including playful, exuberant, and creative language uses and purposes (cf. Buckingham and Sefton-Green 1994). I am well aware, however, that this suggestion runs up against the problem of how to avoid reducing such language uses to merely "school literacies." Perhaps this approach to language and literacy pedagogy is best done in collaboration with artistic and creative groups outside conventional school contexts. For example, performance and techno artists Michael and Ludmila Doneman (<http://mwk.thehub.com.au>) are driving forces in a youth, arts, and training initiative in Brisbane's inner-city Fortitude Valley area that blurs the often artificially drawn lines between play and learning by means of projects based in a telecenter and multimedia work space known affectionately as GRUNT. The kind of training and education envisaged at GRUNT is not designed to make these young people consensual bodies in a regulated world (as school often does); rather, emphasis is on support for enterprise and self-sufficiency, and projects are designed in collaboration with community members, young people, multimedia artists, musicians, and so on. Each project aims to promote a sense of self-identity and interconnectedness with other identities and contexts in a world where many of the young participants seem increasingly to have no place. One project is *Digitarts*,[10] an on-line "new wave" feminist zine written by young women for young women, which explores alternative fashions and expresses different conceptions of female identity through poems, narratives, and digital images. Hotlinks to similar web sites on the internet also define each writer's self and her self connected with others. Other projects include *Famaleez*,[11] a performance-based exploration of "the extremely sensitive issue of alcohol and substance abuse in indigenous communities"; and the two *Virtual Valley* projects. In the second Virtual Valley project, upper primary students from the local Aboriginal (Murri) and Torres Strait Islander Independent Community School, among others, were involved in producing "alternative guides" to local tourist maps of the Valley. These alternative guides were presented as internet pages, and as a booklet to help guide visitors "through a number of interesting sites using maps and postcard images" based on these young people's identities, values, world views, experiences, and ways of locating themselves in time and space within the Valley.[12]

Murri and Torres Strait Islander students would spend half a day each week at GRUNT exploring aspects of identity using conventional artistic means of painting, drawing, and collage, as well as learning technical aspects of web page construction, including: basic HTML and web page design principles, using digital cameras, manipulating digital images and anchoring them to web pages, and using flatbed scanners. Students gathered material for their web pages on walks through the Valley, using digital and disposable cameras, sketch books, and notepads. They began putting together their individual web pages by creating large-scale, annotated collages of aspects of the Valley that were significant to them. These collages comprised photocopies of digital and camera images they had taken of themselves, their friends, family members, and the Valley area, plus drawings and found objects (e.g., food labels, ticket stubs, bingo cards). They were then pared back to key images and passages of text as each student prepared a flowchart depicting the layout and content of their web page. During the last month of the project these flowcharts were used to guide the design and construction of web pages. The result is a series of compelling and evocative readings and writings of everyday cultural (re)productions of the Valley seen through the eyes of these children.[13]

The preceding discussion has focused deliberately on teachers, not because I see them as "guilty" of a range of teaching "sins," but because teachers comprise the most likely and effective agents of change in relation to enhancing language and literacy education. The introduction of any new strategy, idea, policy, syllabus, or program does not guarantee change for better or for worse on its own. It requires, at the very least, active and informed engagement on the part of teachers. And, in addition to producing literate students of one sort or another, schools are also involved in the production of particular kinds of "citizens."

The production of particular kinds of citizens. Schools are public institutions and are expected by society to equip students with the necessary skills, processes, knowledges, and attitudes that will enable them to access personal and social well-being. Teachers need to consider the kinds of citizens they are helping to produce when they implement a new "official" policy or program in their classroom. Cummins and Sayers's (1995, 82) observations about the present role of schooling are startlingly pertinent to current language and literacy education situations in many countries.

Public [and private] schools serve the societies that fund them, and they aim to graduate students with the skills, knowledge, and values necessary to contribute to their societies. In other words, an image of the future society that students will help form is implicit in all the interactions between students and educators in school. The dilemma for educators at the turn of the millennium is that no consensus exists in the broader community about the nature of the society schools should be attempting to promote.

This lack of consensus is a complex issue, and one that is exacerbated by the difficulties attending any attempt to try and predict the futures of current students. Layla is a case in point.

To reiterate, when I first met Layla, she was rated by her year 6 teacher as "average," and my time spent with her in year 7 reconfirmed this assessment. Moreover, Layla indicated that as an adult she would probably become a nurse or "someone who works with animals." She did not seem interested in working in her father's tiling business, or indeed, in any business. If I were to predict Layla's life trajectory four years ago when she was just completing year 7, I would have expected her to remain an average student in high school and to take up a traditionally "feminine" job requiring face-to-face interaction with clients, customers, or patients (cf. Reich's in-person service worker, 1992, 172). Four years later, however, Layla is performing at a level way above average in secondary school, is actively involved in team sports once again, plans on becoming a doctor, and, as I write this, is currently in Japan for two weeks staying with a host family, attending school, and being apprenticed to a range of additional D/discourses. I could never have predicted this path for Layla from the possible Discourse memberships I had identified as coordinating her everyday life at the time of the study. In retrospect it may be possible to identify which Discourses laid the foundations, as it were, for such dramatic changes in Layla's school performance and aspirations.[14]

Without question, all four young people have changed over the past five years since I first met them during a pilot study. Nicholas now wants to be a composer instead of a lawyer, and with the help of a group of friends has already sung his own compositions during church services. Jacques appears to be less anxious about secondary school than he was about primary school;

among other things, a teacher has helped Jacques to enjoy and be successful in mathematics. He says he may even stay on and complete year 12. Hannah has appeared in the chorus of a number of school musicals, is doing extremely well at school, and at the moment is deciding between becoming an actress or a marine biologist. In sum, the unexpectedness of Layla's current trajectory and the changes in the lives of the other study participants certainly challenges Delpit's (1993,1995) claims that Gee's D/discourse theory is dangerously deterministic.

Thus, it seems to me that trying to *predict* the social outcomes obtained by introducing certain approaches to language and literacy teaching (cf. New London Group 1996) is a difficult, if not impossible, task. Nevertheless, this does not mean that educators can teach only for the present, or worse, with eyes fixed unrelentingly on a particular past. One possible approach is to equip students with a repertoire of potentially transportable skills and processes in, knowledge of, and understandings about language and social practices, coupled with the provision of opportunities and contexts that require students to adapt these skills, understandings, and so on to meet a diverse range of purposes. In so doing, students are also provided with opportunities for developing metalevel understandings of language. In addition, discussing possible ways of enhancing classroom language and literacy practices is not a matter of simply superimposing the findings from my four case study participants' everyday practices onto existing classroom practices. This study was not designed to develop, implement, and evaluate a program of work that would claim to address all of the issues raised in preceding chapters. The diverse array of Discourses coordinating and constituting present classroom language and literacy practices, teachers, and their students call for more complex responses than "interventionist" programs (e.g., Reading Recovery, Support-a-Reader). Thus, what follows is largely speculative in terms of language and literacy education in Queensland primary schools and elsewhere, and my teaching and research experiences yet to come. The remainder of this chapter is less a discussion of actualities, and more a process of setting future teaching and research agendas for myself and perhaps for others.

Possible approaches to enhancing language and literacy classroom practices. Although a larger aim of this study was to inform and enhance current language and literacy education, I did not assume there would be any clear cut "answers" to problems uncovered in the course of investigating the everyday lives of Nicholas, Jacques, Layla, and Hannah. I was, instead, interested in investigating the range of these four students' social and language practices, and how these compared with the (reduced) range of language practices admitted into classrooms. The ideas offered in this section are merely possible starting points among many for enhancing the range of language practices made available to students, and the ways in which they are made available, in classrooms.

To begin with, teachers can draw on a number of existing exemplars in which various educators have explored ways of teaching (about) language and literacy that contextualize language use within social practices. These approaches include self-reflexive or metalevel thinking processes in their curricula or programs so that students are actively engaged in learning about their worlds, as well as about the ways in which each class member is coordinated by the social and language practices of their families, their school, and the various social groups to which they lay claim. Luke and Freebody (1997), for example, outline one useful approach to literacy events in classrooms (see earlier).

Charles Bazerman (1992), as another example, wrestles particularly with the complexities of classroom language and literacy practices and the situated, multiple, and shifting contexts that are coordinated and negotiated within them. For Bazerman, enhancing classroom practices is not so much about finding better ways to teach text processing, but about developing metalevel understanding of the classroom as a complex social construction set within an institutional framework. Such understandings—insofar as they can be made conscious—may enable teachers and students, according to Bazerman, to become aware of (at the very least) their own socially constructed identities, subjectivities, and roles (see also Buckingham and Sefton-Green 1994). Bazerman, unfortunately, does not offer specific teaching strategies for developing students' metalevel understandings of language practices. Possible ways of facilitating metalevel language and literacy understandings may be made available by means of ethnographic approaches to language and literacy education. A raft of studies that have monitored and evaluated the use of ethnographic processes in primary school classrooms are now available,[15] and these studies have contributed directly to the ideas I discuss briefly below.

Students could be provided with opportunities for being apprenticed (in ways approximating Rogoff's sense of apprenticeship as closely as possible within the constraints of the classroom) to suitably modified ethnographic ways of collecting information and interpreting it in relation to patterns of social practices. Modifications would likely include: focusing on one or two specific dimensions of—or concepts held by—a particular group of people, a teacher-set timeline for collecting data, the teacher providing a database from which to launch investigations, data may need to be brought to the classroom in the form of guest speakers and borrowed or found artifacts rather than having students work exclusively "in the field," etc. I would not expect students' findings to be theoretically sophisticated; nevertheless, this kind of approach has been used successfully with even year 1 students who have investigated, for example, the kinds of texts produced in the course of certain social practices (e.g., being a school principal, being a shopkeeper, being a bus driver. See, for example, Heath 1983, 315–342). "Student as ethnographer" approaches have been shown repeatedly to enhance among other things students' conventional school-based assessment scores, even when such students are perceived by many to be most at risk as learners.[16] Perhaps adopting explicitly social and collaborative (rather than principally linguistic and/or direct teaching) approaches to language and learning in classrooms might create opportunities for countering the formulaic turn genre approaches to language education seem to have taken in Queensland primary schools. For example, teachers adopting a social and collaborative approach might have students explore a range of social practices and their accompanying texts that students themselves have collected or nominated. These explorations might meaningfully link these properties to past, present, and possible future social purposes and practices.

For example, Neil Anderson (1995), teaching at Monkland State Primary School, involves his year 5 students in—among myriad other things—scripting, producing, and advertising short animated movies created using Microsoft's *3-D Movie Maker* CD-ROM. Students also use desktop publishing software to create movie posters advertising their movies and invitations to their movie's world premiere. In this small country town, going to the cinema or watching videos is an important part of many of these students' lives. It is difficult, however, to assess the extent to which students regarded this work as purposeful and meaningful, although I am convinced that many of them developed at least some metalevel understandings of the language practices involved in producing and promoting a movie. Indeed, six or so students I spoke with commented on how making a movie changed the way they thought about television and films. They also commented on the kinds of language they had needed in order to "advertise" and promote their movie effectively (see also Knobel and Lankshear 1997).

Cummins and Sayers (1995) document a host of collaborative and interactive community projects that are mediated by electronic technologies and that span continents and levels of schooling (see also McWhirter 1996a, 1996b; Salza 1995). These kinds of projects, I am convinced, hold much potential for generating contexts and purposes for producing meaningful texts and for amplifying primary school students' opportunities for participating in a range of webs of interactive relationships. Accordingly, part of the future agenda I have set for myself as one outcome of the present study includes working with teachers and primary school students and using key concepts and methods from critical literacy, new technologies studies, and ethnography to develop effective approaches to language and literacy pedagogy. This work would make use of C. Wright Mills's (1959) concept of "sociological imagination." To have sociological imagination is to be able to relate biography and structure, which may be a condition for larger social imagining (cf. Lankshear 1997a; Searle 1993). This includes a sense of self as constituted by interactive webs of social relations and practices. I suspect this can be done with varying degrees of sophistication at all levels of primary schooling.

Although some would argue that these approaches are idealistic, documented outcomes of such pedagogy suggest otherwise.[17] Thus, as an educator interested in maximizing students' life chances and their general quality of life, I hold fast to sound educational practices such as those signposted above that aim for such outcomes. Nevertheless, as already mentioned, I am also well aware that there are a number of problems inherent in ethnographic or "sociologically imaginative" approaches to language education, not least of which is the danger that over-use may turn these approaches into just another way of "doing school." In addition, these kinds of projects may not always capture students' interests or imaginations, particularly when the ethnographic projects are designed by the teacher to meet particular syllabus directives and specific teaching agendas (cf. Morgan 1994). This is indeed a potential problem requiring further consideration and investigation.

So far I have discussed a number of possible ideas aimed at enhancing language and literacy education in classrooms. To finish here, however, would be to overlook a significant dimension of language and literacy education; that is, teacher education and the social construction of certain kinds of primary school teachers.

Implications for Teacher Education

In Queensland, there are two major institutions responsible for language and literacy teacher education: the universities, which provide undergraduate and postgraduate training, and Education Queensland. The respective education offices for Catholic, Lutheran, and other independent schools in Queensland also provide professional in-service opportunities. However, the following discussion focuses on Education Queensland because it is responsible for the majority of practicing teachers in this state.

Recent times have witnessed the introduction of a host of diagnostic and intervention programs and tests designed to "catch" and "fix" primary school students in year 2 and year 6 who are experiencing difficulties in reading and writing. These programs and batteries of tests include: the Year 2 Diagnostic Net, the Year 6 Test, Reading Recovery, and Support-A-Reader (and the next few years will see the introduction of national benchmark ascertainment protocols in years 3, 5, and 7 as described in chapter 1). Ironically, however, these various diagnostic and remedial packages are grounded chiefly in practices that value code-breaking rather than text use or text analysis (e.g., the focus is on accuracy in reading aloud, alphabet letter identification, word and single image matching, and scribing decontextualized dictations).

Implementation of these intervention and diagnostic programs has been dictated by political rather than by educational processes, with little teacher consultation. Consequently, large amounts of funding have been made available for training teachers as Reading Recovery specialists, and for resourcing intervention programs developed in response to the outcomes of the Year 2 Diagnostic Net and Year 6 Test. Ironically, little funding has been allocated to continuing English syllabus in-servicing programs, despite the recency of its implementation. The syllabus appears to be rapidly becoming a poor cousin in language and literacy stakes in Queensland, and teachers have already expressed confusion as to which documents they are to be held accountable to. This confusion can only increase with the introduction of benchmarking protocols and responsibilities.

Thus, teacher education in universities may hold possibilities for addressing some of the theoretical and pedagogical tensions that exist in language education in Queensland (cf. Freebody 1993). For example, teacher educators, especially those working at undergraduate levels, could work towards providing student-teachers with the wherewithal to critique and modify where necessary current moves in language and education in Queensland and elsewhere. This includes the need for them to have a sound sociocultural theory of language and literacy, and a concomitant theory of how best to teach language and literacy in primary school classrooms.

D/discourses, social change, and student-teachers. Like classroom teachers, student-teachers are coordinated and constituted by a diverse array of Discourses and any suggestions for enhancing language and literacy education must necessarily take these into account. Accordingly, it seems to me that student-teachers may also benefit from opportunities to investigate language and literacy pedagogy in explicitly social, rather than only textual, ways. One possible approach may be to involve student-teachers in investigating interrelationships among the individual, discourses, and the social (i.e., Discourses). This could be done by a number of means, including: short-term individual or small group studies of primary school students' language practices, or student-teachers' analyses of case studies of students similar to those generated in this book.

For example, I am already using all four cases from the present study in lectures and tutorials to encourage student-teachers to think about the range of language and social practices their own students may bring to the classroom, and how this compares with the range promoted in, say, the Queensland English syllabus, or with the proficiencies identified on the Year 2 Diagnostic Net Reading and Writing Developmental Continua or the new Benchmark Statements, or with the types of exercises set for the Year 6 Test.

In my teaching, I aim to engage student-teachers in developing their own metalevel understandings of classrooms as socially constructed contexts, and how the Discourses coordinating classroom practices also coordinate what counts as "being literate." This is not a straightforward matter, given the complexities and constraints characterizing primary teacher education as currently configured in many Australian universities. Moreover, it is difficult to know the degree to which these student-teachers would use metalevel and sociocultural understandings of language and social practices obtained at university in their own classrooms. Nevertheless, this remains an avenue worth pursuing in my subsequent teaching and research.

In addition, numerous educators have trialed collaborative working relationships among schools and faculties of education, with mixed degrees of success. Perhaps one of the most promising models of such collaboration is that enacted by the Santa Barbara Classroom Discourse Group and a number of schools throughout Santa Barbara.[18] Although the university students involved in these collaborations are generally postgraduate students, I believe there is much in this model that could be transferred successfully to undergraduate teacher education. In the Santa Barbara Classroom Discourse Group model, teachers, lecturers, and university students work towards a common aim of establishing effective learning opportunities for primary and secondary school students that link in various ways with the wider community. Emphasis is on inquiry and analysis rather than on content in these classrooms.

For example, in one grade 5 class, students are equipped with ethnographic strategies for gathering and sorting information about themselves and their communities, and provided with historiography techniques for documenting changes in (role-played or imagined) groups or practices over time (Lin 1993). There are exciting possibilities within this model for developing critical social literacy strategies with these primary school students, who hail from diverse cultural and experiential backgrounds. Moves in this direction are underway, for example, with the Tolerance Project which includes investigating different "points of view" in event reporting (e.g., Yeager, Floriani, and Green 1997).

Other programs, such as those reported by Heath and McLaughlin (1994), model effective ways of working with inner city students' funds of knowledge and their everyday lives within particular communities. Graduate students are also involved in these programs, and learn much in the process.

Student-teachers may also benefit from learning experiences similar to those outlined earlier for primary school students whereby student-teachers are provided with opportunities for exploring everyday language practices in a wide range of contexts. This may include, for example, finding ways of apprenticing student-teachers to meaningful ways of teaching language and literacy in a period marked by a proliferation of computer-mediated communication and information sharing. The International Education and Research Network (I*EARN) and its community oriented projects, as more examples, appear to hold much potential for facilitating such apprenticeships in teacher education courses (cf. Salza 1995).

There are, however, a number of drawbacks and constraints accompanying these kinds of collaborations. Often they are extremely labor intensive for everyone involved, and usually require long-term commitments from schools and university departments and stability of conditions and personnel. Funding is also an issue to be considered; at present in Queensland and elsewhere in Australia, classroom teachers receive payment for each student-teacher they have in their class. The kind of collaboration I have in mind would not work under this existing model. Despite these problems, I am convinced there is room in Brisbane and elsewhere for developing fruitful collaborative interrelationships among primary school students, classroom teachers, student-teachers, and university teachers. This is an important ongoing agenda for my own continuing work within language and literacy education.

A (PROVISIONAL) CONCLUSION

Recent state-mandated approaches to language and literacy education such as Reading Recovery, the Year 2 Diagnostic Net, the Year 6 Test, and the years 3 and 5 benchmarks and aspects of the Queensland English syllabus jar with current and widespread sociocultural understandings of language literacy, and what it means to be literate in present times. Approaches to language and literacy education that are out of touch with "new times" face serious problems of legitimation. In addition, already marginalized groups will be even more disadvantaged by quick fix reading and writing diagnoses and "a national crusade for education standards" (Clinton 1997 n.p.) that continue to promote literacy "excellence" as an economic and moral imperative. Indeed, "[i]n an economic climate that, rightly or wrongly, equates literacy with economic productivity and in a cultural climate that equates literacy with moral virtue—economically and culturally marginal groups are all too easily written off in terms of literacy 'deficits' or 'lacks' " (Luke and Freebody 1997, 221).

Within this concluding chapter I have attempted to sketch some ideas for further work in a number of feasible directions within language education in Queensland and perhaps elsewhere. None of the ideas I present poses as an answer to the dilemmas raised in trying to explore—possibly somewhat idealistically—what exemplary language and literacy practices in classrooms might look like. Perhaps the only possible response to make is that any investigation into language and social practices is necessarily complex. This, I believe, has been a strength of the present study. Investigations of language and social practices, I have found, are at once frustrating and intriguing, and there is always room for pushing beyond current formulations of language as a social practice in our attempts to more fully understand ourselves as social beings who construct and are constructed by the language we use in our everyday lives.

Endnotes

1. Claims and interpretations that could not be supported in these ways were abandoned or cast as suppositions. This is yet another hidden aspect of research and reporting.

2. See, for example, among many others: Christian-Smith ed. 1993; Davies 1989, 1993, 1997; Delamont 1990; Gilbert 1991, 1992; Gilbert and Taylor 1991; Graddol and Swann 1989; Henriques et al. 1984; McLaren 1993; McRobbie 1994; Swann 1993; Walkerdine 1981, 1985.

3. In developing his theory of D/discourses, Gee draws explicitly on the work of social psychologists such as Scribner and Cole, Vygotsky, Wertsch, and cognitive scientists such as Knorr-Cetina, Churchland, and Johnson, to name a few. To this list I would also add: Brown and Gilligan 1992; Lave and Wenger 1991; Moll 1992; Rogoff 1990, 1995; Rogoff and Lave 1984; Walkerdine 1985, 1988, 1996a.

4. See, for example, among many others: Breen et al. 1994; Cairney, Lowe, and Sproats 1994; Cazden 1988; Cook-Gumperz 1993; Davies 1997; Delgado-Gaitan 1990, 1993; Freebody, Ludwig, and Gunn 1996; Gutierrez, Rymes, and Larson 1995; Heath 1982, 1983; Heath and McLaughlin 1994; Hull and Rose 1994; Lesko 1988; McLaren 1993; Michaels 1986; Moll 1992; Rose 1989.

5. Interestingly, only Nicholas among his mates seemed to be able to — or want to —move freely through the various constellations of students in year 7 and other grade levels.

6. Previously known as the "Department of Education, Queensland."

7. See, for example, among many others: Bigum and Green 1992; Cummins and Sayers 1995; Freebody 1992; Lankshear 1997a, 1997b; New London Group 1996; Taylor and Saarinen 1994; Walkerdine 1990.

8. See, for example: Anderson 1995; Bigum and Green 1992; Bigum and Kenway 1997.

9. See, for example: Fitzclarence, Green, and Bigum 1994; Green, Reid, and Bigum 1997; Smith and Curtin 1997.

10. <http://digitarts.va.com.au>

11. <http://www.ps.odyssey.com.au/GRUV/contact/confama.htm>
12. <http://www.ps.odyssey.com.au/GRUV/vvalley/welcome.htm>
13. <http://www.ps.odyssey.com.au/GRUV/vvalley/phase2.htm>
14. In addition, the degree to which participating in this project has impacted on Layla can never be ascertained, but neither can it be dismissed entirely.
15. See, for example, among many others: Darder 1991; Green and Yeager 1995; Heath and McLaughlin 1994; Heath and Mangiola 1991; Moll 1992; Thomas and Maybin 1997; Torres 1997.
16. See, for example among others: Anderson and Irvine 1993; Egan-Robertson and Bloome eds. 1997; Green and Yeager 1995; Heath 1983; Heath and Mangiola 1991; Hull and Rose 1994; Irvine and Elsasser 1988.
17. See, for example, the important work already done by: Michael and Ludmila Doneman (<http://mwk.thehub.com.au>); Chris Searle and his school community (1993); teachers documented by Cummins and Sayers (1995); and project leaders reported by Howard Rheingold (1994).
18. See, for example: Floriani 1993; Green and Yeager 1995; Lin 1993; Putney 1996; Santa Barbara Classroom Discourse Group 1994.

REFERENCE LIST

Alloway, N., B. Davies, P. Gilbert, R. Gilbert, and D. King 1996. *Boys and Literacy: Meeting the Challenge*. Canberra: Commonwealth of Australia.

Anderson, G. and P. Irvine 1993. Informing critical literacy with ethnography. In *Critical Literacy: Politics, Praxis, and the Postmodern*, eds. C. Lankshear and P. McLaren. Albany, NY: State U. of New York. 81–104.

Anderson, N. 1995. *When Technology and Equity Become Partners*. Special Program Schools Scheme. Brisbane: Wide Bay S.P.S.S. Regional Project.

Arnett, J. 1995. Adolescents' uses of media for self-socialisation. *Journal of Youth and Adolescence*. 24(5): 519–533.

Aronowitz, S. and W. DiFazio 1994. *The Jobless Future: SciTech and the Dogma of Work*. Minneapolis, MN: U. of Minnesota Press.

Baker, C. 1991a. Reading the texts of reading lessons. *Australian Journal of Reading*. 14(1): 5–20.

———1991b. Classroom literacy events. *Australian Journal of Reading*. 14 (2): 103–108.

———1996. Transcription and representation in literacy research. In *Handbook of Research on Teaching Literacy Through the Communicative and Visual Arts*, eds. J. Flood, S. Heath, and D. Lapp. New York: Macmillan. 110–120.

Baker, C. and P. Freebody 1989. *Children's First Schoolbooks: Introductions to the Culture of Literacy*. Oxford: Blackwell.

Baker, D. 1997. Response. Good news, bad news, and international comparisons: Comment on Bracey. *Educational Researcher*. 26(3): 16–18.

Barton, D. 1994. *Literacy: An Introduction to the Ecology of Written Language*. Oxford: Blackwell.

Baynham, M. 1995. *Literacy Practices: Investigating Literacy in Social Contexts*. London: Routledge.

Bazerman, C. 1992. Where is the classroom? In *Learning and Teaching Genre*, eds. A. Freedman and P. Medway. Portsmouth, NH: Boynton/Cook. 25–30.

Beaumont, S. 1995. Adolescent girls' conversations with mothers and friends: A matter of style. *Discourse Processes*. 20: 109–132.

Beckford, J. 1975. *The Trumpet of Prophecy: A Sociological Study of Jehovah's Witnesses*. London: Blackwell.

Bennett, A. 1993. Review of *Social Linguistics and Literacies: Ideology in Discourses* by J. Gee. *Language in Society*. 22(4): 572–576.

Berman, S. 1993. *Catch Them Thinking in Science: A Handbook of Classroom Strategies*. Sydney: Harker Brown Education.

Bigum, C. and B. Green 1992. Technologizing literacy: The dark side of the dream. *Discourse: The Australian Journal of Educational Studies*. 12(2): 4–28.

Bigum, C. and J. Kenway 1997. New information technologies and the ambiguous future of schooling—some possible scenarios. In *International Handbook of Educational Change*, eds. A. Hargreaves, A. Lieberman, M. Fullan, and D. Hopkins. Toronto: OISE.

Birch, I. and D. Smart 1990. Economic rationalism and the politics of education in Australia. In *Education Politics for the New Century: The Twentieth Anniversary Yearbook of the Politics of Education Association*, eds. D. Mitchell and M. Goertz. London: Falmer Press. 137–152.

Black Voices. Featuring theatre companies working with Aboriginal young people. (cited 9 October, 1997).
<http://www.ps.odyssey.com.au/ps/GRUV/black/blkhome.htm>

Bleicher, R. 1993. Learning Science in the Workplace: Ethnographic Accounts of High School Students as Apprentices in University Research Laboratories. Unpublished doctoral thesis. Santa Barbara: U. of California at Santa Barbara.

Bloome, D. 1989. Beyond access: An ethnographic study of reading and writing in a seventh grade classroom. In *Classrooms and Literacy*, ed. D. Bloome. Norwood, NJ: Ablex. 53–106.

Bloome, D. and A. Egan-Robertson 1993. The social construction of intertexuality in classroom reading and writing lessons. *Reading Research Quarterly*. 28(4): 304–333.

Bloome, D., D. Sheridan, and B. Street 1993. *Reading Mass-Observation Writing: Theoretical and Methodological Issues in Researching the Mass-Observation Archive*. Mass-Observation Archive Occasional Paper No. 1. Sussex: U. of Sussex.

Bloome, D. and E. Theodorou 1988. Analyzing teacher-student and student-student discourse. In *Multiple Perspective Analyses of Classroom Discourse*, eds. J. Green and J. Harker. Norwood, NJ: Ablex. 217–248.

Bourdieu, P. 1977. Cultural reproduction and social reproduction. In *Power and Ideology in Education*, eds. J. Karabel and A. Halsey. New York: Oxford U. Press.

Bowers, J. and K. Iwi 1993. The discursive construction of society. *Discourse and Society*. 4(3): 337–393.

Bracey, G. 1997. Rejoinder. On comparing the incomparable: A response to Baker and Stedman. *Educational Researcher*. 26(3): 19–26.

Breen, M., W. Louden, C. Barratt-Pugh, J. Rivalland, M. Rohl, M. Rhydwen, S. Lloyd, and T. Carr 1994. *Literacy in Its Place: An Investigation of Literacy Practices in Urban and Rural Communities*. Canberra: Department of Employment, Education and Training.

Brodkey, L. 1992. Articulating poststructural theory in research on literacy. In *Multidisciplinary Perspectives on Literacy Research*, eds. R. Beach, J. Green, M. Kamil, and T. Shanahan. Urbana, IL: NCRE/NCTE. 293–318.

Brown, L. and C. Gilligan 1992. *Meeting at the Crossroads: Women's Psychology and Girls' Development*. Cambridge: Harvard U. Press.

Brown, P. and S. Levinson 1987. *Politeness: Some Universals in Language Usage*. Cambridge: Cambridge U. Press.

Brown, M., S. Leavold, D. Tate, and S. Wright eds. 1994. *Literacies and the Workplace: A Collection of Original Essays*. Deakin, VIC: Deakin U. Press.

Buchbinder, D. 1994. Mateship, *Gallipoli* and the eternal masculine. In *Representation, Discourse and Desire: Contemporary Australian Culture and Critical Theory*, ed. P. Fuery. Melbourne: Longman Cheshire. 115–137.

Buckingham, D. and J. Sefton-Green 1994. *Cultural Studies Goes to School: Reading and Teaching Popular Media*. London: Taylor and Francis.

Burbules, N. 1997. Misinformation, messed-up information and mostly useless information: How to avoid getting tangled up in the world wide web. Invited presentation to the Faculty of Education, Queensland U. of Technology. Brisbane, 15 July.

Burbules, N. and T. Callister 1996. Knowledge at the crossroads: Some alternative futures of hypertext learning environments. *Educational Theory*. 46(1): 23–50.

Cairney, T., K. Lowe, and R. Sproats 1994. *Literacy in Transition: An Evaluation of Literacy Practices in Upper Primary and Junior Secondary Schools*, Vol. 1–3. Canberra, ACT: Department of Employment, Education and Training.

Cameron, D. 1985. *Feminism and Linguistic Theory*. London: Macmillan.

——— ed. 1990. *Feminist Critique of Language*. London: Routledge.

Carnoy, M. 1993. Multinationals in a changing world economy: Whither the nation-state? In *The New Global Economy in the Information Age: Reflections on Our Changing World*, eds. M. Carnoy, M. Castells, S. Cohen, and H. Cardoso. University Park, PA: Pennsylvania State U. Press. 45–96.

Carr, J. 1996. The Queensland English Syllabus for Years 1 to 10 and its implementation. *English in Australia*. 116: 38–42.

Carrington, K. and A. Bennett 1996. "Girls' mags" and the pedagogical formation of the girl. In *Feminisms and Pedagogies of Everyday Life*, ed. C. Luke. Albany, NY: State U. of New York. 142–166.

Carspecken, P. 1996. *Critical Ethnography in Educational Research: A Theoretical and Practical Guide*. New York: Routledge.

Cazden, C. 1988. *Classroom Discourse: The Language of Teaching and Learning*. Portsmouth, NH: Heinemann.

———1993. A Report on Reports: Two Dilemmas of Genre Teaching. Paper presented at Working with Genre III. Strictly Genre? Literacies, Communities, Schools. Literacy and Education Research Network National Conference. Sydney, May 21–23.

Christian-Smith, L. 1993. *Texts of Desire: Essays on Fiction, Femininity and Schooling*. London: Falmer Press.

Christie, F. 1987. Genres as choice. In *The Place of Genre in Learning: Current Debates*, ed. I. Reid. Typereader Publications No. 1. Deakin, VIC: Centre for Studies in Literacy Education. 22–34.

───── 1989. Genres as social processes. Paper presented at the Literacy and Education Research Network Working With Genre Conference. Sydney, 25–26 November.

───── ed. 1990. *Literacy for a Changing World*. Hawthorn, VIC: Australian Council for Educational Research.

───── and J. Rothery 1989. Genres and writing: A response to Michael Rosen. *English in Australia*. 91: 8–12.

Clinton, W. 1997. Text of the state of the union address. *Washington Post*. February 5. Downloaded 20 February, 1997: <http://www.washingtonpost.com/wp-srv/national/longterm/union/uniontext.htm>

Clough, P. 1992. *The End(s) of Ethnography: From Realism to Social Criticism*. Newbury Park, CA: Sage.

Coffey, A. 1996. The power of accounts: Authority and authorship in ethnography. *Qualitative Studies in Education*. 9(1): 61–74.

Collins, J. and S. Michaels 1986. Speaking and writing: Discourse strategies and the acquisition of literacy. In *The Social Construction of Literacy*, ed. J. Cook-Gumperz. Cambridge: Cambridge U. Press. 207–222.

Connell, R. 1995. *Masculinities*. St Leonards, NSW: Allen and Unwin.

Cook-Gumperz, J. ed. 1986. *The Social Construction of Literacy*. Cambridge: Cambridge U. Press.

Cook-Gumperz, J. 1993. Dilemmas of identity: Oral and written literacies in the making of a basic writing student. *Anthropology and Education Quarterly*. 24(4): 336–356.

Cook-Gumperz, J. and J. Gumperz 1992. Changing views of language in education. In *Multidisciplinary Perspectives on Literacy Research*, eds. R. Beach, J. Green, M. Kamil, and T. Shanahan. Urbana, IL: NCRE/NCTE. 151–179.

Cope, B. and M. Kalantzis eds. 1993. *The Powers of Literacy: A Genre Approach to Teaching Writing*. London: Falmer Press.

Cranny-Francis, A. 1992. The value of 'genre' in English literature teaching. *English in Australia*. 99: 27–48.

Cummins, J. and D. Sayers 1995. *Brave New Schools: Challenging Cultural Illiteracy Through Global Learning Networks*. New York: St. Martin's Press.

Curriculum Corporation 1994. *A Statement on English for Australian Schools*. Carlton, VIC: Curriculum Corporation.

———1997a. Improving the Literacy and Numeracy Skills of Young Australians—A National Plan. Canberra, ACT: Curriculum Corporation (draft).

———1997b. Years 3 and 5 Literacy (Writing, Spelling, Reading). Professional Elaboration for Ascertaining and Making Judgements About Student Achievements. Canberra, ACT: Curriculum Corporation (draft).

Darder, A. 1991. *Culture and Power in the Classroom: A Critical Foundation for Bicultural Education*. New York: Bergin and Garvey.

Davies, B. 1989. *Frogs and Snails and Feminist Tales: Preschool Children and Gender*. Sydney: Allen and Unwin.

———1993. *Shards of Glass: Children Reading and Writing Beyond Gendered Identities*. Sydney: Allen and Unwin.

Davies, B. 1997. *Power/Knowledge/Desire: Changing School Organisation and Management Practices*. Canberra, ACT: Department of Employment, Education, Training and Youth Affairs.

Dawkins, J. 1991. *Australia's Language: The Australian Language and Literacy Policy*. Canberra, ACT: Australian Government Publishing Service.

de Certeau, M. 1984. *The Practice of Everyday Life*. Berkeley, CA: U. of California Press.

Delamont, S. 1990. *Sex Roles and the School*, 2nd ed. New York: Routledge.

——— 1992. *Fieldwork in Educational Settings*. London: Falmer Press.

Delgado-Gaitan, C. 1990. *Literacy for Empowerment: The Role of Parents in Children's Education*. London: Falmer Press.

——— 1993. Researching change and changing the researcher. *Harvard Educational Review*. 63(4): 389–411.

Delpit, L. 1993. The politics of teaching literate children. In *Freedom's Plow: Teaching in the Multicultural Classroom*, eds. T. Perry and J. Fraser. New York: Routledge. 285–295.

——— 1995. *Other People's Children: Cultural Conflict in the Classroom*. New York: The New Press.

del Rio, P. and A. Alvarez 1995. Tossing, praying, and reasoning: The changing architectures of mind and agency. In *Sociocultural Studies of Mind*, eds. J. Wertsch, P. del Rio, and A. Alvarez. Cambridge: Cambridge U. Press. 215–248.

Department of Education, Queensland 1994. *English in Years 1 to 10 Queensland Syllabus Materials: English Syllabus for Years 1 to 10*. Brisbane: Department of Education.

———1996. *Talking—Our Way Into Literacy*. Brisbane: Department of Education (draft).

Der Derian, J. 1997. The simulation triangle. *21.C: Scanning the Future*. 24: 18–25.

Digitarts. <http://digitarts.vaa.com.au> (cited 9 October, 1997).

Doneman, M. and L. Doneman 1997. MWK 1.6 Pty Ltd: Convergence on a Shoestring. Brisbane, Australia. <http://mwk.thehub.com.au> (cited 3 October, 1997).

Egan-Robertson, A. and D. Bloome eds. 1997. *Students as Researchers of Culture and Language in Their Own Communities*. Cresskill, NJ: Hampton Press.

Emerson, R., R. Fretz, and L. Shaw 1996. *Writing Ethnographic Fieldnotes*. Chicago: U. of Chicago Press.

Erickson, F. 1992. Ethnographic microanalysis of interaction. In *The Handbook of Qualitative Research in Education*, eds. M. LeCompte, W. Millroy, and J. Preissle. San Diego, CA: Academic Press. 201–225.

———1996. Ethnographic microanalysis. In *Sociolinguistics and Language Teaching*, eds. S. McKay and N. Hornberger. Cambridge: Cambridge U. Press. 283–306.

Fairclough, N. 1989. *Language and Power*. London: Longman.

———1992. *Discourse and Social Change*. Oxford: Polity Press.

———1995. *Critical Discourse Analysis: Papers in the Critical Study of Language*. London: Longman.

———1996. Critical discourse analysis in the 1990s: Challenges and responses. In *Proceedings of the First International Conference on Discourse Analysis*, ed. E. Pedro. Lisbon: U. of Lisbon. 289–302.

Famaleez. Contact: Indigenous and Cross-Cultural Projects. <http://www.ps.odyssey.com.au/GRUV/contact/confama.htm> (cited 9 October, 1997).

Fasold, R. 1990. *The Sociolinguistics of Language*. Oxford: Basil Blackwell.
———1992. Sociolinguistics in linguistics. In *Sociolinguistics Today: International Perspectives*, eds. K. Bolton and H. Kwok. London: Routledge. 351–355.
Fetterman, D. 1989. *Ethnography: Step by Step*. Newbury Park, CA: Sage.
Figueroa, E. 1994. *Sociolinguistic Metatheory*. Oxford: Pergamon.
Fine, M. 1993. *Framing Dropouts: Notes on the Politics of an Urban Public High School*. Albany, NY: State U. of New York Press.
Fishman, J. 1972a. The relationship between micro- and macro-sociolinguistics in the study of who speaks what language to whom and when. In *Sociolinguistics: Selected Readings*, eds. J. Pride and J. Holmes. Harmondsworth: Penguin Education. 15–31.
———1972b. *The Sociology of Language: An Interdisciplinary Social Science Approach to Language in Society*. Rowley: Newbury House.
Fitzclarence, L., B. Green, and C. Bigum 1994. Stories in and out of class: Knowledge, identity and schooling. *After Postmodernism: Education, Politics and Identity*, eds. P. Wexler and R. Smith. London: Falmer Press. 131–155.
Floriani, A. 1993. Negotiating what counts: Roles and relationships, texts and contexts, content and meaning. *Linguistics and Education*. 5(2/3): 241–274.
Foucault, M. 1967. *Madness and Civilization*. London: Tavistock.
———1972. *The Archaeology of Knowledge*. London: Tavistock.
———1977. *Discipline and Punish*. London: Allen Lane.
Freebody, P. 1992. A socio-cultural approach: Resourcing four roles as a literacy learner. In *Prevention of Reading Failure*, eds. A. Watson and A. Badenhop. Sydney: Ashton Scholastic. 48–60.
———1993. Review of the Queensland School Curriculum: English. *Report of the Review of the Queensland School Curriculum*. Part A. Brisbane: Department of Education.
———1994. *Literacy Education: The Changing Interface of Research, Policy and Practice*. Brisbane: Faculty of Education, Griffith U.
Freebody, P., C. Ludwig, and S. Gunn 1996. *Everyday Literacy Practices In and Out of Schools in Low Socio-Economic Urban Communities*. Vol. 1. Canberra, ACT: Commonwealth Department of Employment, Education and Training.

Freebody, P. and A. Luke 1990. Literacies programmes: Debates and demands in the classroom. *Prospect: A Journal of Australian TESOL*. 11: 7–16.

Freebody, P. and A. Welch eds. 1993. *Knowledge, Culture and Power: International Perspectives on Literacy as Policy and Practice*. London: Falmer Press.

Garner, H. 1995. *The First Stone: Some Questions About Sex and Power*. Sydney: Picador.

Gee J. 1989. Literacy, discourse, and linguistics: An introduction. *Journal of Educational Review*. 58: 159–212.

———1990. *Social Linguistics and Literacies: Ideology in Discourses*. London: Falmer Press.

———1991a. What is literacy? In *Rewriting Literacy: Culture and the Discourse of the Other*, eds. C. Mitchell and K. Weiler. New York: Bergin and Garvey. 3–12.

———1991b. The narrativization of experience in the oral style. In *Rewriting Literacy: Culture and the Discourse of the Other*, eds. C. Mitchell and K. Weiler. New York: Bergin and Garvey. 77–102.

———1992a. Social gravity: Discourses and education. Paper presented at the Working Conference on Critical Literacy, Griffith U. Brisbane, 29 June–3 July.

———1992b. *The Social Mind: Language, Ideology, and Social Practice*. New York: Bergin and Garvey.

———1992/3. Literacies: Tuning into forms of life. *Education Australia*. 19–20: 12–13.

———1993a. Postmodernism and literacies. In *Critical Literacy: Politics, Praxis and the Postmodern*, eds. C. Lankshear and P. McLaren. Albany, NY: State U. of New York Press. 271–296.

———1993b. Critical literacy/socially perceptive literacy: A study of language in action. *Australian Journal of Language and Literacy*. 16(4): 333–356.

——— 1993c. Quality, science and the lifeworld. *Critical Forum*. 2(3): 13–14.

———1994a. *Quality, Science and the Lifeworld: The Alignment of Business and Education*. Focus Paper No. 4. Leichhardt, NSW: Adult Literacy and Basic Skills Coalition.

———1994b. New alignments and old literacies: Critical literacy, postmodernism and fast capitalism. In *Thinking Work: Theoretical Perspectives on Workers' Literacies*. Vol. 1, ed. P. O'Connor. Leichhardt, NSW: Adult Literacy and Basic Skills Coalition. 82–104.

———1994c. Discourses: Reflections on M. A. K. Halliday's 'Toward a language-based theory of learning.' *Linguistics and Education*. 6: 33–40.

———1996a. *Social Linguistics and Literacies: Ideology in Discourses*, 2nd ed. London: Falmer Press.

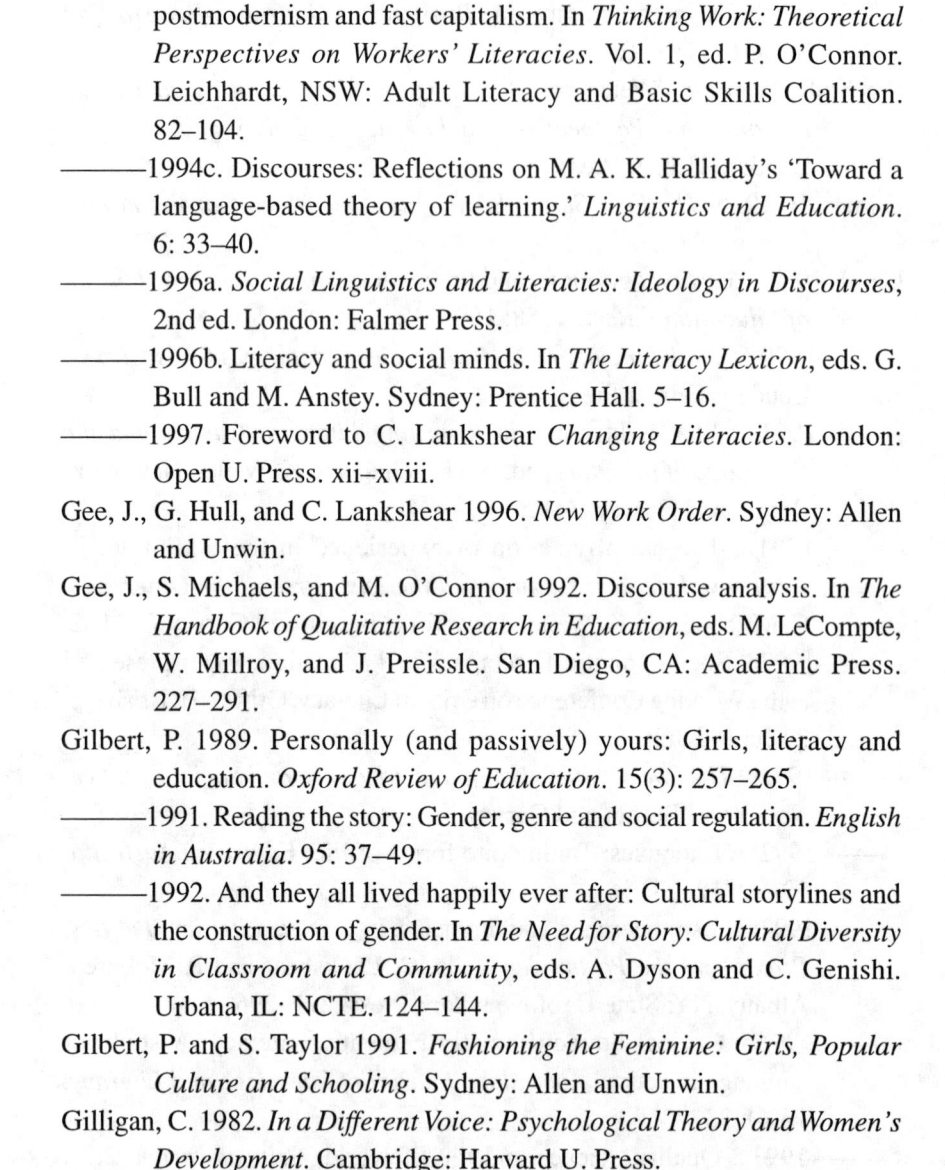

———1996b. Literacy and social minds. In *The Literacy Lexicon*, eds. G. Bull and M. Anstey. Sydney: Prentice Hall. 5–16.

———1997. Foreword to C. Lankshear *Changing Literacies*. London: Open U. Press. xii–xviii.

Gee, J., G. Hull, and C. Lankshear 1996. *New Work Order*. Sydney: Allen and Unwin.

Gee, J., S. Michaels, and M. O'Connor 1992. Discourse analysis. In *The Handbook of Qualitative Research in Education*, eds. M. LeCompte, W. Millroy, and J. Preissle. San Diego, CA: Academic Press. 227–291.

Gilbert, P. 1989. Personally (and passively) yours: Girls, literacy and education. *Oxford Review of Education*. 15(3): 257–265.

———1991. Reading the story: Gender, genre and social regulation. *English in Australia*. 95: 37–49.

———1992. And they all lived happily ever after: Cultural storylines and the construction of gender. In *The Need for Story: Cultural Diversity in Classroom and Community*, eds. A. Dyson and C. Genishi. Urbana, IL: NCTE. 124–144.

Gilbert, P. and S. Taylor 1991. *Fashioning the Feminine: Girls, Popular Culture and Schooling*. Sydney: Allen and Unwin.

Gilligan, C. 1982. *In a Different Voice: Psychological Theory and Women's Development*. Cambridge: Harvard U. Press.

———1990. Teaching Shakespeare's sister: Notes from the underground of female adolescence. In *Making Connections: The Relational World of Adolescent Girls at Emma Willard School*, eds. C. Gilligan, N. Lyons, and T. Hanmer. Boston: Harvard U. Press. 6–29.

Giroux, H. 1993. Literacy and the politics of difference. In *Critical Literacy: Politics, Praxis and the Postmodern*, eds. C. Lankshear and P. McLaren. New York: State U. of New York Press. 367–378.

———1995. Language, difference, and curriculum theory: Beyond the politics of clarity. In *Critical Theory and Educational Research*, eds. P. McLaren and J. Giarelli. New York: State U. of New York Press. 23–38.

———1996. *Fugitive Cultures: Race, Violence, and Youth*. New York: Routledge.

———1997a. *Channel Surfing: Race Talk and the Destruction of Today's Youth*. New York: St Martin's Press.

———1997b. Youth and the politics of representation: Response to Thomas Hatch's 'If the "kids" are not "alright," I'm "clueless",' *Educational Researcher*. 26(4): 27–30.

Giroux, H., C. Lankshear, P. McLaren, and M. Peters 1996. *Counternarratives: Cultural Studies and Critical Pedagogies in Postmodern Spaces*. New York: Routledge.

Goodson, I. 1995. *The Making of Curriculum: Collected Essays*, 2nd ed. London: Falmer Press.

Goffman, E. 1967. *Interaction Ritual*. New York: Anchor Books.

———1974. *Frame Analysis*. New York: Harper and Row.

Gotfrit, L. 1991. Women dancing back: Disruption and the politics of pleasure. In *Postmodernism, Feminism, and Cultural Politics: Redrawing Educational Boundaries*, ed. H. Giroux. Albany, NY: State U. of New York Press. 174–195.

Gowen, S. 1991. Beliefs about literacy: Measuring women into silence/hearing women into speech. *Discourse & Society*. 2(4): 439–450.

Graddol, D. and J. Swann 1989. *Gender Voices*. Oxford: Blackwell.

Graff, H. 1987. *The Labyrinths of Literacy: Reflections on Literacy Past and Present*. Philadelphia, PA: Falmer Press.

Green, B., J. Reid, and C. Bigum 1997. Teaching the Nintendo generation? Children, computer culture and popular technologies. In *Wired Up: Young People and the Electronic Media*, ed. S. Howard. London: Taylor and Francis.

Green, J. 1977. Pedagogical style differences as related to comprehension: Grades 1 through 3. Unpublished doctoral dissertation. Berkeley, CA: U. of California.

———1990. Reading is a social process. In *Social Context of Literacy*, eds. J. Howell, A. McNamara, and M. Clough. Selected papers from the 15th Australian Reading Association Conference. Canberra, ACT. 7–10 July. 104–123.

Green, J. and C. Dixon 1993. Talking knowledge into being: Discursive practices in classrooms. *Linguistics and Education.* 5(3/4): 231–239.

Green, J., M. Franquiz, and C. Dixon 1997. The myth of the objective transcript: Transcribing as a situated act. *TESOL Quarterly.* 31(1): 172–176.

Green, J. and C. Harker eds. 1988. *Multiple Perspective Analyses of Classroom Discourse.* Norwood, NJ: Ablex.

Green, J. and L. Meyer 1991. The embeddedness of reading in classroom life: Reading as a situated process. In T*owards a Critical Sociology of Reading Pedagogy: Papers of the XII World Congress on Reading*, eds. C. Baker and A. Luke. Amsterdam: John Benjamins. 141–160.

Green, J. and C. Wallat 1981. Mapping instructional conversations: A sociolinguistic ethnography. In *Ethnography and Language in Educational Settings*, eds. J. Green and C. Wallat. Norwood, NJ: Ablex. 161–205.

Green, J., R. Weade, and K. Graham, 1988. Lesson construction and student participation: A sociolinguistic analysis. In *Multiple Perspective Analyses of Classroom Discourse*, eds. J. Green and J. Harker. Norwood, NJ: Ablex. 11–48.

Green, J. and B. Yeager 1995. Constructing literate communities: Language and inquiry in bilingual classrooms. In *Celebrating Difference, Confronting Literacies*, ed. J. Murray. Carlton South, VIC: Australian Reading Association. 97–112.

Guba, E. and Y. Lincoln 1988. Naturalistic and rationalistic enquiry. In *Educational Research, Methodology, and Measurement: An International Handbook*, ed. J. Keeves. Oxford: Pergamon Press. 81–85.

Gumperz, J. 1971. On the ethnology of linguistic change. In *Sociolinguistics*, ed. W. Bright. Proceedings of the UCLA Sociolinguistics

Conference. Los Angeles: Center for Research in Languages and Linguistics. 25–49.
———1972. Introduction, pp. 1–25 in *Directions in Sociolinguistics: The Ethnography of Communication*, eds. J. Gumperz and D. Hymes. New York: Holt, Rinehart and Winston.
———1982a. *Discourse Strategies.* Cambridge: Cambridge U. Press.
———ed. 1982b. *Language and Social Identity.* Cambridge: Cambridge U. Press.
———and D. Hymes eds. 1972. *Directions in Sociolinguistics: The Ethnography of Communication.* New York: Holt, Rinehart and Winston.
Gutierrez, K. 1993. How talk, context, and script shape contexts for learning: A cross-case comparison of journal sharing. *Linguistics and Education.* 5(3/4): 335–365.
Gutierrez, K., B. Rymes, and J. Larson 1995. Script, counterscript, and underlife in the classroom: James Brown versus Brown v. Board of Education. *Harvard Educational Review.* 65(3): 417–445.
Gutierrez, K. and L. Stone 1997. A cultural-historical view of learning and learning disabilities: Participating in a community of learners. *Learning Disabilities: Research and Practice.* 12(2): 123–131.
Hall, S. 1991. Brave new world. *Socialist Review.* 21(1): 57–64.
Halliday, M. 1978. *Language as Social Semiotic.* London: Edward Arnold.
———1985. *An Introduction to Functional Grammar.* London: Edward Arnold.
Haraway, D. 1991. *Simians, Cyborgs and Women: The Reinvention of Nature.* New York: Routledge.
Harris, K. 1979. *Education and Knowledge: The Structured Misrepresentation of Knowledge.* London: Routledge and Kegan Paul.
Hasan, R. and G. Perrett, 1994. Learning to function with the other tongue: A systemic functional perspective on second language teaching. In *Perspectives on Pedagogical Grammar*, ed. T. Odlin. Cambridge: Cambridge U. Press. 179–226.
Hatch, E. 1992. *Discourse and Language Education.* New York: Cambridge U. Press.
Heath, S. 1982. What no bedtime story means: Narrative skills at home and school. *Language and Society.* 11: 49–76.

———1983. *Ways With Words: Language, Life and Work in Community and Classrooms*. Cambridge: Cambridge U. Press.

———1992. The multicultural classroom: Readings for content-area teachers. In *Socio-Cultural Contexts of Language Development: Implications for the Classroom*, eds. P. Richard-Amato and M. Snow. Longman: New York. 102–125.

Heath, S. and L. Mangiola 1991. *Children of Promise: Literate Activity in Linguistically and Culturally Diverse Classrooms*. Washington, DC: National Education Association of the United States.

Heath, S. and M. McLaughlin 1994. Learning for anything everyday. *Journal of Curriculum Studies*. 26(5): 471–489.

Henriques, J., W. Hollway, C. Urwin, C. Venn, and V. Walkerdine 1984. *Changing the Subject*. New York: Methuen.

Heras, A. 1993. The construction of understanding in a sixth-grade bilingual classroom. *Linguistics and Education*. 5(3/4): 275–299.

Heritage, J. 1984a. *Garfinkel and Ethnomethodology*. Cambridge, MA: Polity Press.

Heritage, J. 1984b. *Recent Developments in Conversation Analysis*. Warwick Working Papers in Sociology. Coventry: U. of Warwick.

Herrnstein, R. and C. Murray 1994. *The Bell Curve*. New York: The Free Press.

Hinkson, J. 1991. *Postmodernity: State and Education*. Deakin, VIC: Deakin U. Press.

Hirsch, E. 1987. *Cultural Literacy: What Every American Needs to Know*. Boston: Houghton Mifflin.

Hodge, R. and G. Kress 1988. *Social Semiotics*. Cambridge, UK: Polity Press.

Howe, N. and B. Strauss 1993. *13th Gen: Abort, Retry, Ignore, Fail?* New York: Vintage Books.

Hull, G. 1993. Hearing other voices: A critical assessment of popular views on literacy and work. *Harvard Educational Review*. 63(1): 20–49.

Hull, G. and M. Rose 1994. 'This wooden shack place:' The logic of unconventional reading. In *Theoretical Models and Processes of Reading*, 4th ed, eds. R. Ruddell, M. Ruddell, and H. Singer. Newark, DE: International Reading Association. 231–243.

Hymes, D. 1971. Sociolinguistics and the ethnography of speaking. In *Social Anthropology and Language*, ed. E. Ardener. London: Tavistock Publications. 47–94.

———1972. Models of the interaction of language and social life. In *Directions in Sociolinguistics: The Ethnography of Communication*, eds. J. Gumperz and D. Hymes. New York: Holt, Rinehart and Winston. 35–71.

———1974. *Foundations in Sociolinguistics: An Ethnographic Approach*. Philadelphia, PA: U. of Pennsylvania Press.

———1996. *Ethnography, Linguistics, Narrative Inequality: Toward an Understanding of Voice*. London: Taylor and Francis.

Irvine, P. and N. Elsasser 1988. The ecology of literacy: Negotiating writing standards in a Caribbean setting. In *The Social Construction of Written Communication*, eds. B. Bennett and D. Rubin. Norwood, NJ: Ablex. 304–320.

Janks, H. and R. Ivanic 1992. Critical language awareness and emancipatory discourse. In *Critical Language Awareness*, ed. N. Fairclough. London: Longman. 305–331.

Jones, A. 1986. At school I've got a chance: Ideology and social reproduction in a secondary school. Unpublished doctoral thesis. Auckland U. Auckland.

———1993. Becoming a 'girl': Post-structuralist suggestions for educational research. *Gender and Education*. 5(2): 157–166.

Kamler, B. 1994. Resisting oppositions in writing pedagogy or what process-genre debate? *Idiom*. 2: 14–18.

Kantor, R., J. Green, M. Bradley, and L. Lin 1992. The construction of schooled discourse repertoires: An interactional sociolinguistic perspective on learning to talk in preschool. *Linguistics and Education*. 4(2): 131–172.

Kellner, D. 1991. Reading images critically: Towards a postmodern pedagogy. In *Postmodernism, Feminism, and Cultural Politics: Redrawing Educational Boundaries*, ed. H. Giroux. New York: State U. of New York Press. 60–82.

———1995. *Media Culture: Cultural Studies, Identity and Politics Between the Modern and the Postmodern*. London: Routledge.

Kemp, D. 1997. *The National Literacy Policy for Australia: Commonwealth Program of Action for Literacy and Language Education.* Belconnen, ACT: Language Australia.

Kempe, A., M. Anstey, G. Bull, and P. White-Davison 1995–6. *Literacy in the National Curriculum: Professional Development for Teachers.* Toowoomba, QLD: Darling Downs Council of the Australian Reading Association and the U. of Southern Queensland.

Kincheloe, J. and P. McLaren, 1994. Rethinking critical theory and qualitative research. In *Handbook of Qualitative Research*, eds. N. Denzin and Y. Lincoln. Thousand Oaks, CA: Sage. 139–157.

Kincheloe, J., S. Steinberg, and A. Gresson eds. 1996. *Measured Lies: The Bell Curve Examined.* New York: St. Martin's Press.

Knapp, P. 1989. A context for genre theory. Paper presented at the Literacy and Education Research Network Conference. U. of Technology. Sydney, 25–26 November. 45–48.

Knobel, M. 1997. Language and Social Practices in Four Adolescents' Everyday Lives. Unpublished doctoral thesis. Brisbane: Faculty of Education, Queensland U. of Technology.

Knobel, M. and C. Lankshear 1995. *Learning Genres: Prospects for Empowerment.* Brisbane: National Language and Literacy Institute of Australia Child Literacy Research Node of Queensland.

———1997. Ways with windows: What different people do with the same equipment. In *Language, Learning and Culture: Unsettling Certainties. Conference Proceedings.* Joint national conference of the Australian Association for the Teaching of English, the Australian Literacy Educators' Association, and the Australian School Library Association. Darwin, 8–11 July. 182–202.

Krashen, S. 1982. *Principles and Practice in Second Language Acquisition.* Hayward, CA: Alemany Press.

———1985. *Inquiries and Insights.* Hayward, CA: Alemany Press.

Kress, G. 1985. *Linguistic Processes in Sociocultural Practice.* Deakin, VIC: Deakin U. Press.

———1987. Genre in a social theory of language: A reply to John Dixon. In *The Place of Genre in Learning: Current Debates*, ed. I. Reid. Deakin, VIC: Deakin U. Press. 35–45.

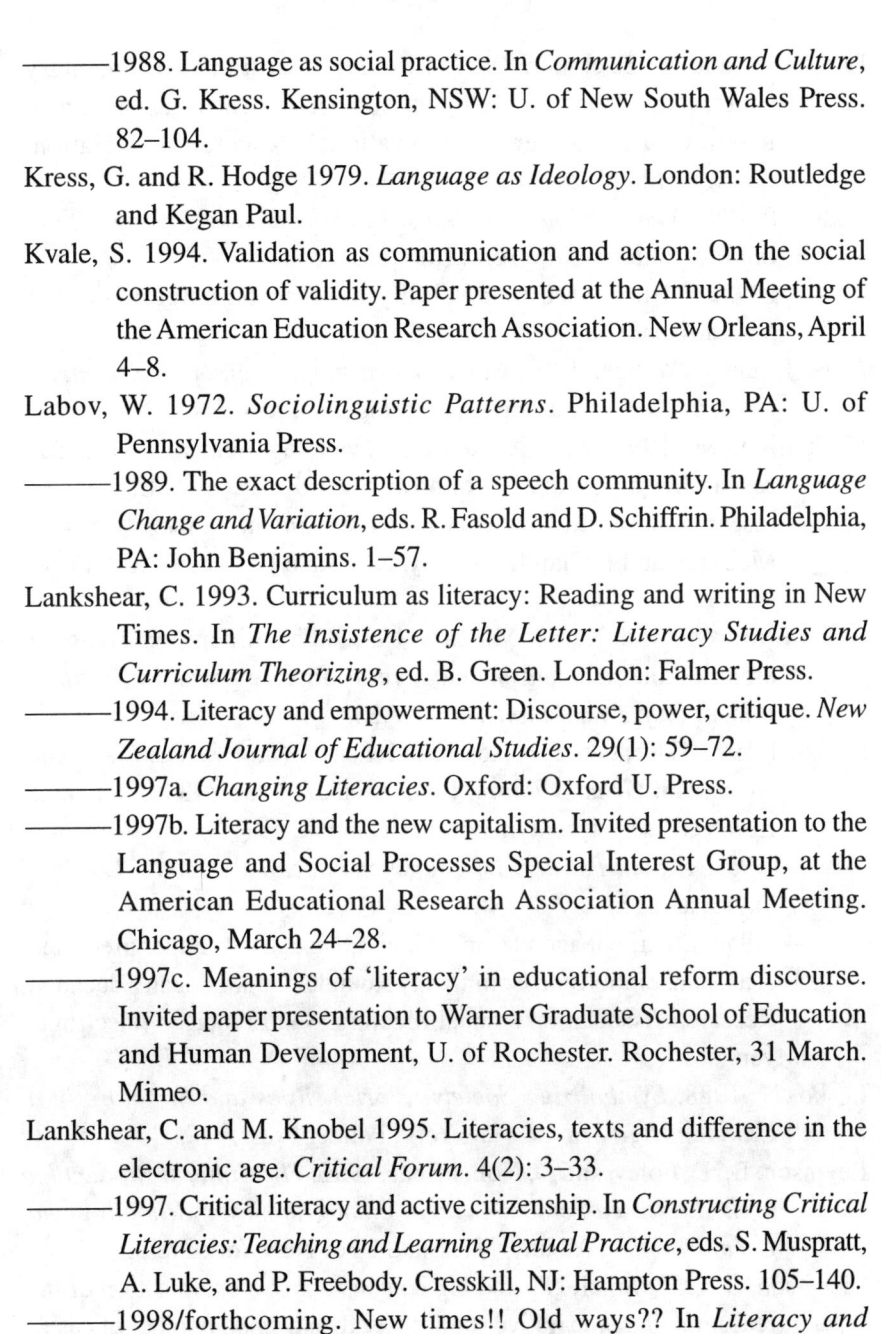

———1988. Language as social practice. In *Communication and Culture*, ed. G. Kress. Kensington, NSW: U. of New South Wales Press. 82–104.

Kress, G. and R. Hodge 1979. *Language as Ideology*. London: Routledge and Kegan Paul.

Kvale, S. 1994. Validation as communication and action: On the social construction of validity. Paper presented at the Annual Meeting of the American Education Research Association. New Orleans, April 4–8.

Labov, W. 1972. *Sociolinguistic Patterns*. Philadelphia, PA: U. of Pennsylvania Press.

———1989. The exact description of a speech community. In *Language Change and Variation*, eds. R. Fasold and D. Schiffrin. Philadelphia, PA: John Benjamins. 1–57.

Lankshear, C. 1993. Curriculum as literacy: Reading and writing in New Times. In *The Insistence of the Letter: Literacy Studies and Curriculum Theorizing*, ed. B. Green. London: Falmer Press.

———1994. Literacy and empowerment: Discourse, power, critique. *New Zealand Journal of Educational Studies*. 29(1): 59–72.

———1997a. *Changing Literacies*. Oxford: Oxford U. Press.

———1997b. Literacy and the new capitalism. Invited presentation to the Language and Social Processes Special Interest Group, at the American Educational Research Association Annual Meeting. Chicago, March 24–28.

———1997c. Meanings of 'literacy' in educational reform discourse. Invited paper presentation to Warner Graduate School of Education and Human Development, U. of Rochester. Rochester, 31 March. Mimeo.

Lankshear, C. and M. Knobel 1995. Literacies, texts and difference in the electronic age. *Critical Forum*. 4(2): 3–33.

———1997. Critical literacy and active citizenship. In *Constructing Critical Literacies: Teaching and Learning Textual Practice*, eds. S. Muspratt, A. Luke, and P. Freebody. Cresskill, NJ: Hampton Press. 105–140.

———1998/forthcoming. New times!! Old ways?? In *Literacy and Schooling*, eds. F. Christie and R. Misson. London: Routledge.

Larson, J. and N. Peckham 1997. Literacy Learning in Elementary Classrooms: Rhetoric or Reality? Paper presented at the annual meeting of the American Educational Research Association. Chicago, March 24–28.

Lather, P. 1991. *Getting Smart: Feminist Research and Pedagogy With/in the Postmodern*. New York: Routledge.

——1993. Fertile obsession: Validity after poststructuralism. *The Sociological Quarterly*. 34(4): 673–693.

Lave, J. and E. Wenger 1991. *Situated Learning: Legitimate Peripheral Participation*. Cambridge: Cambridge U. Press.

LeCompte, M. 1995. Some notes on power, agenda, and voice: A researcher's personal evolution toward critical collaborative research. In *Critical Theory and Educational Research*, eds. P. McLaren and J. Giarelli. Albany, NY: State U. of New York Press. 91–112.

LeCompte, M. and K. de Marrais 1992. The disempowering of empowerment: From social revolution to classroom rhetoric. *Educational Foundations*. 6(3): 5–33.

Lemke, J. 1993. Education, cyberspace, and change. *The Arachnet Electronic Journal on Virtual Culture*. 1(1). (cited 22, March 1994) Available from: <listserv@kentvm.edu> File: lemke v1n1.

——1995a. *Textual Politics: Discourse and Social Dynamics*. London: Taylor and Francis.

——1995b. Emergent agendas in collaborative activity. Paper presented at a Collaboration and Community Roundtable. American Education Research Association Annual Meeting. San Francisco [electronic version].

Lesko, N. 1988. *Symbolizing Society: Stories, Rites and Structure in a Catholic High School*. New York: Falmer Press.

Levinson, B., D. Foley, and D. Holland eds. 1996. *The Cultural Production of the Educated Person: Critical Ethnographies of Schooling and Local Practice*. Albany, NY: State U. of New York Press.

Lieberson, S. 1992. Small N's and big conclusions: An examination of the reasoning in comparative studies based on a small number of cases. In *What Is a Case? Exploring the Foundations of Social Inquiry*, eds. C. Ragin and H. Becker. Cambridge: Cambridge U. Press. 105–118.

Lin, L. 1993. Language of and in the classroom: Constructing patterns of social life. *Linguistics and Education.* 5(3/4): 367–409.

Lincoln, Y. and E. Guba 1990. Judging the quality of case study reports. *Qualitative Studies in Education.* 3(1): 53–59.

Luke, A. 1992a. The body literate: Discourse and inscription in early literacy training. *Linguistics and Education.* 4: 107–129.

———1992b. Stories of social regulation: The micropolitics of classroom narrative. In *The Insistence of the Letter: Literacy and Curriculum Theorizing,* ed. B. Green. London: Falmer Press. 137–153.

———1993. Genres of power? Literacy education and the production of capital. In *Literacy in Society,* eds. R. Hasan and G. Williams. London: Longman.

Luke, A. and P. Freebody 1997. Shaping the social practices of reading. In *Constructing Critical Literacies: Teaching and Learning Textual Practice,* eds. S. Muspratt, A. Luke, and P. Freebody. Cresskill, NJ: Hampton Press.

Luke, C. 1993. Television curriculum and popular literacy: Feminine identity politics and family discourse. In *The Insistence of the Letter: Literacy Studies and Curriculum Theorizing,* ed. B. Green. London: Falmer Press. 175–194.

———1997. Media literacy and cultural studies. In *Constructing Critical Literacies: Teaching and Learning Textual Practice,* eds. S. Muspratt, A. Luke, and P. Freebody. Cresskill, NJ: Hampton Press.

Lumby, C. 1996. *Bad Girls: The Media, Sex and Feminism in the 90s.* Sydney: Allen and Unwin.

Macedo, D. 1993. Literacy for stupidification: The pedagogy of big lies. *Harvard Educational Review.* 63(2): 183–206.

———1994. *Literacies of Power: What Americans Are Not Allowed to Know.* Boulder, CO: Westview Press.

Macken, M. 1990. *A Genre-Based Approach to Teaching Writing. Years 3–6; An Approach to Writing K–12. Book 1: Introduction.* Literacy and Education Research Network and the Directorate of Studies. Sydney: NSW Department of School Education.

Macpherson, J. 1983. *The Feral Classroom: High School Students' Constructions of Reality.* Melbourne: Routledge and Kegan Paul.

Martin, J. 1985. *Factual Writing: Exploring and Challenging Social Reality.* Deakin, VIC: Deakin U. Press.

———1992. *English Text: System and Structure.* Philadelphia, PA: John Benjamins.

———1993. Genre and literacy modeling context in educational linguistics. *Annual Review of Applied Linguistics.* 13:141–172.

Martin, J., F. Christie, and J. Rothery 1987. Social processes in education: A reply to Sawyer and Watson (and others). In *The Place of Genre in Learning: Current Debates,* ed. I. Reid. Typereader Publications No. 1. Deakin, VIC: Centre for Studies in Literacy Education. 58–82.

Martin, J. and J. Rothery 1993. Grammar: Making meaning in writing. In *The Powers of Literacy: A Genre Approach to Teaching Writing,* eds. B. Cope and M. Kalantzis. London: Falmer Press. 137–153.

McLaren, P. 1991a. Post-colonial pedagogy: Post-colonial desire and decolonized community. *Education and Society.* 9(2): 135–158.

———1991b. Schooling the postmodern body: Critical pedagogy and the politics of enfleshment. In *Postmodernism, Feminism, and Cultural Politics: Redrawing Educational Boundaries,* ed. H. Giroux. Albany, NY: State U. of New York Press. 144–174.

———1993. *Schooling Is a Ritual Performance: Towards a Political Economy of Educational Symbols and Gestures,* 2nd ed. New York: Routledge.

McNeill, D. and P. Frieberger 1993. *Fuzzy Logic: The Discovery of Revolutionary Computer Technology And How It Is Changing Our World.* New York: Simon and Schuster.

McRobbie, A. 1991. *Feminism and Youth Culture: From 'Jackie' to 'Just Seventeen.'* London: Macmillan.

———1994. *Postmodernism and Popular Culture.* London: Routledge.

McWhirter, D. 1996a. *Using Telecommunications as a Tool in the Classroom: The Global Student Newspaper.* Southport, QLD: St Hilda's School.

———1996b. *A Range of Responses—Student On-Line Discussion I*EARN.TC.* Southport, QLD: St Hilda's School.

Merriam, S. 1988. *Case Study Research In Education: A Qualitative Approach.* San Francisco: Jossey-Bass.

———1997. *Qualitative Research and Case Study Applications in Education*. San Francisco: Jossey-Bass.

Michaels, S. 1986. Narrative presentations: An oral preparation for literacy with first graders. In *The Social Construction of Literacy*, ed. J. Cook-Gumperz. Cambridge: Cambridge U. Press. 94–116.

Mills, C. 1959. *The Sociological Imagination*. London: Oxford U. Press.

Milroy, J. 1992. The theoretical status of sociolinguistics. In *Sociolinguistics Today: International Perspectives*, eds. K. Bolton and H. Kwok. London: Routledge. 356–361.

Milroy, J. and L. Milroy 1985. Linguistic change, social network and speaker innovation. *Journal of Linguistics*. 21: 339–384.

Moll, L. 1992. Literacy research in community and classrooms: A sociocultural approach. In *Multidisciplinary Perspectives on Literacy Research*, eds. R. Beach, J. Green, M. Kamil, and T. Shanahan. Urbana, IL: NCRE/NCTE. 211–244.

Moraes, M. 1996. *Bilingual Education: A Dialogue with the Bakhtin Circle*. Albany, NY: State U. of New York Press.

Morgan, W. 1994. 'Clothes wear out learning doesn't'—Realising past and future in today's critical literacy curriculum. Keynote address for the Australian Association for English Teachers National Annual Conference. Perth, July.

Morine-Dershimer, G. 1985. *Talking, Listening and Learning in Elementary Classrooms*. New York: Longman.

Myers, J. 1992. The social contexts of school and personal literacy. *Reading Research Quarterly*. 27(4): 297–327.

National Commission on Excellence in Education 1983. *A Nation At Risk. The Imperative for Educational Reform*. Washington, DC: U.S. Department of Education.

New London Group 1996. A pedagogy of multiliteracies: Designing social futures. *Harvard Educational Review*. 66(1): 60–92.

Ochs, E. 1979. Transcription as theory. In *Developmental Pragmatics*, eds. E. Ochs and B. Schieffelin. New York: Academic Press. 43–72.

O'Connor, M. and S. Michaels 1993. Aligning academic task and participation status through revoicing: Analysis of a classroom discourse strategy. *Anthropology and Education Quarterly*. 24(4): 318–335.

O'Connor, P. ed. 1994a. *Thinking Work: Theoretical Perspectives on Workers' Literacies*. Leichhardt, NSW: Adult Literacy and Basic Skills Action Coalition.

———1994b. Fears, fantasies and futures in workers' literacy. In *Literacies and the Workplace: A Collection of Original Essays*, eds. M. Brown, S. Leavold, D. Tate, and S. Wright. Deakin, VIC: Deakin U. Press. 55–102.

O'Neill, W. 1970. Properly literate. *Harvard Education Review*. 40(2): 260–263.

O'Sullivan, T., J. Hartley, D. Saunders, M. Montgomery, and J. Fiske 1983. *Key Concepts in Communication*. Deakin, VIC: Methuen.

Ozolins, U. 1993. *The Politics of Language in Australia*. Cambridge: Cambridge U. Press.

Papert, S. 1993. *The Children's Machine: Rethinking School in the Age of the Computer*. New York: HarperCollins.

Pecheux, M. 1982. *Language, Semantics and Ideology*. London: Routledge and Kegan Paul.

Pennycook, A. 1994. *The Cultural Politics of English as an International Language*. London: Longman.

Perelman, L. 1992. *School's Out: A Radical New Formula for the Revitalization of America's Educational System*. New York: Avon Books.

Popkewitz, T. 1991. *A Political Sociology of Educational Reform: Power/Knowledge in Teaching, Teacher Education, and Research*. New York: Teachers College Press.

Poster, M. 1995. *The Second Media Age*. Oxford: Polity Press.

Poynton, C. 1985. *Language and Gender: Making the Difference*. Deakin, VIC: Deakin U. Press.

Psathas, G. and T. Anderson 1990. The 'practices' of transcription in conversation. *Semiotica*. 78(1/2): 75–99.

Putney, L. 1996. You are it: Meaning making as a collective and historical process. *The Australian Journal of Language and Literacy*. 19(2): 129–143.

Reich, R. 1992. *The Work of Nations: Preparing Ourselves for 21st-Century Capitalism*. New York: Vintage Books.

Reid, I. ed. 1987. *The Place of Genre in Learning: Current Debates*. Deakin, VIC: Deakin U. Press.

Rheingold, H. 1994. *The Virtual Community: Finding Connection in a Computerized World*. London: Secker and Warburg.
Richards, C. 1993. Taking sides? What young girls do with television. In *Reading Audiences: Young People and the Media*, ed. D. Buckingham. Manchester: Manchester U. Press. 24–47.
Richardson, P. 1992. Language as personal resource and as social construct: Competing views of literacy pedagogy in Australia. In *Learning and Teaching Genre*, eds. A. Freedman and P. Medway. Portsmouth, NH: Boynton/Cook. 117–142.
Rogoff, B. 1984. Introduction: Thinking and learning in social context. In *Everyday Cognition: Its Development in Social Context*, eds. B. Rogoff and J. Lave. Cambridge: Harvard U. Press. 1–8.
———1990. *Apprenticeship in Thinking: Cognitive Development in Social Context*. New York: Oxford U. Press.
———1995. Observing sociocultural activity on three planes: Participatory appropriation, guided participation, apprenticeship. In *Sociocultural Studies of Mind*, eds. J. Wertsch, P. del Rio, and A. Alvarez. Cambridge: Cambridge U. Press. 139–164.
Rogoff, B. and J. Lave eds. 1984. *Everyday Cognition: Its Development in Social Context*. Cambridge: Harvard U. Press.
Roman, L. 1992. The political significance of other ways of narrating ethnography: A feminist materialist approach. In *The Handbook of Qualitative Research in Education*, eds. M. LeCompte, W. Millroy, and J. Preissle. San Diego, CA: Academic Press. 555–594.
———1996. Spectacle in the dark: Youth as transgression, display, and repression, *Educational Theory*. 46(1): 1–22.
Rose, M. 1989. *Lives on the Boundary: The Struggles and Achievements of America's Underprepared*. London: Collier Macmillan.
Rushkoff, D. 1996a. *Media Virus: Hidden Agendas in Popular Culture*, 2nd ed. New York: Ballantine Books.
———1996b. *Playing the Future: How Kids' Culture Can Teach Us to Thrive in an Age of Chaos*. New York: HarperCollins.
Salza, D. 1995. *Clean Water for Nicaragua: Integrating Telecommunications and Service Learning into the Curriculum*. Yorktown Heights, NY: I*EARN Telecommunications Network.

Santa Barbara Classroom Discourse Group 1992. Constructing literacy in classrooms: Literate action as social accomplishment. In *Redefining Student Learning: Roots of Educational Change*, ed. H. Marshall. Norwood, NJ: Ablex. 119–150.

———1994. Constructing literacy events in classrooms: Literate action as social accomplishment. In *Theoretical Models and Processes of Reading*, 4th ed, eds. R. Ruddell, M. Ruddell, and H. Singer. Newark, DE: International Reading Association. 124–154.

———1995. Event mapping. Mimeo.

Schiffrin, D. 1994. *Approaches to Discourse*. Oxford: Blackwell.

———1996. Narrative as self-portrait: Sociolinguistic constructions of identity. *Language in Society*. 25(2): 167–203.

Searle, C. 1993. Words to a life-land: Literacy, the imagination, and Palestine. In *Critical Literacy: Politics, Praxis, and the Postmodern*, eds. C. Lankshear and P. McLaren. Albany, NY: State U. of New York Press. 167–192.

Searle, J. 1994. *Pathways to Active Literacy: A Professional Development Program for Senior Secondary and Technical Teachers*. Brisbane: Department of Education, Queensland and TAFE-TEQ, Department of Employment, Vocational Education, Training and Industrial Relations.

Shepard, L. and C. Bliem 1995. Parents' thinking about standardized tests and performance assessments. *Educational Researcher*. 24(8): 25–31.

Shuman, A. 1993. Collaborative writing: Appropriating power or reproducing authority? In *Cross-Cultural Approaches to Literacy*, ed. B. Street. Cambridge: Cambridge U. Press. 247–271.

Simon, R. and D. Dippo 1986. On critical ethnographic work. *Anthropology and Education Quarterly*. 17(4): 195–202.

Smith, D. 1990. *The Conceptual Practices of Power: A Feminist Sociology of Knowledge*. Boston: Northeastern U. Press.

Smith, R. 1995. Schooling and the formation of male students' gender identities. *Theory and Research in Social Education*. 24(1): 54–70.

Smith, R. and P. Curtin 1997. Children, computers, and life online: Education in a cyberworld. In *Page to Screen: Taking Literacy into the Electronic Era*, ed. I. Snyder. Sydney: Allen and Unwin. 211–233.

Stake, R. 1985. Case study. In *Research, Policy, and Practice*, eds. J. Nisbet, J. Murray, and S. Nisbet. London: Kogan Page. 277–285.
——1995. *The Art Of Case Study Research*. Thousand Oaks, CA: Sage.
Stedman, L. 1997a. International achievement differences: An assessment of a new perspective. *Educational Researcher*. 26 (3): 4–15.
——1997b. Response: Deep achievement problems: The case for reform still stands. *Educational Researcher*. 26 (3): 27–29.
Steedman, C. 1981. Schools of writing. *Screen Education*. 38: 5–13.
Stenhouse, L. 1985. A note on case study and educational practice. In *Field Methods in the Study of Education*, ed. R. Burgess. London: Falmer Press. 263–271.
Stevenson, P. 1994. Making Space: For those who invent tomorrow. A report on the feasibility of a multi-purpose youth facility for Brisbane. Funded by the Department of Tourism, Sport, and Racing, Queensland, and the Academy of Arts, Queensland U. of Technology, Brisbane.
Stone, A. 1996. *The War of Desire and Technology at the Close of the Mechanical Age*. Cambridge: MIT Press.
Street, B. 1984. *Literacy in Theory and Practice*. Cambridge: Cambridge U. Press.
Swann, J. 1993. *Girls, Boys and Language*. Oxford: Blackwell.
Tannen, D. 1994. *Gender and Discourse*. Oxford: Oxford U. Press.
Taylor, T. and D. Cameron 1987. *Analyzing Conversation: Rules and Units in the Structure of Talk*. Oxford: Pergamon Press.
Taylor, M. and E. Saarinen 1994. *Imagologies: Media Philosophy*. New York: Routledge.
Thomas, K. and J. Maybin 1997. Investigating language practices in a multilingual London community. In *Students as Researchers of Culture and Language in Their Own Communities*, eds. A. Egan-Robertson and D. Bloome. Cresskill, NJ: Hampton Press. 218–254.
Torres, M. 1997. Celebrations and letters home: Research as an ongoing conversation of students, parents, and teacher. In *Students as Researchers of Culture and Language in Their Own Communities*, eds. A. Egan-Robertson and D. Bloome. Cresskill, NJ: Hampton Press. 90–130.

United States Congress 1994. *Goals 2000: Educate America Act*. Washington, DC: Government Printing Office.

van Dijk, T. 1993. Principles of critical discourse analysis. *Discourse and Society*. 4(3): 249–283.

———1996. Discourse, cognition and society. *Discourse and Society*. 7(1): 5–6.

Vilko, A. 1994. Homespun life: Metaphors on the course of life in women's autobiographies. *Cultural Studies*. 8(2): 269–277.

Vingerhoets, R. 1993. *Earn and Learn*. Mt Waverley, VIC: Dellasta.

Virtual Valley. Brunswick and Beyond. Phase 1. (cited 9 October, 1997). <http://www.ps.odyssey.com.au/GRUV/vvalley/welcome.htm>

Virtual Valley. Brunswick and Beyond. Phase 2. (cited 9 October, 1997). <http://www.ps.odyssey.com.au/GRUV/vvalley/phase2.htm>

Walker, J. 1988. *Louts and Legends: Male Youth Culture in an Inner-City School*. Sydney: Allen and Unwin.

Walkerdine, V. 1981. Sex, power and pedagogy. *Screen Education*. 38: 14–24.

———1985. On the regulation of speaking and silence: Subjectivity, class and gender in contemporary schooling. In *Language, Gender and Childhood*, eds. C. Steedman, C. Urwin, and V. Walkerdine. London: Routledge and Kegan Paul. 203–241.

———1988. *The Mastery of Reason: Cognitive Development and the Production of Rationality*. London: Routledge.

———1990. Difference, cognition, and mathematics education. *For the Learning of Mathematics*. 10(3): 51–56.

———1996a. *Daddy's Girl: Young Girls and Popular Culture*. London: Macmillan.

———1996b. Subject to change without notice: Psychology, postmodernity and the popular. In *Cultural Studies and Communications*, eds. J. Curran, D. Morley, and V. Walkerdine. London: Arnold. 96–118.

Wallace, C. 1992. *Reading*. Oxford: Oxford U. Press.

Walton, C. 1993. Aboriginal education in northern Australia: A case study of literacy policies and practices. In *Knowledge, Culture and Power: International Perspectives on Literacy as Policy and Practice*, eds. P. Freebody and A. Welch. London: Falmer Press. 55–81.

Ward, C. and J. Daley 1993. *Learning to Learn: Strategies for Accelerating Learning and Boosting Performance*. Christchurch: C. Ward and J. Daley.

Watch Tower Bible and Tract Society of Pennsylvania 1971. *Theocratic Ministry School Guidebook*. Brooklyn, NY: Watch Tower Bible and Tract Society of New York.

Weiler, K. 1995. Remembering and representing life choices: A critical perspective on teachers' oral history narratives. In *Critical Theory and Educational Research*, eds. P. McLaren and J. Giarelli. Albany, NY: State U. of New York Press. 127–144.

Winters, K. 1996. *America's Technology Literacy Challenge*. Washington, DC: Office of the Under Secretary, U.S. Department of Education. Available from <acw-l@unicorn.acs.ttu.edu> [cited 17 February 1996].

Williams, G. 1993. Using systemic grammar in teaching young learners: An introduction. In *Literacy Learning and Teaching: Language as Social Practice in the Primary School*, ed. L. Unsworth. Melbourne: Macmillan. 197–254.

Willis, P. 1977. *Learning to Labour*. Farnborough: Saxon House.

Wittgenstein, L. 1953. *Philosophical Investigations*. London: Basil Blackwell and Mott.

———1958. *Preliminary Studies for the 'Philosophical Investigations' Generally Known as The Blue and Brown Books*. Oxford: Blackwell.

Yeager, B., A. Floriani, and J. Green 1997. Learning to see learning in the classroom: Developing an ethnographic perspective. In *Students as Researchers of Culture and Language in Their Own Communities*, eds. A. Egan-Robertson and D. Bloome. Cresskill, NJ: Hampton Press. 180–217.

Yin, R. 1989. *Case Study Research: Design and Methods*, rev. ed. Newbury Park, CA: Sage.

———1994. *Case Study Research: Design and Methods*, 2nd ed. Newbury Park, CA: Sage.

Yukawa, M. 1993. Wetware. In *Mondo 200: A User's Guide to the New Edge*, eds. R. Rucker, R. U. Sirius, and Queen Mu. London: Thames and Hudson. 280.

Zeller, N. 1995. Narrative strategies for case reports. *Qualitative Studies in Education*. 8(1): 75–80.

INDEX

Aboriginal (Murri) and Torres Strait Islander Independent School students, 227
Anderson, Neil, 232
Apprenticeship
    Rogoff's theory, 95–96, 99, 118, 121, 200, 214, 219, 232, 239
    cultural apprenticeship, 95, 121–122, 178, 213
    Gee's concept, 41, 95, 210, 214, 219
Acquisition
    Gee's concept, 41, 43, 219
    and Nicholas, 78
    Rogoff's concept, 95, 99
    and Jacques, 121
Bazerman, Charles, 231
Bennett, Adrian, 49–51, 153, 215
Black Voices, 201
Bloome, David, 18, 52, 54
Blyton, Enid, 177, 183, 185
Bowers, John, 28–29, 30, 66
Boys and Literacy, 219
Carspecken, Phil, 14–15, 71
Circle of friends, 129, 130, 132–134, 143, 154
    and their language games, 129–132
    membership criteria, 133–134
Citizen, 6, 17
    production of, 150, 217, 228–230
Clinton, Bill, 4, 69, 197, 238
Coding practices, 193, 221
Communicative validity, 13, 14–15
Contexts, 7, 64

Coordinations, 45, 47, 78, 152, 173, 180, 187
    between specific discourses, 45, 86, 93, 141, 142, 166
    institutional, 140–141
Critical, 68
    practices, 227
Critical Discourse Analysis, 25, 30–33
Culture, 51
Cummins, Jim, 220, 233, 239
Curriculum Corporation, 2, 3, 17, 199
Data analysis, 51–65
    categories, 53, 68
    example, 60–65
    interaction units, 54, 55, 61
    mapping data, 213–214
    message units, 54, 55, 61
    see Events, Event mapping
Dawkins, John, 199
Davies, Bronwyn, 219
Delpit, Lisa, 47–48, 230
Digitarts, 201, 227
Dippo, Donald, 8
D/discourses, 7–9, 18–27, 33–47, 65, 207–216
    and event mapping, 59, 207–208, 217
    and social groups, 44–45, 78, 236–237
    and institutions, 44–45, 78
    and social practice, 28
    and student teachers, 235–237
    as socially constituted and constituting, 33

business, 117–119, 123, 147, 199, 223
coordinations, 45, 47, 78, 152, 173, 180, 187
criticisms of Gee's theory, 47–51, 152, 215–216
discourse and Discourse, 39–40
forms of life, 35, 75, 127
Gee's theory, 6–7, 22, 26, 33, 51, 83, 117, 136, 212–215
interpretations, 157, 214, 218
joker, 110–113, 126, 134
mateship, 79–84, 86
membership, 36–37, 181–184, 212
model student, 164–167, 181
nice girl, 141, 150, 164, 181, 210
primary and secondary, 40–44, 79, 86, 93–97, 138, 150, 166, 178, 183, 213
research and literacy education, 216–238
subdiscourse, 37, 86, 89, 93, 137–140, 212–213
student, 78–79, 85, 93–97, 110, 112, 149, 164, 166
technological, 151, 224
teengal, 139–143
theories of, 29, 208–211
Discourse analysis procedures, 7, 22, 53–68, 207–208
Doing school, 77, 187–206
classroom language practices, 151
Doneman, Ludmila and Michael, 227, 240
Earn and Learn, 119, 123, 143
Education as reproduction, 172
Education Queensland, 220
Education reform, 21, 25
Email as discourse, 148, 151
Ethnography, 8, 181
Ethnography of communication, 25, 27, 51
Events, 7, 53

Event mapping, 7, 53–58, 207–208
and discourses, 57–58, 207–208, 217
example of, 54, 56, 60
Everyday, 16
Fairclough, Norman, 30
Famaleez, 227
Fasold, Ralph, 66
Floriani, Ana, 102
Foucault, Michel, 32
Freebody, Peter, 188, 191, 193, 221–223
Freiberger, Paul, 67
Gee, James Paul, 25–26, 34–51, 93, 96, 198, 205, 212–216
see also Acquisition; Apprenticeship; D/discourses; Learning
Genre theory, *see* Language and literacy education
Gilbert, Pam, 172
Gotfrit, L., 186
Green, Judith, 7, 22, 26–27, 51–55, 67, 68, 207
see also Santa Barbara Discourse Group; Event mapping
GRUNT, 227–228
Guba, Egon, 15, 71
Guided participation, 89, 118, 121
Rogoff's theory, 95–96
Hannah, 157–184, 191, 195, 196, 198, 199, 202, 214, 216
and her mother, 166, 174–176, 177–179, 180–181
characterization of, 157–160
compared with Layla, 164, 169, 181, 183
compared with Nicholas, 193, 198
drama group, 168, 170–171
family life, 157–158
in school, 159–160
living in the country, 167, 176–177

self sufficiency, 164–165, 182
skits, 167–170, 171–178, 189
themes or forms of life, 160
Heath, Shirley Brice, 42–43, 188, 232, 236, 239
Herrnstein, Richard, 5
Hirsch, E.D, 5
Hymes, Dell, 22–24, 25, 27, 66
Identity (social), 29, 31, 35–37, 46, 53, 110–113, 140, 150, 154, 172, 179–181, 212, 223, 225, 227
Ideology, 38
I*EARN, 237
Individual, 28, 216
  and schools, 217
  construction of, 27–29
  individualism, 150, 155
  speaking, 27, 142
Interactional sociolinguistics, 25, 50
Interactive webs of relationships, 140, 142, 152, 183, 215, 233
Interpretation of data, 72–78, 83–86, 93–97, 110–113, 118, 140–143, 151–153, 182, 208–211
  see also Data analysis; Trustworthiness; Communicative validity
Intervention programs, 190, 191, 230, 234, 235, 237
Iwi, Kate, 28–29, 30, 66
Jacques, 101–124, 187, 195, 200, 208, 209, 211, 214, 217, 218, 219, 224, 225, 239
  and his mother, 107, 113, 114
  characterization of, 101–103, 113–115
  compared with Layla, 145
  everyday life outside of school, 113–122
  family life, 112–115
  in school, 101–103, 113, 189
  themes or forms of life, 103
Jehovah's Witness, 113–115, 121, 223

Kincheloe, Joe, 15
Knowledge, 57, 188, 197
  funds of knowledge, 211, 236–237
  school knowledge, 5
Krashen, Stephen, 41
Kress, Gunther, 29–31, 39, 45
Kvale, Steinar, 13–14
Language and literacy, 5, 202
  and schooling, 218–230
  and social change, 94, 196, 224
  classroom language practices, 146, 217–234
  language use and social practice, 29, 34, 44, 152, 199, 201, 203, 217, 224, 230
  male and female patterns, 209–210
  playful language practices, 225–226
  purposeful language practices, 147, 190–192, 224
  real world language practices, 146, 203, 223, 225
  research, 200, 216
  technological literacies, 90–93, 151, 156, 202, 237
  ways of being literate, 222
Language and literacy education, 2, 10, 193, 205, 218–228, 230
  and discourse, 33, 207–238
  as apprenticeship, 146, 239–241
  Australian, 189–190, 203, 205
  effective approaches, 227, 230–235
  genre theory, 9, 93, 163, 189–190, 193, 197, 205
  social outcomes, 230
Lankshear, Colin, 2, 3, 6, 21, 201, 202, 205, 206
Lather, Patti, 14, 15
Layla, 125–156, 188, 191, 195, 199, 209, 210, 216, 223, 224, 226, 229
  and her mother, 125, 126
  as a student, 143–151
  characterization of, 125–128

compared with Hannah, 151, 164, 169, 181, 183
compared with Jacques, 127, 134
compared with Nicholas, 127, 135, 138
family life, 125–126
in school, 127
themes or forms of life, 127
Learning
Gee's theory of, 41–42, 42–45, 214
See also Apprenticeship
Lemke, Jay, 16, 32, 48–49, 51, 140
Lesko, Nancy, 141, 150
Life chances, 16
Lin, Lichu, 54, 236
Lincoln, Yvonna, 15, 71
Literacy, *see* Language and literacy
Literacy in the National Curriculum, 219
Luke, Allan, 171, 221–222
Mates, 79–86
Membership, 57
negotiating, 79–83, 133–135, 183–184
social groups, 38, 40, 44, 52, 152
discourse, 36–37, 51, 181–184, 212
see also D/discourse
McLaren, Peter, 15, 111, 171, 186, 190
McLaughlin, Milbrey, 236
McNeill, David, 67
Macpherson, James, 85, 111
McRobbie, Angela, 140, 152, 179, 214
Meaning and meaning-making, 37
Merriam, Sharan, 8
Metacognitive strategies, 106, 110
Meta(con)textual commentary, 102, 104
Metalanguage, 89, 146, 236
Mills, Charles Wright, 233
Mothers of case study participants, 98

see also Hannah, Jacques, Layla, Nicholas
Mucking around, 85, 183
Murray, Charles, 5
Narratives and identity, 174–181
National Literacy Goal, Australia, 2
New London Group, 2, 6, 230
Nicholas, 73–99, 188, 191, 195, 198, 201, 209, 215, 223, 224–225, 226, 229
and his mother, 74, 86–90, 94, 201
characterization of, 73–75
compared with Hannah, 198
compared with Layla, 127, 135, 138, 139
event map, 60–65
family life, 73–74, 86–89
homework, 77, 86–89
in school, 74–83
rubber wars, 60–65, 75–76, 80
themes or forms of life, 75
O'Neill, Wayne, 205, 222
Participatory appropriation, 96, 118, 119, 121
Rogoff's theory, 96
Pathways to Literacy, 219
Popkewitz, Thomas, 4, 5, 197
Popular culture, 139, 142, 152
adolescents, 129
shared knowledge of, 132
socializing influence, 129, 132, 142
see also D/discourse; teen gal
Pragmatic practices, 221
Professional development programs, 218–220
Quantification of classroom work, 76
Queensland English syllabus, 9, 93, 124, 189, 193, 197, 218
Reader resources, 221–222
Reich, Robert, 97, 118, 123, 151, 197, 201
Reporting, 71–73
key to codes used, 71

narrative approach, 72–73
see also Snapshots
Research design, 7–15
  case study, 7–9, 13, 14
  ethnography, 8
  methodology, 22–29
  methods of data collection, 9–13
  observations, 11, 12
  participant selection, 10, 18
  reporting, 71-73
  trustworthiness and communicative validity, 13–16
Richards, Chris, 133, 142
Rogoff, Barbara, 95–96, 99, 118, 214
  see also Acquisition; Apprenticeship; Guided participation; Participatory appropriation
Roman, Leslie, 155, 179
Rushkoff, Douglas, 142
Saarinen, Esa, 200–201, 206, 224, 225
Santa Barbara Discourse Group, 7, 22, 26, 51–58, 68, 236
  See also Green, Judith
Sayers, Dennis, 220, 233, 239
Schooling
  and society, 217, 228
  and the individual, 217
  normative and regulatory role 171, 189, 192, 217
Schriffin, Deborah, 29, 180
Sheridan, Dorothy, 18
Simon, Roger, 8
Snapshots
  as narrative approach to reporting, 72, 73
  Hannah, 160, 161, 167–168, 175
  Jacques, 103–104, 115
  Layla, 128, 143–144
  Nicholas, 75–76, 86–88
Social networks, 34, 140, 214–215
  see also Interactive webs of relations

Social cognition, 210
Social practice, 16, 235
  and discourse, 29–34
  and language use, 29
  see also D/discourse; Language and literacy
Sociolinguistics, 22–29, 216
  critical discourse analysts, 25, 30–33
  ethnographers of communication, 25, 27, 51
  interactional sociolinguists, 25, 27, 51
Sociological imagination, 233
Standards, 2–3, 11, 25, 45, 97, 190, 204, 208
  Benchmarks, 2–3, 17, 204
  USA, 3–4
Stine, R.L, 174, 176, 185
Street, Brian, 18
Students as ethnographers, 232
Systemic functional linguistics, 30, 205
Talking—Our way into Literacy, 220
Taylor, Mark, 200–201, 206, 224, 225
Teachers
  and adolescents, 187–193
  authority and power relations, 132, 138
  and student roles, 202, 225
  education, 235–237
Teaching practices, 187–193
  collaboration with universities, 236
  community-based, 227–228, 237
  examples of effective practice, 230–234, 238–242
  transmission models, 197
Text meaning practices, 221
Theocratic school, 119–120, 121
Transcription conventions, 69
Trustworthiness (of interpretations), 13–15

Van Dijk, Teuwen, 31, 33
Vingerhoets, Rob, 123
Virtual Valley projects, 201, 227–228
Walkerdine, Valerie, 188
Wallace, Catherine, 222
Walton, Christine, 38, 43
Wannabes, 132, 135, 155
Watch Tower Bible and Tract Society of Pennsylvania, 119, 121
Wetware, 206
Wittgenstein, Ludwig, 16, 35, 39
Working man/worker, 115–119
Yin, Thomas, 8, 9, 73
Zeller, Nancy, 72

COUNTERPOINTS

Studies in the Postmodern Theory of Education

General Editors
Joe L. Kincheloe & Shirley R. Steinberg

Counterpoints publishes the most compelling and imaginative books being written in education today. Grounded on the theoretical advances in criticalism, feminism and postmodernism in the last two decades of the twentieth century, Counterpoints engages the meaning of these innovations in various forms of educational expression. Committed to the proposition that theoretical literature should be accessible to a variety of audiences, the series insists that its authors avoid esoteric and jargonistic languages that transform educational scholarship into an elite discourse for the initiated. Scholarly work matters only to the degree it affects consciousness and practice at multiple sites. Counterpoints' editorial policy is based on these principles and the ability of scholars to break new ground, to open new conversations, to go where educators have never gone before.

For additional information about this series or for the submission of manuscripts, please contact:

>Joe L. Kincheloe & Shirley R. Steinberg
>637 West Foster Avenue
>State College, PA 16801